THE ARTS

IN

AMERICA

The Colonial Period

THE ARTS IN AMERICA

The Colonial Period

LOUIS B. WRIGHT   GEORGE B. TATUM

JOHN W. McCOUBREY

ROBERT C. SMITH

SCHOCKEN BOOKS · NEW YORK

CONTENTS

LIST OF ILLUSTRATIONS

xii

xiv

DIAGRAMS IN TEXT

FROM WILDERNESS TO REPUBLIC

1607–1787

by Louis B. Wright

THE evolution of thirteen separate and distinct English colonies into a nation with a republican government was a slow and arduous process that consumed the energies of its people and left little time for the development of a taste for the fine arts and all that an interest in the arts implies. Yet within the span of one hundred and eighty years, these disparate English colonies had grown into a fully-developed nation with a constitution that would weld them together and give them a lasting coherence. This nation had also developed a certain amount of sophistication, a few urban centers of cultivation, and a group of leaders of remarkable cultural attainments. With still unrealized natural resources of incredible richness, the country had a potential of future greatness that some patriots were ready to proclaim to all the world. Timothy Dwight, later to become president of Yale, delivered himself of a paean in praise of his land in 1787:

> *Columbia, Columbia, to glory arise,*
> *The queen of the world, and the child of the skies!*
> *Thy genius commands thee; with rapture behold,*
> *While ages on ages thy splendors unfold.*
> *Thy reign is the last and the noblest of time,*
> *Most fruitful thy soil, most inviting thy clime;*
> *Let the crimes of the East ne'er encrimson thy name,*
> *Be freedom, and science, and virtue thy fame.*

In his vision Dwight foresaw the United States as a land where learning and the arts would flourish with renewed vigor.

> *New bards and new sages, unrivaled shall soar*
> *To fame, unextinguished, when time is no more;*
> *To fame, the last refuge of virtue designed,*

> *Shall fly from all nations the best of mankind;*
> *Here, grateful to heaven, with transport shall bring*
> *Their incense, more fragrant than odours of spring.*
> *Nor less shall thy fair ones to glory ascend,*
> *And Genius and Beauty in harmony blend;*
> *The graces of form shall awake pure desire,*
> *And the charms of the soul ever cherish the fire;*
> *Their sweetness unmingled, their manners refined,*
> *And virtue's bright image, enstamped on the mind. . . .*

Other enthusiastic prophets dreamed of a perfect blend of freedom, learning, and the arts in the pure air of America. Although the vision of a perfect combination of democracy and the arts was only a poet's dream in 1787, and would remain imperfectly realized in the generations to come, the vision was there and it revealed a hope that would remain constant through the years. And by 1787 enough progress had been made to suggest that the United States was a country where all of the arts might one day flourish.

The characteristics of a people, artistic and otherwise, depend upon many factors, and no one has yet discovered what nucleus in their genes accounts for the particular qualities that distinguish one group from another. In the evolution of the American people, many complex and diverse influences exerted themselves. Environment undoubtedly played a large part in determining the qualities of American taste and its manifestation in the various regions of the country. Traditional values that immigrants brought with them from their countries of origin were also important. Religious attitudes, particularly doctrines that emphasized the outward expression of social relationships and social views, had a far greater influence than modern Americans are likely to remember. The diversity of peoples and regional differences in geography and climate played their part. All of these things influenced the development of American attitudes toward the arts in all of their manifestations, from the decorations of the humblest cottage to the best of original creations in painting, sculpture, letters, and architecture.

Much ink has been wasted in lamenting the lack of artistic interest in the early days of America, the poverty of literature, and the general bleakness of life when measured against European standards of the 17th and 18th centuries. Modern armchair critics of life in the colonial period who seem puzzled by the lack of a positive aesthetic in the early years of settlement betray their own failure to understand the conditions that the first immigrants faced when they landed on these shores and the difficulties that they had to overcome before they could achieve a stable social order. Because this background of struggle and hardship is so often forgotten in discussing the aesthetic problems of the colonial period, it is well to recapitulate briefly the history of the growth of a settled society in the thirteen original colonies, particularly as it affected aesthetic progress.

THE SOUTH AND ITS SOCIETY

Most of the Englishmen who made the first permanent settlement at Jamestown in 1607 were unconscious of their high destiny as the forerunners of empire. Their motives in coming were various but inevitably human. Most of them had dreams of quick wealth, which they would acquire by discovering gold; others came for the sake of adventure, for theirs was an age when young men went on quests almost as fantastic as the search for the Holy Grail; still others had been shipped off by their families as a good riddance—for America already was looked upon as a solution for the problem of family ne'er-do-wells, and it would become the home of many a remittance man. Not many if any of the "First Supply," as Captain John Smith described the men who came in the *Susan Constant* and her two sisterships, planned to make a permanent career of Virginia. Whatever the Virginia Company which had sent them out might think, they intended to get rich quickly, satisfy their curiosity about the New World, and return to their homes in England.

If the early efforts at colonization seem to us naïve and inept, we would do well to remember that the English were as yet almost totally without experience in such ventures. A few Englishmen, it is true, had settled estates in Ireland, but the Irish experience was not applicable to conditions three thousand miles away on the other side of a stormy ocean, and few had any knowledge even of the settlement of "plantations" in Ireland. The early

5

immigrants into Virginia had only the vaguest notions of the climate, of the products of the country, of the hazards from pestilence and savages, and of the labor required to reduce a forested terrain to productive farmland. Many of the potential settlers had no conception of hard work of any sort. They were technically gentlemen, men of a class unaccustomed to working with their hands, and Captain John Smith bitterly complained about the difficulty of getting these soft-handed gentry to chop down trees and perform other laborious work necessary to making a dent in the wilderness.

After the first shock of discovery that hard labor was essential, and that no man need expect to escape his obligation to work, the pioneers at Jamestown fell to their tasks and built themselves shelters and stockades against the Indians. Thus an English "town" on the periphery of a vast continent had its beginning, but Jamestown would remain little more than a symbol of town life as Virginia developed a distinctly rural economy.

The kind of huts that the first settlers built were of the sort that Englishmen had known since primitive times. Crotched trees served for framing, and wattles (willow rods or withes of other trees) woven together and daubed with mud made the walls, with a thatched roof to keep out the rain. A mud-and-stick chimney at one end conducted the smoke from the fireplace of the more pretentious houses. In others an aperture in the roof sufficed for the escape of smoke from a stone hearth on the floor. Crude wooden bunks served for beds; benches made of half-hewn logs supplied the place of both chairs and tables. Such huts were not luxurious but they were sufficient to protect the occupants against the worst of the weather. Not for many years would Englishmen build log cabins. These were an innovation of Scandinavians from the heavily wooded regions of Northern Europe, or of Germans from the Black Forest. Englishmen reproduced the kind of structures they had known at home. These were strictly utilitarian and they demonstrated a conservative adherence to ancient traditions of building that had persisted in rural England since Saxon times.

When the Jamestown settlers had established themselves more securely, they built better houses, some of brick and some of timber, and they placed them close together in a compact village for protection against the Indians. With a whole continent before them, they laid out streets of row houses; for protection was more important than privacy. Town life, however, did not develop in Virginia. As the settlers grew bolder, they moved out along the waterways and established isolated plantations. Each planter could have his own dock on a stream deep enough for ocean-going vessels and could trade directly with England.

John Rolfe, who had married Pocahontas, daughter of Powhatan, the most powerful of the Indian potentates, demonstrated in 1614 that tobacco could be grown successfully and profitably. His marriage had brought at least a temporary peace with the Indians, and Virginians saw themselves on the way to a prosperous agrarian economy. The tobacco that Rolfe planted was not the bitter Virginia variety but a sweeter tobacco, the seed of which he had obtained from the West Indies or South America. Rapidly, tobacco planting came to occupy the interest of the settlers. The price at first was high, and everybody tried to grow as much tobacco as he could. Settlers who had little land planted tobacco even in their dooryards at Jamestown.

The discovery was soon made that tobacco exhausted the soil after six or seven years' planting on the same ground. Hence it became necessary for a planter to have sufficient land to enable him to clear fresh fields for tobacco at intervals while the exhausted fields lay fallow and regained their strength through successive crops of weeds that rotted on the land. This need of always having new fields in reserve meant that planters must inevitably be land-hungry; they had to obtain and hold the largest number of acres possible. Since the individual plantations frequently were of a vast extent, the planters found themselves living in relative isolation from their neighbors. The separate plantations became self-contained units, with the owner's house set amidst a complex of outbuildings. An excellent example can be seen to this day at "Shirley" on the James River, with its schoolhouse, servants' quarters, barns, smokehouses, and other necessary structures. The plantation economy of both Virginia and Maryland, characterized by widely separated self-contained establishments of individual planters trading directly with England, prevented the growth of towns. In the colonial period, only the tiny capitals of Williamsburg and Annapolis in Virginia and Maryland achieved anything approaching an urban culture.

Elsewhere in the southern colonies a different but related type of agrarian society developed. The Carolinas, which were not settled until the later years of the 17th century, had a diverse population ranging from poor yeoman farmers in the back country to rich grandees in the tidewater sections. Unlike the Chesapeake Bay colonies, the Carolinas did not depend upon tobacco or upon any single crop. Tidewater Carolina grew rice in great abundance and later found the growth and preparation of indigo a profitable industry. In the upcountry, farmers raised cattle and grain crops. The very name of one South Carolina town in the Piedmont, Cowpens, the site of a famous Revolutionary battle, is indicative of the chief occupation of the inhabitants. The wealthy planters of tidewater Carolina established comfortable homes on their plantations and built handsome town houses in Charleston and Wilmington. Because of the heat and the mosquitoes on their river estates, they lived in their town houses in the summer and moved out to the country in the winter. This seasonal migration from town to country profoundly affected the kind of social life characteristic of tidewater Carolina. The Carolina planters also frequently combined the occupations of farming and trade. No one in Carolina, or elsewhere in the agrarian colonies for that matter, was so foolish as to look askance at money derived from the market place. The so-called "taint of trade" was a concept still far in the future, when degeneracy would overtake the descendants of the vigorous colonials.

In the Chesapeake Bay region the 17th and early 18th centuries were years of struggle against both wilderness and savages. The Virginia colony was nearly wiped out on Good Friday, 1622, when the Indians made a concerted attack on outlying farms and slaughtered more than three hundred men, women, and children. A similar massacre occurred in 1644 with the loss of more than five hundred lives. But gradually settlers cut down the forest, subdued the Indians, and began to erect houses that were something more than mere protection against the elements and the savages. By the end of the first quarter of the 18th century, handsome dwelling houses were beginning to dot the land along waterways of Virginia and Maryland.

From the earliest days of settlement until the end of the colonial period, the problem of an adequate supply of labor, both skilled and unskilled, continually troubled all of the colonies, but particularly the agrarian regions. Farm work was laborious and required long hours in the burning sun of summer. Much of it was tedious and monotonous, and some of it entailed intense discomfort and even danger. Although the Indians had grown tobacco with relative ease, the cultivation of this crop as an article of commerce kept laborers extremely busy throughout the summer. Seedlings had to be transplanted from beds to open fields; the tender young plants had to be hoed constantly to keep weeds and grass from smothering them; the ripe leaves had to be plucked and cured in barns over slow fires; the cured tobacco had to be packed in hogsheads and rolled to the docks. The planter could not rest in peace even when the crop was stowed on board a ship bound for London or Bristol because he realized no profit until his factor on the other side of the Atlantic received and sold the cargo. Even more troublesome was the cultivation of rice and indigo in the Carolinas. Rice grew in steaming lowland fields that had to be flooded during the growing season. Laborers in the rice fields endured mosquitoes and risked fever; they had to avoid poisonous snakes and sometimes scarcely escaped drowning. The preparation of indigo plants to make them into marketable raw dye was a messy, stinking task. None of these farming operations could attract laborers who could find anything better to do.

During the 17th century, the majority of laborers were indentured white servants, that is, individuals who bound themselves to serve for a definite period of time, ranging ordinarily from four to seven years, to pay for their passage across the Atlantic. Some convicts were also shipped to the colonies and sold to planters for a period of years. Thousands of indentured servants poured into the Chesapeake Bay colonies to work on the tobacco plantations. Before they could be acclimatized, many of them died. The death rate among convicts who had been weakened by months in prison and by jail fever was even higher. Despite the mortality among them, white indentured servants made up the principal labor supply in the years before 1700. Not only did they do the heavy work of unskilled laborers but from their ranks came craftsmen of all varieties and even schoolmasters. They continued to be an important element in the economy of the southern colonies until the end of the colonial period. An indentured Scotsman, John Harrower, who came to Virginia just before the Revolution, kept a journal in which he told of his experiences as a schoolmaster near Fredericksburg. His life was not hard; he ate with his master's family and participated in their pleasures and in some of their entertainment. But such an idyllic existence was not the lot of laborers. If they survived their years of bondage, they could take up land of their own and become independent farmers. Since that is what they did, as a rule, no free supply of labor in any quantity existed.

Many of these indentured servants had been yeoman farmers, or the sons of yeoman farmers in England, and they had the independent spirit of free Englishmen. By the time they were free, they had learned how to farm in the new country and were prepared to become landed proprietors, if only on a small scale. Eventually a number of them achieved prosperity and some few rose to prominence. These farmers had some knowledge of various crafts and helped to supply the need for skilled workers: carpenters, brickmakers, bricklayers, plasterers, tanners, leather-workers, and a variety of other occupations. Most of them were not the best of their kind, for they had not served long apprenticeships in a craft, and though their handiwork might be adequate, it was rarely distinguished. The lack of fine craftsmen is one reason for the simplicity of early American design and the emphasis upon strictly utilitarian qualities.

In 1619 occurred an event that vastly altered the labor pool in the English colonies. In that year a Dutch man-of-war tied up at Jamestown and sold to the planters twenty Negroes, the forerunners of a stream of slaves to follow. Whether these first twenty Negroes were sold as slaves for life or as indentured servants is a moot question, but there is no doubt that they turned the planters' attention to a new source of unskilled labor. Nevertheless, it was not until near the end of the century that Negro slavery became an important factor in the labor supply. In 1672 Charles II granted a charter to the Royal African Company which greatly stimulated the slave trade. It received a further impetus in 1697 when this company's monopoly was broken and the way was opened for colonials themselves, both North and South, to engage in the profitable trade. Steadily during the 18th century the number of slaves in all of the agrarian colonies increased. Competition with slave labor was hard on white landowners with small holdings who found themselves pushed into the back country where they could engage in subsistence farming. By the end of the colonial period Negro slaves supplied almost all of the unskilled labor on the large plantations. Many planters also had slaves trained in various skills, from fiddle-playing to carpentry. Like the white indentured servants, these craftsmen were frequently ill-trained and the quality of their work was often short of perfection. But they managed to do creditable carpentry, bricklaying, house-painting, and decorating, and to supply other skills when professional craftsmen from overseas were unavailable.

By the mid-18th century an affluent agrarian aristocracy had developed in the region south of Pennsylvania. The great planters lived in fine houses in considerable style, enjoyed contacts with correspondents overseas, primarily in England, sometimes sent their children abroad to be educated, occasionally made trips overseas themselves on business or pleasure, and were an intelligent and sophisticated class. Both consciously and unconsciously this aristocracy found a rationale of conduct in the way of life of the English "county families." Colonial planters may have come of humble origins themselves, but having acquired land—always the symbol of gentility—and having achieved prosperity, they set about imitating as best they could the behavior of the English country gentry. Indeed there is evidence that they idealized the English gentry and perhaps struggled harder to achieve that ideal than if they had been to the manor born. The development of this aristocracy had significant implications for the future of America because its better elements, while attaining great power, socially, economically, and politically, also believed that they had an obligation to cultivate their minds, to develop their intellectual powers, and to utilize their intelligence in the service of their country. They were convinced that privilege carried with it responsibility to society. The manifestation of these beliefs is evident in the careers of men who came to the fore as leaders during the American Revolution: Richard Henry Lee, George Mason, Washington, Jefferson, and a host of others.

These men also set an example in taste which had a far-reaching influence. After the birth of the nation, the enormous prestige of Washington alone was sufficient to cause many people to imitate him in all that he did or possessed. Gouverneur Morris realized this when he wrote to Washington: "I think it of very great importance to fix the taste of our country properly, and I think your example will go very far in that respect. It is therefore my wish that everything about you should be substantially good and majestically plain, made to endure. . . ."

The Virginia and Maryland aristocracy was distinctly an agrarian society. Although some of the great planters had town houses in Williamsburg and Annapolis, and at intervals during the year these little capitals fluttered with social activity, the essential life of these colonies was lived on the land.

The prominence of the aristocratic families should not be allowed to obscure the fact that in both colonies the interior was peopled with small farmers, farmers who in England would have been classified as yeomen, and that they occupied an increasingly important economic and political position as the 18th century wore on. They were on the frontier and were helping to open up a back country that was already attracting the speculative interest of the wealthy men of the colonies. By the time of the Revolution land speculation had become a dominant preoccupation of the wealthy.

The isolation of the Chesapeake Bay planters forced them to take strenuous measures to maintain the civilized way of life of the social class to which they aspired. They were determined not to be barbarized by frontier conditions, and they were eager for their children to have the kind of schooling that would make them a credit both to their families and to the commonwealth. To that end they employed tutors and set up plantation schools. John Harrower, the indentured schoolmaster of Colonel William Daingerfield's children at Fredericksburg, tells in his *Journal* how Colonel Daingerfield himself rode through the neighborhood advertising the services of the schoolmaster so that others might take advantage of the opportunity. And Harrower was allowed to keep the fees for himself. Some children at a very early age were sent to England for their education so that they could acquire a background of cultivation unobtainable on a river plantation. William Byrd II, for example, spent much of his childhood and youth in English schools. Although colonial parents were not all convinced that education in England was a good thing for sons who ran the risk of being spoiled for plantation life by the pleasures of London, they were not willing for their children to grow up uncouth and unlettered. They gathered little libraries of general interest and utility and shared the books with their neighbors. They also cultivated the art of conversation, and from the conversation of their elders children learned much. Hospitality was traditional and "visiting" was one of the social amenities. Children, like their parents, enjoyed the talk of visiting friends and neighbors or of the chance traveler from afar, who was always welcome, whatever his status, for he brought news from a world beyond the bend in the river.

At Williamsburg and Annapolis, the little provincial capitals, one could occasionally see plays and enjoy musical concerts. After the middle of the 18th century, traveling troupes of actors enacted the plays of Shakespeare there and the works of later dramatists like Congreve, Vanbrugh, and Farquhar. Addison's *Cato*, curiously, was a favorite piece, and some of the politicians borrowed oratorical phrases from its swelling rhetoric. At Williamsburg and Annapolis one could also buy a weekly newspaper and, if inspired by the Muse of poetry or stirred by the spirit of controversy, one could contribute to its columns. Life in the Chesapeake Bay colonies consisted of something more than hard work seasoned with frivolity.

In South Carolina, where the great planters frequently combined the business of a merchant with their agricultural pursuits, the aristocracy developed a more urban point of view. Summer found them living in close social contact in their town houses, which were built on the edge of Charleston's harbor. Ships from England and the West Indies swung at anchor there, waiting for cargoes of rice, indigo, turpentine, rosin, and other products of the pine forests needed as ships' stores overseas. Wealth came rapidly to these South Carolina merchants and their houses reflected their affluence. Built high and narrow, three and four stories from street level, they were characteristically only one room wide so that breezes from the sea or land could blow through the open windows. Verandas upstairs and down, shaded by liveoaks and hackberries, looked out upon the bay. Charleston adapted to its hot climate, and the inhabitants of the tall houses could enjoy a summer of comfort and pleasure.

For their entertainment, Charlestonians in the later 18th century had an excellent theatre and perhaps better music than any other city in the English colonies. The Saint Cecilia Society sponsored both amateur and professional concerts. The town also had a good newspaper, the *South Carolina Gazette*, founded by one of Benjamin Franklin's apprentices. Few other localities demonstrated a greater interest in books. In 1748 a group of citizens founded the Charleston Library Society, which within two years had one hundred and thirty members who kept up with the most recent European publications. Some of the Charleston gentry were devoted readers of the classics. A contributor to the *South Carolina Gazette* declared that only a genius could write good English unless he had a foundation in the Greek and Roman classics. When the Charleston Library Society decided to stop buying editions of the ancient classics, Christopher Gadsden was so incensed that he resigned. Both Charles Cotesworth Pinckney and Thomas Pinckney were noted for their attainments as classical scholars. Charleston society in the 18th century was noteworthy for its cultivation, its intellectual interests, and its elegance.

An aristocracy without wealth could not have existed, but a wealthy society is not necessarily an aristocracy. The affluence of the aristocracies of the southern colonies was a means to an end, and that end was a life of cultivation and grace. The wealth of the great planters—a wealth based on credit rather than ready money—gave them the means to build handsome houses, fill them with good furniture, have their portraits painted, and lead lives that went beyond mere getting and spending. Not every planter, to be sure, was a paragon of gentility, but a persistent ideal of conduct influenced the whole of the upper class and made possible the development of a milieu where good taste prevailed.

Although various elements had gone into the composition of the population of the southern colonies, its dominant ruling class was, as already noted, a homogeneous society that took the English country gentry for its model. That is not to say that it reproduced slavishly the social characteristics of its prototype in the mother country, for there were obvious variations from English life, but the southern aristocracy looked to England and its upper class for guidance in all matters of taste.

The ruling class of the southern colonies was also fairly homogeneous in religion, for the Church of England was the established religion in Virginia and the Carolinas during most of the colonial period. In Maryland some of the leaders belonged to a strong Catholic minority. In South Carolina, French Huguenots were numerous but they were assimilated into the Anglican establishment. North Carolina had an infusion of Quakers and

Dissenters of various types, but the tidewater aristocrats around Wilmington for the most part were Anglicans. In all of these colonies, the back country was peopled with Presbyterian Scots and other Dissenters, but they were not as yet socially dominant.

Whatever the personal behavior of these southern colonial aristocrats, they subscribed to the established religion and believed that they ought to set an example by attending service. They built simple churches out of wood or brick that were usually architecturally pleasing. The services therein were also simple, for rural conditions made simplicity imperative. Country churches could not support the pomp and circumstance of vested choirs and elaborate rituals. From the beginning the establishment was Low Church. But the church had no prohibitions against luxury, as had the Quakers and the Puritans (at least nominally), and no sumptuary laws attempted to regulate dress, decoration, or display of any kind. If an occasional cleric inveighed against luxury, it was merely a personal judgment, not an ecclesiastical position. In short, the religious doctrines subscribed to by the ruling class were favorable to the development of tastes that condoned luxury and admitted that comfort, grace, and beauty were desirable.

Evidence of the quality of the civilization developed by the ruling class in the Chesapeake Bay colonies and the Carolinas may be found in the inventories of their estates, in newspapers, advertisements, and letters, and in surviving examples of their household goods and dwellings. The Henry Francis du Pont Winterthur Museum and the collections at Williamsburg, Virginia, provide visual evidence of the taste of this civilization, all of which shows how thoroughly Anglicized was the material manifestation of their culture. Abundant illustration will also be found in the later chapters of this book. Colonial mansions were not without decoration, but they rarely contained interiors that were beyond the capacity of local craftsmen. We know that planters on occasion bought indentured servants with special skills needed in building and decorating, but by and large the work was done by native artisans, both Negro and white. The scarcity of skilled labor placed a premium on simplicity, usually to the benefit of design.

The houses of the poorer farmers and workmen were structurally simple and bare of unnecessary details. The smallest house might be a one-

15

room rectangle made of timber with a chimney at one end and a covered porch behind. A somewhat more commodious house might be a long rectangular structure of two stories with a chimney at each end. As the family increased, an ell might be added. The furniture and decorations were plain and strictly utilitarian. Robert Beverley in 1705 complained that Virginians were so dependent upon England that they imported even their woodenware, but later a considerable amount of plain houseware was made locally—such as pine or oak benches, tables, chairs, and bed frames. The quality of local craftsmanship and the necessity of ensuring maximum utility dictated plainness of design and execution. The best furniture, however, was brought from overseas.

The southern colonies were not the only ones with an agrarian economy, but they were the only colonies where the planters became an aristocratic ruling class with the means and the judgment to develop sophisticated tastes. The greatest farming region in the English colonies developed in Pennsylvania, which became the granary of the New World. But Pennsylvania's best farmers were predominantly Germans of peasant stock who had no interest in, and indeed were hostile to, aristocratic pretensions. They were not without skill in useful crafts, and they had a sense of design, but their concern was with strictly utilitarian construction. They erected sturdy stone houses and built magnificent barns so that wagons could gain access on two or three levels. They were the inventors and builders of the Conestoga wagons—strong and capacious for hauling farm products across country to the Philadelphia markets. They also created the long rifle later to be known as the Kentucky rifle, a beautiful and accurate weapon which helped the frontiersmen win a foothold in the earliest West. Folk arts flourished among these German farmers. They decorated pottery, did elaborate needlework, including colorful patchwork quilts, and were skillful cabinet-makers. But though they might embellish household objects and the interiors of their houses with pattern and color, their interest was concentrated upon utility. If they grew prosperous, they might add acres to their farms, rooms to their houses, and more cubic area to their barns, but they retained essentially the point of view and the taste of the German peasant. Sophistication was beyond them.

NEW ENGLAND AND THE MIDDLE COLONIES

In contrast to the agrarian civilization of the South was the evolution of a commercial society in the North, with the gradual growth of towns and cities which fostered the beginnings of urban culture. Many factors of background, religion, education, occupations, and environment went into the development of this civilization, which was far more diverse than that of the South.

The settlers who landed at Plymouth in December, 1620, were an industrious and pious group of Separatists who had lived for some years in Holland without absorbing any of the characteristics of their Dutch hosts. Indeed, one influence which moved them to leave Holland was the fear lest their children would not retain their English ways as their fathers had succeeded in doing. They were simple folk, artisans and farmers, who were willing to suffer hardships in order to remain separate from the Established Church. Even their leaders were of humble origin. William Brewster had been postmaster and bailiff at Scrooby Manor in Nottinghamshire, and William Bradford, who wrote *Of Plymouth Plantation*, a prose epic of their experiences, had been a poor farmer. Yet both of these leaders were men of learning and cultivation. Brewster was a graduate of Cambridge University and Bradford was well versed in ancient and modern languages.

The Plymouth colonists lived by farming, fishing, and fur-trading. Their houses were simple structures like English farmhouses of the day but built of wood. Their church was as plain as their dwellings. They affected simple dress and looked upon ostentation in any matter as ungodly. Yet they achieved a dignity that was monumental, perhaps magnified in retrospect by the scriptural cadences of William Bradford's magnificent prose narrative. Their later impact upon the American imagination has been far greater than their social and cultural impact upon their own time, for their chief contribution to New England's evolution was the precedent they established for independent congregational church government.

Of the English colonists who settled on the Atlantic seaboard before the middle of the 17th century, none exerted a more far-reaching influence on the future development of the country than those who came to Massachusetts Bay between 1630 and 1640. The leaders of these people were Puritans who wanted to establish a godly commonwealth uncontaminated by the evils of the Old World, but religion was not the only motive that sent them forth from England into the wilderness of the North Atlantic region. Conditions in East Anglia, where most of the leaders of the migration to Massachusetts lived, were not propitious in the 1630's. Profits from both farming and sheep-raising were falling, and trade was at a standstill. A depression that affected all of England was felt with peculiar force in the eastern counties. Puritanism had gained great strength in this part of England, and the faithful were growing ever more restive under the increasing pressure of the ecclesiastical power of Canterbury. For depressed Puritans the future looked gloomy, both materially and spiritually.

One of the Puritans who was peculiarly unhappy was John Winthrop, squire of the manor of Groton in Suffolk. He was distressed over his debts and the fact that his expenses continued to outrun his income, as he wrote to his son Henry, already settled in Barbados. The growing cost of living and rising prices were alarming others besides John Winthrop, but as a country gentleman who was expected to keep a certain state, he was especially embarrassed by the prospect of accumulating financial difficulties. The religious situation also depressed him. The Bishop of London and Chancellor of Oxford was William Laud, soon to be Archbishop of Canterbury. Working closely with the King, Laud was making an effort to rid from office every Puritan who could be eliminated. Winthrop saw little hope of political or economic improvement, or of spiritual happiness for himself and his fellow religionists. The possibility of a commonwealth of the godly on the other side of the Atlantic was therefore particularly appealing to him and a like-minded group who received a charter in 1629 authorizing a colony in the Massachusetts Bay region.

The charter of the Massachusetts Bay Company was unlike that of any other previous venture in that it permitted the incorporators to take the charter with them and to establish control of the government in the New World instead of in London. Winthrop and his colleagues had shrewdly insisted upon this provision so that they could dictate the quality of the emigrants and the nature of the government. They were taking no chances that this new migration of the chosen of God into the Promised Land should be contaminated with faithless ne'er-do-wells recruited by greedy London entrepreneurs.

One of Winthrop's colleagues in organizing the enterprise was Thomas Dudley, who had served as steward to the Earl of Lincoln and had proved his business ability by accumulating a fortune of his own. He was also an exceedingly pious Puritan and something of a religious poet. In one of his poems he had urged that men of God "in courts and churches" maintain a watch "O'er such as do a toleration hatch." Winthrop himself was an authoritarian who distrusted those who talked of liberty, and he insisted upon the unquestioning subjection of the populace to the will of the magistrates. There would be no malcontents to "hatch a toleration" if Winthrop and Dudley had their way. The members of the company elected Winthrop governor and Dudley deputy-governor. Gathering a body of emigrants whose religion was pure, Winthrop and Dudley in the summer of 1630 sailed with them to Massachusetts Bay. Many of the new settlers came from East Anglia, and John Cotton, the vicar of St. Botolph's Church at Boston in Lincolnshire, preached the farewell sermon before their departure. It was not without significance, therefore, that the settlers named one of their towns Boston. Three years after the Winthrop group sailed, Cotton himself fled from the ecclesiastical oppression of England to the more congenial atmosphere of New England.

During the decade after 1630, the immigrants who flowed into the Massachusetts Bay colony were so numerous that the movement is known as the Great Migration. By 1640 something like fourteen thousand had come to Massachusetts, two thousand to Connecticut, and a few hundred to Rhode Island. Not all of these were Puritans, for the leaders soon discovered that it was not economically feasible to insist upon strict religious orthodoxy for every worker. Even a pagan could be a hewer of wood and a drawer of water. But the dominant group held religious views consistent with those of Winthrop and Dudley.

The non-Puritan settlers in New England were more numerous than one is sometimes led to believe, and Winthrop's brethren had to contend with some ungodly folk. By the middle of the century, what is now Maine and New Hampshire was dotted with tiny fishing villages, offshoots of the great fishery in Newfoundland where more than ten thousand Englishmen spent a part of the year fishing and curing their catch. A few independent Englishmen had also found a foothold elsewhere in New England. One Captain Wollaston with a small company made a settlement approximately on the site of modern Quincy, and there Thomas Morton, an uninhibited lawyer from Clifford's Inn, set up a Maypole, to the great scandal of their pious neighbors at Plymouth. Governor Bradford eventually sent Captain Miles Standish to cut down the Maypole, arrest Morton, and ship him off to England. Another group, dispatched by that persistent dreamer of colonial expansion, Sir Ferdinando Gorges, had attempted in 1623 a settlement at Weymouth which had collapsed. But a few hardy souls remained and one of them, an Anglican parson named William Blaxton, planted an apple orchard on what later became known as Beacon Hill, Boston. After Winthrop's Puritans had established their rule, he moved to another place. "I came from England," he said, "because I did not like the Lord Bishops, but I cannot join with you, because I would not be under the Lord Brethren." Not even in New England was it possible for the Lord Brethren to create a commonwealth exclusively of one religious belief, as they soon discovered. But they made a heroic effort to plant what one of them called a "garden of the Lord" which would be free of tempting serpents and troublesome heretics.

The Puritan migration to Massachusetts Bay was a well-organized and a well-financed enterprise, backed by substantial men, many of whom were university trained. A number of them had received degrees at Emmanuel College, Cambridge, then one of the chief intellectual centers of Puritanism. The majority of the clergymen who came to Massachusetts Bay were Emmanuel College graduates.

These earnest Christians were determined that they would establish a religious commonwealth where their faith might flourish in its purest form, but, to ensure the continuity of this godly enterprise, they were also determined to provide proper educational facilities for their children, including a college for the training of ministers. Six years after John Winthrop's first group landed, the settlements were sufficiently well established for the inhabitants to begin thinking of higher education, and in 1636 they founded

Harvard College. No more succinct statement about the origin of the college can be found than the often-quoted passage from *New England's First Fruits:*

> *After God had carried us safe to New England and we had builded our houses, provided necessaries for our livelihood, reared convenient places for God's worship, and settled the civil government, one of the next things we longed for and looked after was to advance learning and perpetuate it to posterity, dreading to leave an illiterate ministry to the churches when our present ministers shall lie in the dust. And as we were thinking and consulting how to effect this great work, it pleased God to stir up the heart of one Mr. Harvard . . . to give the one half of his estate (it being in all about £1,700) towards the erecting of a college, and all his library. After him another gave £300, others after them cast in more, and the public hand of the State added the rest. The college was by common consent appointed to be at Cambridge (a place very pleasant and accommodate) and is called (according to the name of the first founder) Harvard College.*

Although one of the primary purposes of the college was to ensure a learned ministry, it had another declared purpose—to "advance learning and perpetuate it to posterity." Combining the best of the classical tradition with the new Christian humanism of the 16th and 17th centuries, Harvard College became an institution respected both at home and abroad. By the middle of the century a few Puritan families in England were sending their sons to Harvard, where they could drink from a purer fountain of knowledge than they could find at home.

In April, 1635, the citizens of Boston had met and elected Philemon Pormort as teacher of a school which in the following year added a graduate of Emmanuel College, Daniel Maude, as Latin master. This was the beginning of the famous Boston Latin School. Other little towns in Massachusetts were setting up schools, and soon Lynn, Salem, Dorchester, New Haven, and others could boast of "free schools." That meant that the schools were free to the children of the inhabitants of the township; outsiders were required to pay. And all pupils were expected to contribute a fair share of the expense of firewood and other necessities.

The Massachusetts General Court in 1642 ordered the selectmen of the various townships to make inquiries at intervals to see that parents and masters of apprentices were requiring children under their care to "read and understand the principles of religion and the capital laws of the country." The preamble of another act of the General Court in 1647 warned that the "old deluder Satan" wished to hold men in ignorance and keep them from the knowledge of the Scriptures. To outwit Satan's intentions, every town of fifty householders was required to hire a schoolmaster to teach all the children to read and write, and every town of one hundred householders was required to establish a Latin grammar school where the pupils could prepare themselves for the university. Responsible persons were constantly enjoined to see that children learned to read, write, and cipher and had some honest trade to live by. Massachusetts wanted its citizens to be literate, religious, and industrious. This aim became the goal of New England families for generations to come, and this ambition accounts for the spread of New England culture across the American continent.

Another influence of vast import for the cultural development of New England was the establishment of a printing press at Cambridge in 1639, the first in any of the English colonies. By 1640 the press had brought out *The Whole Book of Psalms* and it would continue to print books and pamphlets for years to come. Printers trained at Cambridge went out to other colonies to establish presses. The first attempt, in 1690, to start a newspaper in Boston ended in failure, but by 1704 John Campbell had begun publishing the *Boston News-Letter*, and fifteen years later William Brooker brought out the first issue of the *Boston Gazette*, which had for its printer James Franklin, half-brother of Benjamin Franklin. James Franklin later set up his own paper, the *New England Courant*, which frankly announced as one of its purposes the publication of amusing material "to entertain the town." It flouted the Puritans and angered those high priests of Puritanism, the Mathers, to such a degree that Franklin spent a term in jail and in 1727 thought it best to move on to Newport, where he published for a short time the *Rhode Island Gazette*. The printing presses and newspapers of New England provided an outlet for literary expression and for the voicing of opinions on public affairs. By the time of the Revolution these printing presses would be powerful influences in the shaping of public opinion.

The Englishmen who settled in Massachusetts Bay and elsewhere in New England were varied in background and attainments. At the top were educated men, many with university degrees, some of whom had been members of the country gentry in England. An unusually large number of learned clergymen came to New England because it offered a refuge for those who dissented from the tyranny of Archbishop Laud in the later years of Charles I's reign. Because the lay leaders wanted a religious commonwealth, the clergy in the early days of the settlement of Massachusetts Bay exercised enormous power. If not literally, at least in practice, the colony was a theocracy. Below the gentry and the clergy came a large body of people representing most of the occupations of England: tradesmen, seamen, craftsmen of all sorts, farmers, and laborers. Many of these had the same religious beliefs as the leaders, but many others were lukewarm, if not cold, to Puritan doctrines.

Control of the colony was at first exercised by the governor, deputy-governor, and assistants (or magistrates), but under the charter a General Court had to be held once each quarter at which the "freemen" or shareholders would meet, pass laws, and decide upon the admission of other freemen. A group of 108 settlers applied for admission as freemen in 1630 and were admitted. Winthrop, who was no believer in popular government, became alarmed lest the multitude should gain control, and in 1631 he and the other leaders decided upon a limiting expedient; they decreed that only members of an approved church could be selected as freemen. Five years later another act decreed that no church could be organized without the consent of the Court. A person could not become a church member merely by his own volition. He had to testify that he had experienced conversion, and he then had to be approved by the pastor, officers, and congregation of the church. The obstacles to becoming a church member were so great that the majority of the population remained outside the fold, and the control of the government remained in the hands of the godly minority. Since the population increased faster than church membership, and since people outside of the church communion were constantly agitating for power in their local communities, the authorities in 1662 decided that something needed to be done to increase the number of church members eligible to be freemen and therefore to vote. They hit upon the plan of admitting the children of church members even though they could not testify to conversion. This so-called "Half-Way Covenant" would strengthen the power of the "right people" and keep out the unregenerate multitude. The fact that such an expedient was believed necessary was an indication of the weakening of the theocracy. Although religion remained a powerful influence in New England, a gradual increase in the rate of secularization is noticeable from this time onward as the country became prosperous and as trade with the outside world multiplied nonreligious influences.

Religious dissension wracked the settlements from time to time and caused congregations to break away and seek greener pastures elsewhere. Individuals whose consciences would not permit them to live with their views unspoken sometimes caused trouble. Roger Williams was one of these, and in 1635 the General Court banished him. He fled to Rhode Island and helped establish a colony where a spirit of tolerance would flourish.

Although the religious beliefs of New Englanders varied to a greater degree than one is likely to assume, the Puritan ethic was an influence of enormous importance in every area of life. The emphasis upon the virtues of sobriety, diligence, and thrift helps to account for the quality of New England society and indeed for the dynamic drive that characterized it.

The importance of religion in the early days of the settlement of New England, however, tends to obscure other aspects of the social and economic development of the region. Religion, of course, was not the only concern of the inhabitants. They had come to improve their economic as well as their spiritual lot, and, like intelligent men, they set about making the most of their new environment.

Many of the newcomers were farmers who were distressed to find that except in the river valleys the soil was thin and rocky. Yet the land was sufficiently arable to support subsistence farming everywhere, and farmers soon learned to supplement agriculture with a variety of handicrafts and trades. The ingenious and industrious Yankee had an early birth.

The forests offered one of the first and most important of the country's natural resources. Englishmen were keenly aware of the value of woodlands, for the home country had been seriously deforested because of the demand for timber needed in housing and shipbuilding, the use of wood for fuel, and the requirement of charcoal for forges. Before the settlements in America, Englishmen had imported forest products from the Baltic area, and they were now eager for fresh and cheaper sources of supply. New England had abundant forests of oak, maple, birch, pine, hemlock, and other useful woods. A farmer could rive shingles in his spare time or make barrel staves and hoops, which were in great demand for casks. Conditioned as we are today to the pasteboard packing case, we forget that wooden casks were essential to the life of our ancestors. Every householder had to have barrels and kegs for the storage of grain, meat, and other foodstuffs. Every ship had to have casks for its water as well as for most of the freight stored in its hold. The wine-growers of Europe, the sugar- and molasses-makers of the West Indies, and the fishermen of Newfoundland needed barrels, barrels by the thousands, and New England farmers learned that cooperage—the making of barrels—was an enterprise that could keep them and their families profitably busy during the long dark days of winter. The lowly barrel deserves an honored place with the codfish as a symbol of New England's prosperity.

The abundance of fish along the Atlantic shelf had excited the interest of early explorers; Captain John Smith in *A Description of New England* (1616) had grown ecstatic over the prospect of a great fishery there. He emphasized that the Dutch had shown the way to prosperity by fishing and that Englishmen could learn from them. "This [fishing] is their mine, and the sea the source of those silvered streams of all their virtue," he observed. Not only did Smith's book give currency to the name "New England," but it also brought home to his countrymen the prospect of a new source of wealth. Hence, even before the Great Migration to Massachusetts Bay, English settlers were beginning to set up fishing bases along the New England shore, and from 1630 onward fishing rapidly increased in importance. Gloucester early became an important fishing port, and Marblehead was not far behind. By the mid-18th century Gloucester alone had more than seventy vessels engaged in the fishing trade, and New Hampshire ports sent at least one hundred fishing craft to sea. The cod was the most important fish, but great quantities of mackerel and herring were also taken.

Ironically, Puritan New Englanders, who deplored everything smacking of Popery, made a profit out of the observance of fish days by Catholics in Portugal, Spain, and Italy. Codfish, salted and dried, kept indefinitely and was easily shipped. New England fishermen early discovered that the Latin countries themselves did not produce enough fish to supply the demand which seemed insatiable. Furthermore, since those countries, and the Canary and Madeira Islands, also needed barrels for their wine and oil, the New Englanders opened up a profitable trade in both fish and wood products and brought back wine, silk, and a variety of luxury items.

The mackerel and herring, which abounded in untold numbers and were easily caught, found a market in the West Indies where they were used as cheap food for the slaves who worked in the sugar cane fields. As the production of sugar and molasses increased, the demand for barrels in these islands also grew. Shippers from New England thus had another outlet for their cooperage, and they could always bring back a cargo of molasses which their distilleries could make into rum.

Rum was in demand on the coast of Africa where local African kings and chiefs had long been accustomed to sell to slave-traders the captives whom they took in tribal wars or rounded up as a matter of routine commercial enterprise. Ship captains from Boston and Newport discovered that they could barter rum for slaves and sell these human cargoes at a great profit in the West Indies. Having sold their slaves, they could take on a cargo of molasses for the rum distilleries of Boston, Newport, Providence, and other New England towns. Thus developed the famous triangular trade that made fortunes for many a pious family. Not all slaves, of course, were sold in the West Indies. Some were brought to the northern colonies and retained there, but many others were taken directly to the agricultural colonies of the South and sold to tobacco and rice planters.

Shipping and shipbuilding developed along with fishing, and the shipyards of New England became famous for the quality of the vessels that they turned out. Boston, Dorchester, Salem, Charlestown, Newport, and

Bristol, Rhode Island, made shipbuilding one of their most profitable industries. Newport boasted that its shipyards could build ships better and cheaper than its competitors. Even British magnates ordered vessels of as much as 400 tons built in Rhode Island yards, and some of the fastest slave ships of the mid-18th century came from Rhode Island.

Building and sailing ships brought prosperity to many a New England family. Though Great Britain by means of her Navigation Acts tried to funnel international trade through her own ports, she could not prevent colonial merchants using their own vessels to trade with the British West Indian islands or with the Wine Islands and the Mediterranean countries. Nor could she stop a vast amount of illicit trade with the French islands in the West Indies and with foreign vessels off the fishing grounds of Newfoundland. Few colonial shippers regarded smuggling as a crime, and more than one fortune was made in illicit trade.

Although whaling was not as important an industry in the colonial period as it became in the first half of the 19th century, a number of seafarers from Boston, Newport, Nantucket, and New Bedford found it worth their while to take whales in the North Atlantic. By the end of the period, Newport and Nantucket were sending out more than forty whaling vessels each year. Although most colonial whaling was done offshore or at least in northern waters, a few expeditions ventured into the South Atlantic. Whale oil was valued for lamps and for lubricants. Spermaceti, a thick substance from the head of the sperm whale, was highly valued for candle-making. Aaron Lopez, a Portuguese Jewish merchant of Newport, saw the possibilities in this industry and made a fortune manufacturing spermaceti candles.

With ingenuity and an almost religious concern for diligence that made work an end in itself, New Englanders pursued trade and business and grew rich in the process. Some family dynasties that began in the colonial period have lasted to the present day. For example, from Chad Brown, who landed in Boston in 1638 and later removed to Providence, descended a numerous progeny of industrious and thrifty merchants, some of whom occupied places of first importance in Rhode Island. The brothers James and Obadiah Brown were conspicuous in the mercantile activities of Providence. James, a godly Baptist deacon, had a ship named the *Truth and Delight* on which he himself sometimes sailed as master, carrying foodstuffs to the West Indies and bringing back molasses for his distilleries. He had no compunctions about evading the Molasses Act of 1733 and provided his shipmasters with detailed advice on smuggling. Obadiah expanded the family business, built a chocolate mill, manufactured spermaceti candles, and developed smuggling from French and Spanish West Indian ports into a fine art. The Brown merchant dynasty became one of the most important in colonial America.

Hardly any community in New England lacked a prominent trading family that acquired wealth, built fine houses, and lived in comfort and considerable style. The Hancocks of Boston were particularly conspicuous. In 1735 Thomas Hancock built Hancock House on Beacon Hill, one of the most luxurious residences of the day, filled with fine furniture from England, good books, pictures, and everything that a man of taste would require. Hancock, the grandson of a Cambridge cobbler, ordered one of his London agents to "look into the Herald's office and take out my arms. Let it be [a] well-cut crest and arms in silver fixed to ivory for the use of a counting room." Thomas Hancock, like James and Obadiah Brown, had prospered in part because he had learned to evade the Navigation Acts. His nephew and heir, John Hancock, grew even richer, evaded the Navigation Acts even more skillfully, and became a patriot and signer of the Declaration of Independence.

As wealth from the use of land had made possible the rise of an aristocratic ruling class in the agrarian colonies, so wealth from trade opened the way to the rise of a mercantile aristocracy in the North. Not all of the rich merchants were as pretentious as Thomas Hancock, but few of them eschewed the luxuries and trappings of gentility. In time, some of the merchant and shipping grandees in Boston, Newport, Providence, and Portsmouth grew as proud—and sometimes as arrogant—as any planter on the James or Cooper Rivers. Indeed the magnificence of their dwellings often exceeded those of the Southern aristocrats because they had more means, more ready cash, more experience in the marts of the world, and greater opportunities to buy anything that their wishes might dictate.

Trade and commerce made possible the rise of wealthy families of power and influence in the middle colonies also, for New England had no monopoly of business zeal. The Dutch who first settled New Amsterdam were motivated by a desire to open up the fur trade, which they realized held promise of vast profits. Later, when the English had taken over, New York became an even more important commercial center, with a body of wealthy landlords who held vast baronies in the back country. Landowners, merchants, and lawyers (occasionally combined in the same individual) were the ruling class in New York. Families such as the De Lanceys, Livingstons, Schuylers, and van Cortlandts were dominant in every department of that colony's life.

Still another type of merchant prince developed in Pennsylvania—the rich Quaker, who by religious profession was supposed to follow a life of simplicity, but who sometimes was tempted by the pelf he accumulated to lead a life of conspicuous grandeur. The Quakers, like the Puritans, were motivated by a zeal for industry, thrift, and sobriety that made them highly successful businessmen. Many New Englanders also infiltrated the rich province of Pennsylvania and some settled in Philadelphia. The combined efforts of Quakers, Puritans, and other less religious traders made Philadelphia by the time of the Revolution one of the two or three largest cities in the British Empire.

At Philadelphia's docks, outward-bound ships loaded food-stuffs and grains, hides and leather goods—all the produce of a rich agricultural back-country—products that were in great demand in the West Indies, in the other mainland colonies, and in Great Britain and Europe. Incoming vessels brought the finished products of the mother country—clothing, fabrics, furniture, china, silverware, and household goods of every description. Philadelphia was the most important port on the whole Atlantic seaboard, and it had a fleet of vessels for transocean as well as coastwise traffic. From Philadelphia radiated lines of communication and trade that were among the few influences at work to bring the disparate colonies into contact with one another. By the time of the Revolution, Philadelphia was not only the largest city in the colonies, it was also the most significant cultural center in the British New World, and exhibited a quality of urbanity that even the most dour of the Quaker merchants had difficulty resisting.

Some of them did not resist. For example, Isaac Norris, a very rich merchant, rationalized his desire for luxury and finery by evolving a theory that an individual could justifiably increase his material comforts and worldly show as his prestige and wealth increased. In demonstration of his theory, he ordered from England in 1713 a fine coach, bearing his coat of arms, but at the last minute his Quaker conscience made him recoil from this ostentation and he settled for his initials only on the doors. He ordered liveries for his coachmen and footmen, but they were to be "strong and cheap, either of a dark or sad color . . . or any grave color." Norris was not the only Quaker who rejoiced in the good things of the earth. Many of the wealthy merchants rode in handsome coaches, dressed in rich fabrics, erected great houses, rejoiced in the best furniture and silver that the market could supply—and were a scandal to their country cousins who held to the plain way of living.

THE DOMINANT CULTURE OF BRITAIN

FROM the most distant town in Maine to the latest settlement at the tip of Georgia, the civilization that the colonies developed was thoroughly British. This does not mean that no modifications occurred in the transmission of culture, or that no other influences were felt in the growth of colonial civilization, but it does mean that all other cultures were assimilated into the British before the Revolution and that the British left an inheritance that affected the whole of the social and aesthetic development of the nation.

The capacity of British culture for absorbing and dominating all other cultures in the American colonies—and of retaining its influence throughout later American development—is an extraordinary phenomenon not easily accounted for, even when one allows for the preponderance of British racial stocks and the prevalence of a common language. Many other peoples had poured into the colonies: Dutch, Swedes, Finns, and others into the Hudson and Delaware valleys; French Huguenots in large numbers into South Carolina, New York, Pennsylvania, and to a lesser degree into New England; thousands of Germans into Pennsylvania and thence into the back country of Maryland and down the Great Valley of Virginia into the Carolinas; and many thousands of Negro slaves, particularly into the agricultural regions of the South. All of the colonies also had continuing contacts with the native American Indians. These non-British peoples were not without influence, it is true, for they all left some residual evidence of their presence, but it is astonishing how little effect they had on the totality of the developing civilization.

The Dutch in New York introduced some architectural forms that persisted—the stepped-gable end of a house, for example, and certain styles in brickwork. They were responsible also for the popularity of decorative tiles and a few characteristic types of furniture. During the colonial period the Dutch language prevailed in overwhelmingly Dutch communities, but it was dying out by the Revolution and survives only in a few words which have become "naturalized" in our own tongue. The Swedes and Finns had almost no permanent impact beyond a little folklore, though the Swedes and Germans are credited with teaching frontiersmen how to build log cabins. The Germans bequeathed us the Lutheran Church, a variety of other religious sects, some music, a type of stone barn, and a few characteristic folk arts and customs peculiar to their localities. The French Huguenots brought many crafts and skills—silversmithing, weaving, cabinet-making, painting, and other useful arts—but they were quickly assimilated into the English culture. Even in Charleston, South Carolina, where the Huguenots were most numerous, they joined the Church of England, and in fact practically took it over; one strictly Calvinistic Huguenot church alone persisted in that community. The native Indians contributed many place names, a few words in our vocabulary, a few dishes to our tables (succotash, for example), and not much else. The Negro slave population brought music rhythms, some folklore (as exemplified in stories of Br'er Rabbit and the Fox), a taste for okra (a native African vegetable), and a persistent and tragic racial problem. But the overriding influence in all of the colonies was British culture as modified by local conditions.

An important explanation for this dominant influence was the fact that, owing to the Navigation Acts, Great Britain was the principal source of supply for most things that the colonies imported, from books to furniture. Some luxuries came from other countries by way of Great Britain, and some items came direct from the Wine Islands and the Mediterranean countries, but the great bulk of American imports were from Great Britain. Agents in

London or Bristol carried on the business of the Southern planters, filled their orders for goods, selected items from shops (including such intimate things as clothes and jewels for the planter's wife and daughters—even wedding rings), and recommended schools for their children and sometimes supervised their education in England. Although the urban development of the northern colonies resulted in each town having shops of its own, so that the inhabitants were less dependent upon foreign agents, they were equally beholden to England as the ultimate source of many essential materials.

From England came books for American libraries, periodicals, and newspapers from which colonial newspapers clipped articles for reprinting. One of the most popular works in 18th-century America was the *Spectator Papers*, and colonials were much indebted to Joseph Addison's essays for guidance in conduct and behavior. Colonial libraries were well stocked with books providing advice on conduct, advice that Englishmen had been reading for generations. They also had an abundant supply of books of religious instruction, for the most part devotional works and sermons. Surprisingly, the libraries of William Byrd of Virginia and Cotton Mather of Boston contained many of the same religious works. These were books that had influenced English religious thinking and would continue to influence Englishmen even when they had been translated to the colonies. Of the books in colonial libraries as a whole, utilitarian works made up the largest proportion. These ranged from fundamental works on English law to the latest tract on horse diseases.

Works on architecture helped to shape the taste of American builders; and pattern books for craftsmen showed them how to make anything from a simple chair to elaborate chests of drawers. Most of these works were of English origin, or they were transmitted through English translation and showed an adaptation to conditions in England. English design, of course, had been strongly influenced by countries across the Channel, but the designers and the authors of pattern books in England had adapted what they wanted from Flemish, French, and Italian architects or designers of furniture and household objects; they had made the designs their own. Colonial craftsmen, with considerable originality, frequently made further adaptations to suit their own purposes and materials, but their inspiration was prevailingly British.

THE GROWTH OF TASTE

THE rapid increase in colonial wealth in the 18th century gave rise in all the colonies to an upper class of persons who had sufficient money to buy the best that the English market could supply and to build dwellings that were as comfortable and commodious as those of English gentlemen. Design varied somewhat from region to region, but a common denominator of good taste is evident from Portsmouth to Charleston. This good taste was, as we have said, in part a result of the necessity of sticking to simple lines and simple decorative devices based on classical designs that local carpenters could execute properly.

Wealth made possible the great houses of the colonial period and wealth also provided the means of acquiring the taste that filled these houses with pleasing furniture, good books, and pictures in keeping with the rest of the establishment. The Hancock house in Boston; "Stenton," the Logan house in Philadelphia; "Westover," the Byrd house on the James in Virginia; the Gabriel Manigault mansion in Charleston, all showed similarities that indicated the development of a homogeneous civilization, though one was the residence of a Yankee trader, another the house of a devout Quaker, another the country seat of a Virginia squire, and the last the palatial town house of the descendant of a Huguenot carpenter.

Despite the wars of the 18th century—in fact, in part as a result of those wars—British colonies flourished and grew increasingly prosperous. During the second half of the 18th century, as wealth accumulated, the demand increased for the good things of the world, for material evidence of the individual's standing in his community, and for such amenities as good silver, fine table linen and hangings, well-designed furniture, and pictures. From the beginning, colonials had been anxious to preserve likenesses of their families, and many an itinerant limner had painted pictures that now adorn galleries of American primitives. But after the mid-18th century, the

33

wealthier members of American society showed more sophistication. They wanted their pictures painted by the best artists. Two American portrait painters, John Singleton Copley and Benjamin West, had gone abroad and made reputations. If colonials could not have their portraits painted by Copley or West, they at least hoped to sit to someone of reputation.

Ralph Izard of Charleston, son of an indigo and rice magnate, illustrates the rise of a new type of connoisseur among colonials. From the age of twelve he went to school at Hackney in England and returned to the colonies to marry in 1767 Alice de Lancey, niece of James de Lancey, a former chief justice of New York. Izard, who later became a diplomat of the new nation, traveled widely in Europe, and he and his wife sat to John Singleton Copley, then maintaining a studio in Rome. Izard admired good pictures, fancied himself a judge of painting, and was a patron of the arts. He was so proud and arrogant that when someone suggested that he be presented at the Court of St. James, he declined, because he would bow to no mortal man. Not everyone had the means to be a connoisseur of Ralph Izard's type, but many stay-at-home colonials patronized the arts in a lesser way as the later chapters of this book most amply illustrate.

The wealth of Philadelphia, the diversity of its population, its tolerance, and its contacts through its shipping interests with the world across the seas made it, as we have noted previously, the most sophisticated city in America. In many respects it was like Amsterdam in the 17th century. The American Philosophical Society, organized by Benjamin Franklin and others in 1744, the oldest learned and scientific society in America, had as part of its title the phrase "for promoting useful knowledge." In Philadelphia it drew members from more than one level of society, for at that time Philadelphia had among its citizens more inventive, ingenious, ambitious, and learned men engaged in a wide variety of professions and trades than any other city on the American continent. Membership in the American Philosophical Society was a mark of proficiency in some branch of knowledge rather than a social distinction. A prominent member, Dr. John Morgan, founder of the Pennsylvania Medical School in 1765, was the son of a rich Philadelphia merchant and was himself a grandee, at home in the literary and artistic circles of Rome; yet at meetings of the American Philosophical Society in Philadelphia, he was merely one among a group of eager and curious men from all walks of life. It is small wonder that artists, inventors, and craftsmen found the milieu of a city that could support such a society hospitable and stimulating. Philadelphia became famous for the quality of its crafts. Its silversmiths and its furniture-makers, for example, in the last half of the 18th century rivaled the best of London craftsmen.

Other towns where there was wealth developed both sophisticated taste and skillful craftsmen. Boston, too, had its silversmiths; the best-known was Paul Revere, son of a Huguenot craftsman. It also had excellent makers of furniture and master-builders who possessed judgment and a sense of dignity and proportion. Newport in Rhode Island perhaps exceeded Boston in the skill and artistry of its craftsmen, particularly as evidenced by the furniture that came from their shops. And Newport could boast of the handiwork of the man who has been called the first professional architect in America, Peter Harrison.

By the beginning of the last third of the 18th century, all of the colonies had grown in prosperity and all had a stable and conservative wealthy class capable of building fine houses and maintaining themselves in a style that differentiated them from the multitude. This affluence had modified the sterner Puritan point of view that frowned on extravagance and had even affected the religious insistence upon plainness that traditionally characterized the Quakers. Relaxation into luxury, however, had not come without misgivings and doubts in certain quarters. The conditioning of the thrifty Puritan background left its mark on many an apologetic New Englander, who feared extravagance and ostentatious display as he feared the devil, yet found the temptation of material beauty in his surroundings hard to resist. John Adams, for instance, was strongly moved by the sensuousness of art, yet his feeling of guilt was so great that he had an imperative urge to put such things behind him. Visiting Philadelphia in 1774, he attended the Catholic church there but he wrote his wife immediately afterward: "Here is everything that can lay hold of the eye, ear, and imagination, everything which can charm and bewitch the simple and ignorant. I wonder how Luther ever broke the spell." * Many years later Adams, in writing to Jefferson, reminded him that "Every one of the fine arts from the earliest times has been enlisted in the services of superstition and despotism. The whole world at this day gazes with astonishment at the grossest fictions because they have been immortalized by the most exquisite artists." Adams exemplified the Puritan distrust of the senses and an unqualified adherence to the pragmatic and the utilitarian. But perhaps he did not altogether rule out some eventual enjoyment of the fine arts, for he wrote to his wife Abigail from France: "My sons ought to study mathematics and philosophy, geography, natural history, and naval architecture, navigation, commerce, and agriculture, in order to give their children the right to study painting, poetry, music, architecture, statuary, tapestry, and porcelain." The young nation had a long way to go, Adams believed, before it could afford the luxury of an addiction to the fine arts. That time might come in the days of his grandchildren.

When the Revolution and Independence broke our traditional ties with Great Britain, the way was open for a multiplicity of new influences that would affect every aspect of American life. The alliance with France turned attention to that country, and French fashions dominated American upper-class society for a time. In all of the former colonies, a social upheaval had taken place and new men had come, or were about to come, to the fore. The relative homogeneity of the affluent class that had existed just prior to the Revolution was gone. And gone with it was the related homogeneity of taste. From this time forward Americans for better or worse would be more experimental and more open to new ideas and movements in aesthetics. This new spirit would manifest itself at times in movements like the Greek Revival, which left a heritage of magnificent and stately buildings both private and public, or it would reveal a tendency toward the eccentric and the

---

* For suggestions about John Adams' attitude toward the fine arts, I am indebted to Mr. Wendell Garrett for letting me read an unpublished paper of his, "John Adams and the Limited Role of the Fine Arts." I am also indebted to Mr. Wayne Andrews' discussion of Adams' attitude in *Architecture, Ambition and Americans* (New York, 1947). Spelling, punctuation, and capitalization in the quotations from Adams, and from others in this essay, have been modernized.

amorphous. Yet whatever else the new trends indicated, they would show vigor and strength and give promise of a development that one day might bring about the artistic millenium that Timothy Dwight and other patriots saw in their visions.

ARCHITECTURE

by George B. Tatum

I T MAY be taken for granted that American colonists, like any others, were in some degree dependent upon the countries of their origin for a majority of their customs and attitudes, including those connected with the arts. But this is not to say that buildings erected in the New World were simply provincial (and therefore presumably less desirable) versions of more accomplished originals. To some extent most of them were that, of course; but more often than not they were considerably more.

Because climate and natural resources are only two of the many ways in which the Americas differed from Europe, in the process of adapting Old World practices to the environment of their new homes, the colonists not infrequently evolved variants of European styles that have a distinctive local flavor. For if it is true that behind most colonial artifacts there lies a foreign archetype, it is also to be noted that rarely, if ever, can an American building be mistaken for one of its European models. Nor in such a comparison does all the advantage lie with the mother country; what the colonial craftsman may have lacked in sophistication, he not infrequently made up for by the economy of his design, the vitality of his forms, and the effective use of his materials. In this sense, at least, we may fairly speak of an "American" style of architecture.

As for the merit of things American, architectural and otherwise, attitudes and judgments have understandably varied considerably with the individual and the age. Modern admirers of such early Georgian buildings as the College of William and Mary may need to be reminded that no less an architectural critic than Thomas Jefferson once described both the hospital and college at Williamsburg as "rude, misshapen piles which, but that they have roofs, would be taken for brick-kilns." These and similar comments Jefferson included in his *Notes on the State of Virginia*, published as early as 1785; and by the time Mrs. Louisa Caroline Tuthill brought out her

41

History of Architecture at Philadelphia in 1848 this critical view of early American architecture had been extended to include nearly everything produced during the 18th century, not excepting the buildings designed by Jefferson himself. Since Mrs. Tuthill considered even the churches of New England "outrageous deformities to the eye of taste," she was heartened to find that "they were all of such perishable materials, that they [could] not much longer remain to annoy travellers in 'search of the picturesque.'"

Fortunately, history suggests that such harsh views are usually reserved for art produced in the recent past. Predictably enough, even before the end of the 19th century the process of reappraising the colonial period had already begun, and "good taste" required that the mid-Victorians be ridiculed in the same terms they had applied earlier to their Georgian predecessors. Although architectural considerations probably counted for little in the 1856 decision of the Mount Vernon Ladies' Association to undertake the preservation of Washington's home, the centennial of American independence, celebrated at Philadelphia twenty years later, undoubtedly did much to interest Americans in the arts of their colonial past. The result has been the creation in the United States of numerous house-museums, a variety of local and regional preservation societies, and at the highest level the National Trust for Historic Preservation, chartered by Congress in 1949.

Under these conditions it was perhaps inevitable that history should occasionally be confused with art, and patriotism sometimes pass for aesthetic judgment. And not content with trying to arrest the destruction occasioned by time and neglect, there are even those who would turn back the clock. By definition, a building once destroyed cannot, of course, be "restored." The fact that so many are willing to forget or overlook this fact is no doubt a tribute to the taste and skill of numerous architects and historians, but especially to those associated with Colonial Williamsburg, the inspiration, direct or indirect, of most of the projects of this kind.

Of the numerous factors that hamper our efforts to understand the architecture of the past—let alone recreate it—few are more significant than the changes that have taken place in building practices since the Civil War. Trained in a rigorous system of apprenticeship, often under a deed of indenture, the craftsman of an earlier day had far less need for complete working drawings than does his modern counterpart. Nor did our forebears know the clear distinction between designer and builder now required both by law and professional ethics. More often than not, the wages of the master carpenter seem to have included payment for whatever simple working drawings were required. Responsibility for the basic scheme of the building, on the other hand, can often be traced to the owner or some other talented amateur, for in the 18th century some acquaintance with architecture was more likely to be a part of a gentleman's education than it is today. If Peter Harrison is called the "first American architect," it is largely because, unlike the typical carpenter-architect of the time, he designed buildings for others to execute, and unlike earlier amateurs whose names are usually somewhat loosely associated with a single structure, he was clearly responsible for at least five of the most distinguished buildings of the period. But Harrison had been born in York, England, and from first to last seems to have practiced architecture as an avocation, while deriving his income from his mercantile interests at Newport and, later, from his post as Collector of Customs at New Haven. The first native-born and professionally trained American to practice architecture successfully as a vocation is usually considered to have been Robert Mills. He was not born until 1781, six years after Harrison's death, and did not begin his professional career until the first decade of the 19th century.

American architecture in the 17th and 18th centuries is the story of several styles, rather than of one, for the numerous kindreds and tongues that played a part in the settlement of the New World left their mark upon the architecture of the colonies no less than upon political and social institutions.

THE SPANISH AND THE FRENCH

ALTHOUGH the early architecture of Florida differs from that of California or the Southwest, all three styles share a common origin in the artistic traditions current at the court of Spain in the 17th century and dissemination of these traditions by missionary priests of the Catholic Church.

The Arts in America: The Colonial Period

Florida may have received its name from Ponce de León as early as 1513, but few (if any) surviving buildings in this area can be dated prior to the middle of the 17th century. Of these, the most important is the redoubtable Castillo de San Marcos at St. Augustine (*Plate 1*), now in the care of the National Park Service. Not only is this the outstanding structure of its kind in the United States, but its 40-foot moat, portcullis, and massive walls

44   *Plate 1.* CASTILLO DE SAN MARCOS, ST. AUGUSTINE, FLORIDA. 1672–1756. Principal rooms of the castle are grouped around a central court approximately one hundred feet square, and at each corner, bastions shaped like spear points helped the defenders repel the English in 1702, 1728, and 1740. PHOTOGRAPH, *courtesy* NATIONAL PARK SERVICE, UNITED STATES DEPARTMENT OF THE INTERIOR, WASHINGTON, D. C.

of coquina (a form of limestone) bear favorable comparison with European fortresses of the same period. Obviously the Spanish took seriously their efforts to conquer and hold this portion of their American possessions.

More than half a century passed after Coronado's expedition of 1540–1542 before permanent settlements were made in the region now known as New Mexico. At Santa Fe, the adobe Governor's Palace (*Plate 2*) with its open plaza and long covered porch (*portales*) is at once the most impressive civil monument to this period and very probably the oldest surviving structure built in the United States for white men. In common with other early buildings of New Mexico, the Palace derives its distinctive character from the interpretation of Spanish forms in terms of ancient Pueblo techniques, an instance, rare in American art, when an indigenous culture may be said to have modified significantly the imported European tradition.

ate 2. GOVERNOR'S PALACE, SANTA FE, NEW MEXICO. Erected 1609–1614; rebuilt 1680 and frequently reafter. After housing successive Spanish, Mexican, and American governors for nearly three hundred ars, the palace was restored in 1914 as the Museum of New Mexico. PHOTOGRAPH BY WAYNE ANDREWS

The Arts in America: The Colonial Period

Even when it became apparent that the Southwest would not yield gold in quantity, the area was still regarded as fertile ground for the missionary activities of the Franciscan friars. Of the surviving missions in New Mexico, one of the earliest is the starkly beautiful San Estéban (*Plate 3*) at Ácoma, the site selected by Willa Cather as the setting of *Death Comes for the Archbishop*. Perhaps because the structural problems were too difficult or wood for centering too scarce, the arch was rarely, if ever, used by the Indian builders of this area; instead, the roof was spanned, as here, by strong timbers (*vigas*) supported within by brightly painted corbels and projecting on the exterior to form staccato accents on the plain adobe walls. Only

Plate 3. SAN ESTÉBAN, ÁCOMA, NEW MEXICO. Completed before 1644. Like the soil for the gardens, t heavy timbers for the roof of San Estéban had to be transported by Indian labor to the top of this high mes PHOTOGRAPH BY WAYNE ANDREWS

those who have experienced at first hand the climate of the Southwest can fully appreciate the inviting contrasts offered by the dim and cool interiors of the missions. When reflected by the whitened walls, the strong light admitted through even the few small doors and windows is sufficient to bring to life the bold forms and bright colors employed by the native painters. In their hands, Indian mythology was blended with Christian symbolism to form a local style found in the painted reredos above many a mission altar and most exuberantly expressed in the remarkable murals of San José at Laguna (*Plate 4*).

te 4. INTERIOR OF SAN JOSÉ, LAGUNA, NEW MEXICO. 1699–1706. The murals probably postdate the com-
ion of the church by at least a century. Represented along the nave are the Pueblo symbols of sun, rain,
thunder. PHOTOGRAPH BY LAURA GILPIN

Although considerably later than San Estéban, the exterior of the mission church at Ranchos de Taos (*Plate 5*) best represents the simple dignity of this strongly sculpturesque style. Here the massive walls serve as a foil for the greater delicacy and elaboration of the doorway, a Spanish practice more fully realized in the portals provided by the Mexican sculptor Pedro Huizar for several of the missions located in what is now Texas. Details like the baptistery windows (*Plate 6*) or the principal portal of San José y San Miguel de Aguayo are clearly the work of a skilled artist, and trained craftsmen were also responsible for the designs of the four other missions built near San Antonio during this period. As in the case of Huizar,

48   *Plate 5.* MISSION CHURCH, RANCHOS DE TAOS, NEW MEXICO. *Circa* 1780. The structural properties of ad require the use of thick walls and heavy buttressing. Belfries of the missions may take the form of squ towers, as here, or as simple openings in the façade wall of the church, as at Laguna.
PHOTOGRAPH BY WAYNE ANDREWS

most of the artisans associated with the Texas missions were doubtless trained in Mexico, although the ultimate sources of their style were the baroque forms employed abroad in the service of the Counter Reformation and popularly associated with the name of their principal Spanish exponents, the brothers Churriguera.

ate 6.
PTISTERY WINDOW, SAN JOSÉ Y
N MIGUEL DE AGUAYO, SAN
NTONIO, TEXAS. 1768–1781.
dro Huizar, sculptor.
cularized in 1794 along with
e other Texas missions, San
sé was in ruin at the time of
restoration in 1933.
OTOGRAPH BY WAYNE ANDREWS

9

The Arts in America: The Colonial Period

Time and the Indian attacks that have brought to ruin all of Arizona's other missions have left intact the most important colonial example of the Churrigueresque style in North America. This is San Xavier del Bac near Tucson (*Plate 7*), like the others a Franciscan foundation. San Xavier has been called "the most ambitious of all the Spanish colonial churches," and it would be hard to match elsewhere either the opulent façade with its carved and molded portal or the elaborate baroque decorations of the domed interior.

The latest and most abundant architectural evidence of Spanish colonization is to be found in California. There in restored form survive portions of most of the twenty-one missions founded by the Franciscans between 1769 and 1823. Stylistically, the California missions lie somewhere between the

Plate 7. San Xavier del Bac, Tucson, Arizona. 1784–1797. Of burned brick covered with lime stucco, smooth white walls form a sharp contrast to the dark wood of the balconies and mellow red tones of brick portal. PHOTOGRAPH BY WAYNE ANDREWS

simple dignity of the mission church at Ranchos de Taos and the greater sophistication of San José or San Xavier. Adobe remained the cheapest and most available building material, although kiln-burned bricks were also used in quantity and all-stone buildings were not unknown. The latter was the material chosen for San Juan Capistrano (*Plate 8*), severely damaged by the earthquake of 1812 only six years after its consecration. But even in ruin, the classical details, like its full cruciform plan and domed and vaulted nave, mark San Juan as the work of a trained designer and in many ways the most accomplished of the California missions. Following Mexico's declaration of independence in 1821, the care of all the missions (save Santa

8. SAN JUAN CAPISTRANO, CALIFORNIA. 1797–1806. Designed by Isidoro Aguilar. Originally founded 76 as one of the nine missions established by Father Junípero Serra, the first great *padre presidente* of ornia, the magnificent new church at Capistrano was begun in 1797 under Serra's successor, Fermín cisco de Lasuén. Aguilar, the master stonemason, was a native of Culiacán, Mexico. PHOTOGRAPH BY AM H. JACKSON (*circa* 1890), *courtesy* LIBRARY OF STATE HISTORICAL SOCIETY OF COLORADO, DENVER

51

Barbara) was transferred from the Franciscan Order to diocesan priests, and soon thereafter they began to fall into the disrepair from which only restoration in the present century has rescued them.

Little or nothing remains of the four *presidios* that once sheltered the secular government of early California. Presumably their use of redwood supports, adobe walls, tile roofs, and open courtyards differed principally from the mission buildings in the emphasis given to the requirements of defense. Many of these same features also survive in the farmhouses, built for the most part in the 19th century and therefore somewhat loosely referred to as "Spanish colonial." But whatever the date or name, the one-story plan, long veranda, and open patio of the houses of southern California have been much admired in the 20th century and have helped to inspire the "ranch house" of the modern suburb.

Whereas the single-story house was typical in the southern *rancho* or *hacienda*, the two-story town house (*casa de pueblo*) was favored in the northern settlements of California. Outstanding among these is the house built in 1835–1837 for Thomas O. Larkin, American consul at Monterey, but the area is also rich in other notable examples such as Casa Amesti (*Plate 9*). Double verandas similar to those of the Larkin House or Casa Amesti are also characteristic of many of the plantation houses in the Mississippi Valley, a circumstance that has led to the supposition that Spanish influence also persisted in this area. But similarity does not necessarily imply connection; probably this is another example—by no means uncommon in the history of art—of the rise of parallel forms accounted for by corresponding conditions. But whatever the explanation, it is convenient in a brief discussion such as this to include the architecture of the French colonies with that of the Spanish.

Descending the Mississippi in the wake of La Salle's expedition of 1682, the French established a series of trading posts at strategic points between Canada and the Gulf of Mexico. Flood and fire have aided time in the obliteration of most of the colonial buildings in the Mississippi Valley, but the few remaining examples reveal a vigorous and distinctive architectural style that merits consideration. In such early examples as the so-called

Plate 9. CASA AMESTI, MONTEREY, CALIFORNIA. 1824–1834. Now the property of the National Trust for Historic Preservation, this adobe house is an excellent early example of what has come to be known as the "Monterey style." *Courtesy*, NATIONAL TRUST FOR HISTORIC PRESERVATION, WASHINGTON, D. C. PHOTOGRAPH BY BURGESS, 1961

"Courthouse" at Cahokia, Illinois (*Plate 10*), logs, hewn flat on two surfaces, were set upright in the ground (*poteaux-en-terre*) or upon stone foundations (*poteaux-sur-sole*) and the spaces between filled with a variety of materials, including stones, locally burnt brick, or clay mixed with some binding medium such as moss, grass, or hair. But whatever the specific filling, danger of erosion by the weather made it advisable to cover the exterior walls with lime plaster, a type of surfacing that has continued in favor in many parts of the old Louisiana Territory.

Some relief from the heat, as well as easy access to the several rooms, was provided in the French house by the characteristic veranda (*galerie*), which in many cases was carried around all four sides. Chimneys were

54   *Plate 10.* COURTHOUSE, CAHOKIA, ILLINOIS. *Circa 1737.* This oldest of extant French houses in the Un⟨ited⟩ States was turned into a county courthouse and jail in 1793. After being exhibited at the St. Louis Fai⟨r⟩ 1904 and later at Jackson Park, Chicago, it was rebuilt in 1939 on its original foundations. PHOTOGRA⟨PH⟩ *courtesy* HISTORIC AMERICAN BUILDINGS SURVEY AND LIBRARY OF CONGRESS, WASHINGTON, D. C.

sometimes in the center or more frequently at either end, but the double pitch of the roof, occasioned by the *galerie*, seems to have been a nearly universal feature. For later and more pretentious structures, logs might give way to stone, but the *galerie*, as in the case of the plastered walls mentioned earlier, continued in use until modern times. Both features may be found, for example, in the few houses of New Orleans' Vieux Carré that survived the disastrous fires of 1788 and 1794, as well as in the more pretentious plantation houses of Louisiana (*Plate 11*).

ate 11. HOMEPLACE PLANTATION (KELLER MANSION), HAHNVILLE, LOUISIANA. *Circa* 1800. In common th the walls of the first story, the round piers supporting the *galerie* are of brick covered with stucco, a ture, like the unusual square capitals, shared with Parlange, the much earlier plantation house erected New Roads, Louisiana, in 1750. Except for a large dining room, the first floor of Homeplace Plantation occupied by servants' quarters and service rooms. The kitchen was in a separate building some distance m the house. PHOTOGRAPH, *courtesy* HISTORIC AMERICAN BUILDINGS SURVEY AND LIBRARY OF CONGRESS, SHINGTON, D. C.

THE DUTCH AND FLEMISH

LIKE the French, the Dutch were attracted to America primarily by the hope of profits. To exploit the discovery made by Henry Hudson in 1609, the West India Company was founded in 1621, but some years went by before colonists in any numbers began to reach New Netherlands, as the Dutch possessions in North America were called.

The Dutch have always excelled as builders in brick, and that was doubtless the preferred material in the colonies no less than in the mother country. In the beginning a few bricks may have been imported as ballast, but within a short time native kilns were turning out good quality bricks in a number of sizes and colors. By interspersing the long sides (stretchers) of some bricks with the short ends (headers) of others, walls might be laid in one of several bonds, and still different effects were made possible by glazing the headers, by varying the colors of the bricks, or by altering the character of the mortar joints. As befits the most talented craftsmen in brick, the Dutch have given their name to a particularly effective variant of English bond in which a diapered pattern is achieved in the manner indicated by the accompanying diagram. Old views of New Amsterdam show numerous brick structures lining the streets in neat rows, two-and-one-half to three

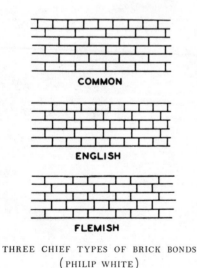

COMMON

ENGLISH

FLEMISH

THREE CHIEF TYPES OF BRICK BONDS
(PHILIP WHITE)

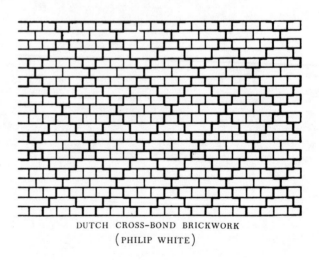

DUTCH CROSS-BOND BRICKWORK
(PHILIP WHITE)

From Hugh Morrison, *Early American Architecture*, New York, 1952.
PHOTOGRAPH, *courtesy* NEW YORK PUBLIC LIBRARY

stories high (*Plate 12*). Especially reminiscent of the medieval architecture of the Low Countries are the crow-stepped gables, a shape perhaps inherent in the brick medium and no doubt of considerable advantage to the chimney sweep who had to climb the steep tile-covered roofs. A similar pattern was

ate 12.
RTION OF VIEW OF
W YORK FROM BROOKLYN
IGHTS. 1716–1718. Drawn by
lliam Burgis (fl. 1716–1731).
obably engraved in London;
ued 1719–1721. In the western
tor can be seen the type of
dieval Dutch house with
pped-gable ends. North of Wall
eet the houses are more English
character, with only here and
re an older Dutch example. At
s period New York was the third
gest city in the colonies.
urtesy, THE NEW-YORK HISTORICAL
CIETY, NEW YORK CITY

followed for Dutch houses in the country, save that the entrance was usually on the side, rather than in the gable end, and the gables themselves were regularly straight, instead of being stepped (*Plate 13*).

Plate 13. DE BRIES HOUSE, EAST GREENBUSH, N. Y. *Circa 1722*. Already a ruin when this picture was tak about 1940, the house that Hendrick de Bries built on the River Road about three miles south of Renssel is an earlier representative of a type of Dutch country dwelling of which the Leendert Bronck House at W Coxsackie, New York (*circa* 1738) is probably the best-known example. Characteristic features include steep roof, iron beam-anchors, "elbows" at the lower corners of the gable ends, and bricks set at ri angles to the sloping sides of the gable. Probably of Flemish origin, this latter feature provided a slopi surface more weather tight than a stepped gable, while at the same time imposing on the bricks along edge a serrated pattern known as "mouse-tooth" (*muisetanden* in Dutch). PHOTOGRAPH BY CORTLANDT V. HUBBARD, PHILADELPHIA

Contrasting sharply with the brick structures of New Amsterdam are the stone or wood-sheathed houses of Long Island, southern New York, and northern New Jersey. These were partly the work of Flemish settlers who continued to favor the distinctive flaring eaves that in the coastal regions of their native land had helped to protect soft clay walls from the destructive effects of the weather. In the 18th century this attractive form was often combined with a double-pitched roof, broken near the ridgepole to produce the "Dutch gambrel," a feature that in company with fieldstone walls has provided—albeit somewhat incorrectly—the modern concept of "Dutch colonial" (*Plate 14*).

te 14. MORRIS GRAHAM HOUSE, PINE PLAINS, NEW YORK. 1772. The comparatively late date for this house
ns reflected in the width of the flaring eaves that now project sufficiently to provide a shallow porch.
sibly of Flemish origin, the "Dutch" gambrel roof is distinguished, as here, by a break nearer the ridge
n in either the "New England" or "Swedish" forms. Several good examples of this type of house still
vive in such communities of New Jersey as Tenafly and Hackensack. PHOTOGRAPH BY CORTLANDT V. D.
BARD, PHILADELPHIA

THE SWEDES AND GERMANS

WHILE the Dutch and Flemish were settling the territory to the north, Swedes and Germans were immigrating in considerable numbers into Pennsylvania, western New Jersey, and northern Maryland. "New Sweden" was chartered in 1638, but we have no certain examples of the "true" log cabin made of round logs with notched and protruding ends that the Swedes are known from literary records to have used at an early date. Several of the more finished type of hewn-log houses are believed to survive from the 17th century, however, and variations of this, as well as of the cruder form, were certainly employed by later German settlers until well into the 18th century (*Plate 15*). It is less certain whether in their use of the log house the Germans were influenced by their Swedish neighbors or were merely continuing a practice derived from their own European homeland.

English sovereignty did not mean an end of German immigration. Encouraged by William Penn and his successors, colonists by the thousands poured into Pennsylvania from the Rhine valley, and today throughout much of Lancaster, Berks, Bucks, Montgomery, and Lehigh Counties, their descendants tend rich farms dominated by capacious stone and timber barns decorated with the "hex" signs associated with the "Pennsylvania Dutch."

Plate 15.
BERTOLET-HERBEIN CABIN, BERKS COUNTY, PENNSYLVANIA. Built between 1737–1745. An entrance on both back and front leads into the large kitchen that extends across one end of the cabin. From this a steep stairway in an outside corner gives access to the attic. The remainder of the first floor is divided laterally into two rooms, the front one of which served as a parlor. Once numerous in Pennsylvania, log houses of this type are now rare. *Courtesy,* HISTORIC AMERICAN BUILDINGS SURVEY AND LIBRARY OF CONGRESS, WASHINGTON, D. C.

The generous proportions that distinguish so much of colonial German architecture received their most impressive American expression in the buildings of the monastic community erected between 1740 and 1750 at Ephrata, Pennsylvania, by the Society of the Solitary, a religious sect founded by the German mystic Johann Konrad Beissel. Now carefully restored and open to the public under state auspices, structures like the *Saal* (community house) or *Saron* (sisters' house) are eloquent witnesses to the ascetic views of their builders, as well as to the medieval architectural practices still current in the rural sections of Central Europe from which they came (*Plate 16*). Scarcely less characteristic are the smaller and somewhat later stone buildings erected at Bethlehem and Nazareth by the *Unitas Fratrum* (commonly called Moravians), a religious group whose members, largely from Bohemia and Moravia, sought asylum in Pennsylvania under the leadership of Count Zinzendorf. At Bethlehem, as at Ephrata, many of the structures give evidence of their Germanic origins by their steep roofs pierced with small dormers, often in several rows.

But important and persistent as were the national traditions of several of the colonies, the architectural future of the North American continent, like its political destiny, lay very largely with the English.

ate 16. THE "SARON" OR SISTERS' HOUSE, EPHRATA, PENNSYLVANIA. 1743. As in the case of this one, most the Society's buildings had walls made of oak logs chinked with clay and faced with poplar clapboards on outside and plaster on the interior. In use until about 1925, the Cloister is now the property of the State of nnsylvania which since 1941 has been occupied with its careful restoration and preservation. PHOTOGRAPH WAYNE ANDREWS

THE LATE MEDIEVAL TRADITION IN THE ENGLISH COLONIES

ONLY in totally reconstructed form, as at Plymouth or Salem, Massachusetts, it is now possible to see the shelters hastily built of easily worked materials by the earliest arrivals in New England. As time and resources permitted, these first crude structures were gradually supplanted by more permanent dwellings constructed in accordance with the medieval practices then still followed in many parts of England, especially the rural areas from which a majority of the colonists had come. Among the several score of surviving New England houses that may fairly be considered to date from the 17th century, that begun by Jonathan Fairbanks in 1636 at Dedham, Massachusetts, appears to be the earliest. Subsequent additions and modifications have considerably altered the original appearance of the Fairbanks House, however, and a better impression of the medieval architecture of New England may be gained from a group of early houses that have been carefully restored in recent years. In Massachusetts alone, a partial list of the most prominent of these would include: the Whipple House at Ipswich (1640), the "Scotch"-Boardman House at Saugus (*circa* 1650), the Turner House ("Seven Gables") at Salem (1668), the Parson Capen House at Topsfield (1683), and the John Ward House (1684), now on the grounds of the Essex Institute at Salem. Second only to Massachusetts is Connecticut, with such notable examples as the Hyland House (1660) at Guilford, the Buttolph-Williams House (*circa* 1690) at Wethersfield, Leffingwell Inn (*circa* 1675) at Norwich, the Swain-Harrison House (*circa* 1680) at Branford, and especially the Stanley-Whitman House at Farmington. Although not so well known as some of those in Massachusetts, the last named of these (*Plate 17*) is perhaps as typical of its time and place as any that could be found. Elsewhere in New England early houses are much more scarce. The oldest house in Portsmouth, and one of the few in New Hampshire that date from the 17th century, is that begun about 1664 by Richard Jackson, a prosperous shipbuilder; and Rhode Island has the Eleazer Arnold House (*circa* 1687) at Lincoln and the Clemence-Irons House (*circa* 1680) at Johnston. A number of the finest New England houses, including the three examples last named, are now owned by the Society for the Preservation of New England Antiquities.

Plate 17. STANLEY-WHITMAN HOUSE, FARMINGTON, CONNECTICUT. *Circa* 1660. Usually considered one of the earliest and best preserved of the "framed overhang" type of Connecticut dwelling, the Stanley-Whitman House was restored by J. Frederick Kelley in 1935 and is now open to the public as the Farmington Museum. The lean-to at the rear is thought to have been added about 1760. PHOTOGRAPH, *courtesy* OF THE FARMINGTON MUSEUM

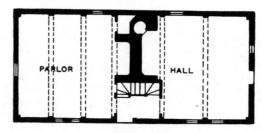

PLAN OF THE PARSON CAPEN HOUSE (PHILIP WHITE, AFTER MILLAR)
From Hugh Morrison, *Early American Architecture*, New York, 1952.
PHOTOGRAPH, *courtesy* NEW YORK PUBLIC LIBRARY

The plan of the Parson Capen House illustrated in the accompanying diagram is also characteristic of New England at this period. In a dwelling of this size the second floor would usually contain two bedrooms for which access was provided by a narrow winding stair backed against the massive chimney and rising from a central vestibule (porch) into which opened the front door. On the right the porch led into the "hall" or general living-room (*Plate 18*). Here was done the spinning, weaving, and candle making; and here the family partook of the meals cooked in the large open fireplace or baked in the adjacent oven. In larger (and often somewhat later) houses there might be a lean-to at the rear where the cooking and many of the other household chores would be done, but even in this case the hall retained much of its earlier medieval function as the center of family life. When the lean-to was part of the original plan, the slope of the rear roof might more readily be continuous, thereby suggesting the profile of the wooden boxes commonly used for salt. From this fact comes the term "saltbox" frequently used to describe houses of this type. On the other side of the porch, opposite the hall, was the parlor, a room reserved for entertaining distinguished callers and for such other solemn and formal occasions as funerals and weddings. Heated by still another fireplace in the capacious chimney and in keeping with its restricted use, the parlor contained the owner's most dignified furnishings, especially any imported from Europe. There would almost certainly be an armchair or two, possibly a gate-leg table, and perhaps a chest of drawers. Here, too, might be found the best bed, for more often than not the parlor doubled as a guest room when important visitors had to be accommodated overnight.

Clearly visible in any room of the New England houses is the sturdy oak frame of hand-hewn timbers that forms the basis of its structural system.

In the center of the hall, for example, the great summer beam supports the joists on which rests the floor above, while in the corners may be seen posts flared at the top to receive the main horizontal timbers (girts) of the second story. Double floors, sometimes with a layer of sand between, offered a measure of insulation from the damp cold of the unfloored and unheated cellar, the usual storage place for vegetables and other foodstuffs. At about

late 18. Hall, From Seth Story House, Essex, Massachusetts. *Circa* 1684. Now installed in the Henry Francis du Pont Winterthur Museum, the large cooking fireplace, plaster walls, and exposed oak frame (himney post, chimney girt, summer beam, and joists) are typical of the period. In addition to the stretcher-sed table and pine bench in the foreground, the room is handsomely furnished with such other characteristic ems as the painted chest of drawers from Connecticut and the "Carver" armchair beside the fireplace. HOTOGRAPH, *courtesy* HENRY FRANCIS DU PONT WINTERTHUR MUSEUM, WINTERTHUR, DEL.

two-foot intervals between the main vertical timbers the builders regularly placed a series of smaller studs, and the spaces between these might be filled with such materials as unburnt brick, clay and straw, or wattle and daub. But whatever the material used for filling, it was usually soft enough to require protection on the interior by plaster or wainscot and on the exterior by horizontal clapboards. The latter was a form of surfacing occasionally found in England but regularly employed in the American colonies.

As yet no one has offered a satisfactory explanation for the original purpose of the projecting second and third stories that contribute so much to the distinctive character of the early houses of New England. When applied to forts and blockhouses, such a feature no doubt afforded some advantages to the defenders, but this can hardly explain the use of the overhang for domestic architecture, especially in the case of the English houses upon which the American variations were patterned. In the 17th century most of the windows seem to have been stationary; those that were movable conformed to the casement type, hinged on one side and glazed with small panes, usually of diamond shape and held together by lead strips. Long subject to a heavy tax, glass used in the American colonies continued to be imported from Europe until well after the Revolution. And since dormers were rare prior to the 18th century, the rooms in the ample garret were lit by windows in the gable ends of the house, under the steeply pitched roof. This latter feature should probably be regarded as a survival from a time when thatch was the customary roofing material, though in the period here under discussion hand-riven shingles were as widely used in New England as were tiles in the colonies settled by the Dutch. As kilns were built and lime mortar became available, most of the great stone chimneys that had supplanted the earlier ones of wood or clay were finished off above the roof line with burnt brick. In this case the chimney tops were usually given a rectangular shape and capped with one or two overhanging courses. Sometimes several pilasters were also added to each side, thereby retaining something of the "clustered" effect frequently associated with medieval practice.

Early methods of architectural framing, so far as the American colonies are concerned, may be studied in their most spectacular form in the roof timbers of the Old Ship Meeting House at Hingham, Massachusetts (*Plate 19*). Here are clearly visible the marks of the broadaxe and adze with which the massive oak beams were hewn by hand on the site, a custom that continued long after the erection of sawmills, doubtless because of the difficulty of transporting timbers of this size. Hand-cut nails secured siding and shingles, but the principal joints of the oak frame were either dovetailed or cut with flange and socket (mortise-and-tenon) held fast by wooden pins (treenails). With its curved struts, tie beams, king posts, and braces, the interior of the Old Ship Meeting House recalls the great halls of medieval Europe, but the severity of its appointments and the simplicity of its exterior design (*Plate 20*) suggest that its dissenting builders took as their models the plain style of Protestant Holland, rather than the more elaborate Gothic forms favored by the Established Church in England.

It is known that a number of New England towns once had similar meetinghouses, but today only that at Hingham survives from the 17th century. And so it is with most other buildings of a public or institutional character in this area. Boston's first town hall (1657) burned in 1711; and the early buildings of Harvard College (*e.g.*, Old College, 1638–1642; "Indian College," 1654; Harvard Hall, 1677; Stoughton, 1699) disappeared long ago.

Although stone was almost too plentiful in New England and brick was manufactured locally at an early date, probably unfamiliarity with the medium and lack of a good adhesive prevented most of the settlers in this region from using either of these materials on a large scale. Wood had been customarily employed for houses in the countries from which a majority of the first New England colonists had come, and without a good supply of lime a durable mortar is impossible. Neither of these conditions was present to the same degree in the South. There the immigrants had been drawn from a variety of English counties, and a lime that was adequate, if not always of the best quality, could readily be obtained by burning oyster shells. This helps to explain why brick is characteristic of the only structures in Virginia that survive from the 17th century, though the use of half-timber construction is known to have been common in that area.

68   *Plate 19.* Roof of The Old Ship Meeting House, Hingham, Massachusetts. 1681. The church at Hingham is presumed to take its name from the resemblance of the framing of the roof to the inverted hull of a ship. Backless wooden benches served until 1755 when the first box pews were installed. The side galleries were added in 1730 and 1775. PHOTOGRAPH BY DOROTHY ABBE

Plate 20. OLD SHIP MEETING HOUSE, HINGHAM, MASSACHUSETTS. 1681. Now considered the oldest church in continuous existence in the United States, this simple frame structure was also used for town meetings until 1780. Congregational in policy, the only denominational affiliation the Old Ship Church has ever known is Unitarian. The present restoration dates from 1930. PHOTOGRAPH BY DOROTHY ABBE

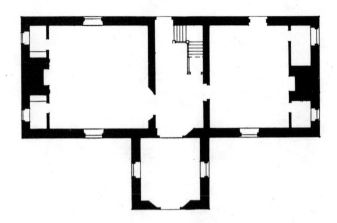

From Thomas T. Waterman, *The Dwellings of Colonial America*, Chapel Hill, 1950.
PHOTOGRAPH, *courtesy* THE UNIVERSITY OF NORTH CAROLINA PRESS

The accompanying plan of the house built in New Kent County, Virginia, for Colonel Joseph Foster about 1690 resembles that of the Parson Capen House in having the first floor occupied by two principal rooms, the hall and parlor. But whereas the northern builder had favored a central chimney for greater warmth, the southern house frequently had its chimneys at either end, thereby making possible better ventilation through a central passageway. At Foster's Castle the principal entrance was through a projecting but enclosed porch, and in more pretentious houses this might be balanced on the other side by a tower containing a stairway. Of the seven examples of the cross-house in Virginia mentioned by Forman, the earliest and most important is that built in Surry County about 1655 by Arthur Allen but known as "Bacon's Castle" from its use in 1676 by the followers of Nathaniel Bacon in their rebellion against Governor Berkeley (*Plate 21*). Among the unusual features of Bacon's Castle are the curving "Flemish" gables and the boldly clustered chimneys with their diamond-shaped stacks, forms found frequently on the late medieval buildings of England but never very common in the colonies.

Virginians also employed the cross-plan when they built their fourth State House at Jamestown in 1685. This structure burned in 1698 and today no civic structures contemporary with Bacon's Castle are extant in the South. At least one church deserves mention, however—the Newport Parish

Plate 21. Bacon's Castle, Surry County, Virginia. *Circa* 1655. The present sash-hung windows are later additions; originally there must have been leaded casements with mullions and transoms, patterned on English models. The enclosed porch and stair tower are also features of the medieval architecture of England.
PHOTOGRAPH BY WAYNE ANDREWS

71

Church (*Plate 22*) at Smithfield, Virginia, begun perhaps as early as 1632. Despite the loss of the original interior, the single west tower and stepped wall-buttresses of the church at Smithfield are sufficient to recall numerous late medieval counterparts among the rural parishes of England. Only by such an occasional ingenuous detail as the brick tracery of the windows do Virginia builders betray their provincial status.

Plate 22. NEWPORT PARISH CHURCH (ST. LUKE'S), ISLE OF WIGHT COUNTY, SMITHFIELD, VIRGINIA. 1632. T crude pediment above the door recalls a similar feature once a part of Bacon's Castle and other details a sufficiently close to those of the ruined brick church at Jamestown (completed 1647) to suggest some conne tion between the two buildings. Research carried out when the church was restored in the 1950's tended confirm the traditional date of 1632 (James Grote Van Derpool in the *Journal of the Society of Architectu Historians*, March, 1958). PHOTOGRAPH, *courtesy* HISTORIC AMERICAN BUILDINGS SURVEY AND LIBRARY CONGRESS, WASHINGTON, D. C.

The date late in the 17th century once generally ascribed to the church at Smithfield seemed to find some confirmation in the stone accents at the corners (quoins) and in the triangular pediment over the doorway of the tower, both features that belong to the architectural vocabulary of the Renaissance, rather than to the idiom of the Middle Ages. Similar classical forms also characterized many of the buildings erected in the middle colonies following the granting of Pennsylvania to William Penn by Charles II in 1681. This was especially true of Philadelphia. In rural areas, houses like that built about 1704 for the prosperous Quaker, William Brinton, clung to earlier practice in their use of steep roofs, casement windows, and asymmetrical plans (*Plate 23*). In fact, some of these features

Plate 23. Brinton House, Dilworthtown, Birmingham Township, Delaware County, Pennsylvania. 1704. Representative of the larger type of dwelling built by prosperous English Quakers, the Brinton House is constructed of stone quarried nearby and laid in courses of random width. Originally the kitchen was in the basement. Restored in 1956 by G. Edwin Brumbaugh, this important early Pennsylvania house is the property of the Chester County Historical Society. *Courtesy,* Historic American Buildings Survey and Library of Congress, Washington, D. C. Photograph by Ned and Lila Goode

survived in modified form throughout the next century in the much-admired Pennsylvania stone farmhouses (*Plate 24*). Even when classical canons of taste were clearly in the ascendancy, the pent roofs that characteristically run across gable ends or between stories of Pennsylvania houses are frequently regarded as a survival from an earlier (*i.e.*, medieval) time when half-timber construction required protection from the weather.

Plate 24. COLLINS HOUSE, WEST GOSHEN TOWNSHIP, CHESTER COUNTY, PENNSYLVANIA. Begun 1727. Between 1758 and 1760 the kitchen wing was added, and from this period date the sash-hung windows and the wooden trim on the front of the house. The first floor of the original house had contained only one room in which was a cooking fireplace and in the northwest corner a stair leading to the second floor. There a small hall opened into two rooms partitioned off with upright poplar boards. Today the Collins House is owned by the Chester County Historical Society. PHOTOGRAPH BY NED AND LILA GOODE

74

THE EARLY GEORGIAN (RENAISSANCE) STYLE (*circa* 1700–*circa* 1750)

POSSIBLY because of the break with Rome under Henry VIII (d. 1547), the revival of interest in Roman architecture that began in Italy in the 15th century reached the British Isles only slowly and at second hand, usually by way of the Low Countries where it was never universally admired or completely understood. Not until the time of Inigo Jones (1573–1652) did English architects supplant the somewhat whimsical treatment of classical motifs prevalent during the reigns of Elizabeth (d. 1603) and James I (d. 1625) by a more faithful adherence to the principles of their Italian predecessors, most notably Andrea Palladio (1518–1580). Indeed, so admired were Palladio's buildings (*Plate 25*) and so much read and copied his *I quattro libri dell' architettura* (first published 1570) that the term "Palladian" is almost synonymous with the Renaissance architecture of England. This is not to suggest that other and later Italian architects were without influence. Presumably, reaction to the austerity imposed by the Puritan Revolution (1642–1649) and the Interregnum (1649–1660) helps

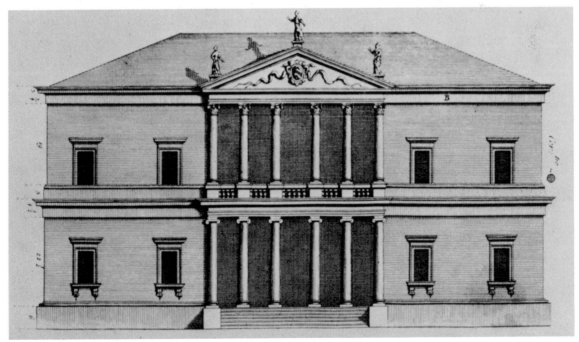

75

Plate 25. DESIGN FOR A HOUSE WITH A DOUBLE PORTICO. From *The Architecture of A. Palladio in Four Books . . .* by Giacomo Leoni, 2 vols., 3d ed., London 1742, Vol. I, Book Two, Plate LVIII. Although the interest of Englishmen in the Italian Renaissance was at least as old as John Shute and the middle of the 16th century, the first English edition of Palladio's work was brought out in 1715 under the supervision of the Venetian architect, Giacomo Leoni (*circa* 1686–1746). *Courtesy,* NEW YORK PUBLIC LIBRARY

to account for the increased favor with which the Stuart Restoration viewed Italian baroque architecture of the 17th century. Though lacking the exuberance of their Italian models, English architects like Sir Christopher Wren (1632–1723) and Sir John Vanbrugh (1664–1726) produced as dramatic designs as the Anglo-Saxon temperament was prepared to accept. Vanbrugh's Blenheim Palace (begun 1705) for the first Duke of Marlborough is one of the few English buildings to which the term "baroque" may be applied without serious qualification, while Wren is best remembered for the more than fifty churches he designed for London following the Great Fire of 1666.

It was, of course, this new Renaissance London of Wren and his followers that the founders of Philadelphia had in mind when they made clear their preference for houses built of brick. In favor of this material was its resistance to fire and decay as well as its widespread use in the Low Countries where many of the Royalists had lived during the Commonwealth and Protectorate. These cultural ties with Protestant and democratic Holland were strengthened still further in 1689 when William, Prince of Orange, became William III of England. In the light of these circumstances some historians have adopted the term "Anglo-Dutch" in speaking of the architecture of this period, while others would identify with the reign of Queen Anne (1702–1714) the simple but symmetrical brick structures relieved by light trim that are characteristic of the first phase of Renaissance classicism in America. But artistic taste is not readily circumscribed by the lives of monarchs, and many of the finest examples of this style fall well into the reigns of Anne's successors. Not until 1719 did William Trent build his fine house in the present city of Trenton, New Jersey. "Stenton" (*Plate 26*), the Germantown residence of James Logan, secretary to William Penn, was begun in 1728; and in Williamsburg, Virginia, it must have been about 1750 before Richard Taliaferro designed the house (*Plate 27*) that still faces the Palace Green. Perhaps we can do no better than retain the more common designation of "Georgian" to identify this whole phase of the Renaissance in the colonies, provided it is remembered that the English interest in Roman classicism—and particularly its genesis—embraced a

ate 26. "Stenton," Philadelphia (Germantown), Pennsylvania. 1728–1734. The sides and rear of
*…*nton lack the symmetry of the façade, a feature not uncommon in Renaissance architecture and one prob-
*…*y reinforced in the colonies by the use of books in which only the front elevations of buildings were
*…*strated. James Logan's fine house is today maintained by the National Society of the Colonial Dames of
*…*erica in the Commonwealth of Pennsylvania. PHOTOGRAPH BY WAYNE ANDREWS

period of considerably greater extent than that represented by the reigns of the first three Georges (1714–1820).

But by whatever name it is called, the characteristics of the colonial style of the first half of the 18th century seem clear enough. As in the examples noted, medieval verticality is modified by a classical emphasis on the horizontal: roofs are lower; a belt course marks the position of the second floor; and a watertable, often of molded brick, caps the basement. In permitting this last feature to project above ground level, Renaissance architects sought not only to insure dryness of the principal rooms but also to enhance their dignity by providing a kind of pedestal upon which they appear to rest. Perhaps nothing divides the classical from the medieval more sharply than this insistence on formal elegance, often at the expense of convenience and utility. In simpler structures like the Wythe House (*Plate 27*) this effect was achieved by little more than a spacing of door and

Plate 27. WYTHE HOUSE, WILLIAMSBURG, VIRGINIA. *Circa* 1750. Presumably designed by Richard Taliaferro (1705–1779), the first owner, the house takes its name from George Wythe (1726–1806), professor of law at the College of William and Mary and husband of Taliaferro's daughter, Elizabeth. Here Jefferson was a frequent visitor, and before the siege of Yorktown the Wythes put their house at the disposal of General Washington. Usually considered the finest colonial dwelling in Williamsburg, the Wythe House was restored in 1939–1940. PHOTOGRAPH BY WAYNE ANDREWS

windows so rigidly symmetrical as to give little indication on the exterior of the size or arrangement of the rooms within. The usual doorway of the period is essentially plain except for the glazed transom, and on the exterior, at least, the classical vocabulary of decorative forms is apt to be limited to an occasional wooden cornice adorned with Roman modillions (brackets). Sash windows regularly take the place of medieval casements, and dormers now become fairly common. With its four rooms and central stair hall (constituting the "double pile" of old accounts) the plan of the Wythe House, illustrated here, may also be considered a logical development from those of the 17th century and typical of its time.

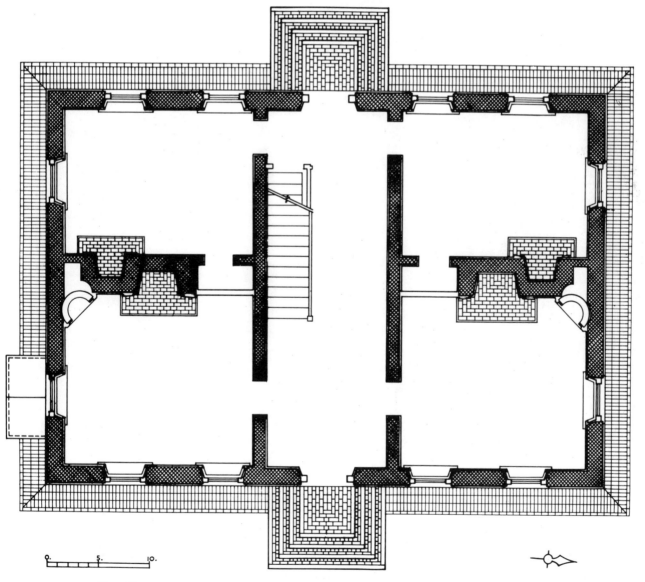

From Marcus Whiffen, *The Eighteenth-Century Houses of Willamsburg*, Williamsburg, 1960. PHOTOGRAPH, *courtesy* COLONIAL WILLIAMSBURG, WILLIAMSBURG, VA.

Although these features of the Early Georgian style are most readily illustrated by the simpler dwellings of the period, they are no less characteristic of the greatest mansions in Virginia. As evidence of this we have the Governor's Palace at Williamsburg (*Plate 28*), begun as early as 1706, as

Plate 28. Governor's Palace, Williamsburg, Virginia. Begun 1706; Henry Cary, "Overseer." After undergoing a variety of alterations and additions, the Palace burned December 23, 1781, while serving as a military hospital during the Revolution. Restored in 1932–1933 by Perry, Shaw & Hepburn, the design of the present building is based principally on three sources: the old foundations as excavated in 1930, a plan drawn by Thomas Jefferson, and an engraving made *circa* 1737 (the so-called "Bodleian Plate"). PHOTOGRAPH BY WAYNE ANDREWS

well as the somewhat later but even more monumental "Stratford" (*Plate 29*), the mansion near Montross built for Thomas Lee (1690–1750) about 1725 to 1730. Austere even in a period when severity of architectural design was the rule, with its Great Hall over 28 feet square and its main story raised nearly 10 feet above ground, "Stratford" would have been impressive at any period; in colonial America it seems to have been unique.

Plate 29. "STRATFORD," WESTMORELAND COUNTY, VIRGINIA. *Circa* 1725–1730. There was English precedent for the H-plan of Stratford, and in Virginia it was forecast to some extent by the Capitol at Williamsburg. But it is the baroque manner of such English architects as Sir John Vanbrugh or Nicholas Hawksmoor that seems echoed most clearly in details like the arched-and-clustered chimneys, as well as in the unusual monumentality of the whole. Restored and cared for by the Robert E. Lee Memorial Foundation, Stratford is open to the public. PHOTOGRAPH BY WAYNE ANDREWS

OLD STATE HOUSE, CONGRESS HALL and TOWN HALL.
Chesnut Street PHILADELPHIA.

Plate 30. STATE HOUSE (INDEPENDENCE HALL), PHILADELPHIA, PENNSYLVANIA. *Circa* 1730–1748; Supreme Court (City Hall) building on far left, 1790–1791; Congress Hall (County Courthouse) on right, 1787–1789. Engraving *circa* 1803 by William Birch (1755–1834) from *The City of Philadelphia in the State of Pennsylvania North America: as it appeared in the Year 1800,* 2d ed., 1804. In this view the State House is shown without Edmund Woolley's tower which had been removed in 1781 because of rotting timbers. When William Strickland designed the present tower in 1828 he included a clock, a feature hitherto located at either end of the main building, as shown here. Old prints such as this provided much of the evidence for the modern restoration of the north doorway and the arcades and dependencies at either end of the central structure, all of which had been considerably altered in the 19th century. Engraving by William Birch, *courtesy* HISTORICAL SOCIETY OF PENNSYLVANIA, PHILADELPHIA

As befits their function, public buildings of the Early Georgian period were frequently more elaborate than their domestic counterparts. Later alterations of Boston's Second Town House (1712) and Faneuil Hall (1740–1742) have obscured their original design, but better evidence is afforded by the State House in Philadelphia (*Plate 30*). In fact, the decorative use of stone for quoins, belt courses, keystones, and panels beneath the windows marks the last of these as one of the most ambitious civic structures of its day. Principal rivals for this distinction would appear to be the earlier (and now totally reconstructed) Capitol at Williamsburg (*Plate 31*) and the contemporary Colony House (*Plate 32*) that Richard

Plate 31. CAPITOL FROM THE SOUTHWEST, WILLIAMSBURG, VIRGINIA. 1701–1705; burned 1747; rebuilt 1751–1753; east wing demolished 1793; west wing burned 1832. As in the case of the Governor's Palace (*Plate 28*), the original foundations and the Bodleian engraving provided the principal evidence for the rebuilding of the Capitol in 1928–1934. Whiffen suggests that such features as the arcades ("piazzas") and apsidal terminations of the wings probably had considerable influence on later civic structures. Henry Cary was the "Overseer." PHOTOGRAPH BY WAYNE ANDREWS

Munday (d. 1740) designed for Newport, Rhode Island, and not even these include the full five-part plan (center section with flanking dependencies) recommended by Palladio and achieved by the Pennsylvania builders. After being subjected to a variety of reconstructions and refurbishings over many years, Independence Hall (as the State House is known) is now being restored by the National Park Service to something approaching its colonial appearance.

Plate 32. Colony House, Newport, Rhode Island. 1739. Richard Munday, builder. Unusual for New the bricks of the Colony House must have been imported, perhaps from Boston or possibly as ballast Bristol. The houses with which Munday's name has been associated are gone, but Trinity Church (1 1726; enlarged *circa* 1762) still stands as a tribute to his taste and builder's skill.
PHOTOGRAPH BY WAYNE ANDREWS

Beginning with Gloria Dei Church or "Old Swedes'" (*Plate 33*), the Georgian form of the ecclesiastical buildings of Philadelphia also developed unevenly but surely in the direction of greater elaboration. For their meet-

Plate 33. GLORIA DEI CHURCH (OLD SWEDES'), PHILADELPHIA, PENNSYLVANIA. 1698–1700. Workmen from Holy Trinity, Wilmington, Delaware (1698–1699), are said to have assisted with the building of Gloria Dei. The simple lines and steep roof of this earliest of Philadelphia's extant churches are characteristic of the period and possibly of the Scandinavian origin of its builders. Several later additions are indicated by the greater elaboration of the south doorway as well as by variations in the character of the brickwork. PHOTOGRAPH, *courtesy* HISTORIC AMERICAN BUILDINGS SURVEY AND LIBRARY OF CONGRESS, WASHINGTON, D. C.

inghouses the Quakers would continue to prefer a plain style (*Plate 34*), but by 1727 the Anglicans had begun the construction of what must be considered the most sumptuous colonial church of the period. Like its contemporaries in Boston (Old North, begun 1723, and Old South, 1729–1730), Christ Church in Philadelphia (*Plate 35*) is a free adaptation of the peculiarly English mingling of baroque and Palladian motifs made popular by the London churches of Sir Christopher Wren. St. James Piccadilly is most frequently mentioned in connection with Old North, and St. Andrew-by-the-Wardrobe seems closest to Christ Church, but at best the similarity is only a general one. Nor is this to suggest that Wren's followers in the colonies were necessarily acquainted with his work at first hand. More

86   *Plate 34.* Exeter Friends' Meeting House, near Stonersville, Berks County, Pennsylvania. 1758. This well-preserved example of a rural Quaker meeting house is the third to serve the area, the first having been a log structure erected in 1726. The interior is finished with carefully made but unpainted woodwork, and sliding panels permit the space to be divided into two rooms. The exterior porch on the east end was added in the 19th century. *Courtesy,* Historic American Buildings Survey and Library of Congress, Washington, D. C. Photograph by Cervin Robinson

Plate 35. Christ Church, Philadelphia, Pennsylvania. 1727–1744; steeple 1754. When first erected, its 196 feet must have made the tower of Christ Church one of the tallest structures in the colonies. Although the urns that decorate the balustrade at the eaves are now cast-iron, they faithfully reproduce the wooden originals ordered from London about 1735. Here worshipped on occasion such notables as Washington and Franklin, and in the burial ground are the graves of seven signers of the Declaration of Independence. PHOTOGRAPH BY CORTLANDT V. D. HUBBARD, PHILADELPHIA

87

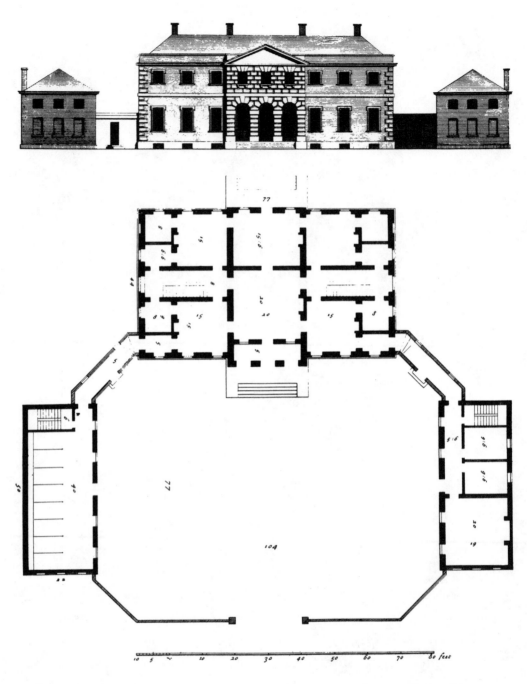

Jacobo Gibbs Architecto   *H. Hulfbergh Sculp:*

Plate 36. Design for a Gentleman's House in Dorsetshire. James Gibbs, *A Book of Architecture*, 2d ed. London, 1739, Plate 58. Containing most of the author's commissions to date and intended from the first as an aid to those desiring architectural advice, the *Book of Architecture* was probably the most popular pattern book of its day. Its handsome but somewhat conservative designs were widely used, not only in the rural sections of England, but also throughout the West Indies and the American colonies as well. *Courtesy*, NEW YORK PUBLIC LIBRARY

frequently, English designs made their way to America by way of such popular builders' guides as the influential *Book of Architecture* (*Plate 36*), first published in 1728 by James Gibbs (1682–1754), a talented admirer of Wren, and one who had himself studied in Italy under Carlo Fontana.

In colonial America, however, few could qualify as practicing architects. The task of selecting English models and adapting them to local use thus fell most frequently to some informed amateur, while the day-to-day supervision of construction and the development of suitable architectural details were left to a master carpenter trained in the apprenticeship system. William Price, a Boston print seller, is usually credited with the design of Old North. In Philadelphia, the names of two professional men are closely associated with the most important structures of the day: Dr. John Kearsley, a physician, served as "supervisor" for the building of Christ Church; and Andrew Hamilton, a lawyer, is said to have developed a design for the State House. Nor do these conditions seem to have differed much in the South. There no less a person than Governor Alexander Spotswood drew the plans for a new church at Williamsburg (*Plate 37*). Despite the somewhat medieval cast of its cruciform plan and steep roof, the restored Bruton Parish Church (originally 1711–1715) must be counted one of the earliest American examples of the use of the Georgian style by the Church of England. A simple modillioned cornice runs along the eaves, and round-topped windows light the plain but spacious interior.

A later date and more professional hand are evident at Christ Church (*Plate 38*) in nearby Lancaster County, a structure remarkable both for the sophistication of its design and the excellence of its preservation. Here classic pediments cap the transept doors above flanking pilasters of molded brick, and a rich cornice, unusual for the time and place, separates slightly flaring eaves from walls of Flemish bond. Local quarries presumably supplied material for keystones, sills, and imposts, but imported Purbeck marble was selected for the aisle floors of Christ Church, as was walnut for the doors and most of the interior woodwork. And in the churchyard is the marble tomb of the donor of all this magnificence, Robert "King" Carter (d. 1732), one of the richest plantation owners of his time.

Plate 37. Bruton Parish Church, Williamsburg, Virginia. 1711–1715; enlarged 1751–1755; steep
added 1769. On March 1, 1711, the minister of Bruton Parish Church reported to the Vestry that "he h
received from the Honble. Alexr. Spotswood a platt or draught of a church." In 1903–1907, under the Re
William A. R. Goodwin, an attempt was made to restore the church to its appearance prior to the changes
1838–1840. This was followed in 1939–1940 by a second restoration under the direction of the architects
Colonial Williamsburg. PHOTOGRAPH BY WAYNE ANDREWS

e 38. CHRIST CHURCH, LANCASTER COUNTY, VIRGINIA. 1732. Its isolated location and the protection
he Carter family have helped to preserve virtually intact this finest of the colonial churches of
inia. Excavations conducted in 1959 established that the main entrance was intended to be on the
and that the churchyard had originally been surrounded by a brick wall, demolished *circa* 1836.
OGRAPH BY WAYNE ANDREWS

The Carter name is also associated with many of the finest early mansions of Virginia. Of these Sabine Hall, built for Landon Carter about 1730 still stands, but Nomini Hall, built about the same time for Robert Carter II, like "King" Carter's own Corotoman (*circa* 1715), burned long ago; and only blackened walls bear witness to the grandeur of "Rosewell" (1726–1730), the superb mansion of the "King's" son-in-law, Mann Page.

Of the great plantation houses in Virginia that still survive, few can equal the mansion begun about 1730 by William Byrd II (d. 1744) on a site overlooking the James River about 25 miles west of Williamsburg. The gates and possibly other of the stone details of "Westover" were imported from England, but a local designer, as yet unidentified, must have been responsible for the handsome proportions of the two façades and the fine de-

92   *Plate 39.* "Westover," Charles City County, Virginia. Begun *circa* 1730. The dependency on the (west), used for the kitchen, seems to antedate the main block and may have been erected about 170 even earlier. The contemporary "flanker" on the east, used by Byrd as his library, was destroyed durin Civil War and rebuilt *circa* 1900. The fact that both the north and south doors appear to follow closel signs in William Salmon's *Palladio Londinensis*, first published in 1734, suggests that the building of V over may have continued somewhat longer than is commonly supposed. photograph, *courtesy* vir DEPARTMENT OF CONSERVATION AND DEVELOPMENT, RICHMOND

tailing of cornice and windows. Now joined by modern "hyphens," the flanking dependencies of Byrd's great house were originally separate from the main block (*Plate 39*).

One of the last and in some respects most satisfying of the early Georgian mansions of Virginia is that begun in 1750–1751 by the Williamsburg builder David Minitree for King Carter's grandson, Carter Burwell. As at "Westover," the dependencies of "Carter's Grove" (*Plate 40*) were originally separate from the main house, and from the remodeling of 1928 date also the steep roof (now eleven feet above the original) and the hipped

Plate 40. "CARTER'S GROVE," JAMES CITY COUNTY, VIRGINIA. 1750–1753; enlarged and refurbished 1928. Unlike Richard Bayliss, who seems to have been a skilled joiner brought over from England specifically to execute the rich interiors, David Minitree, the carpenter in charge of the work at Carter's Grove, was a native of Williamsburg and perhaps a son of the David Minitree (d. 1712), who is known to have been employed on the Capitol. PHOTOGRAPH BY WAYNE ANDREWS

dormers. Richard Taliaferro, mentioned earlier in connection with the Wythe House (*Plate 27*), is considered by some to have been the designer of "Carter's Grove," but the fine entrance hall (*Plate 41*) with its dado, Ionic pilasters, and modillioned cornice seems to have been the work of the English carpenter Richard Bayliss. This practice of reserving the richest details for the interior is not uncommon in the history of architecture. From

Plate 41. ENTRANCE HALL, "CARTER'S GROVE," JAMES CITY COUNTY, VIRGINIA. As in the case of the ways of Westover, the designer of this finest of Virginia entrance halls seems to have borrowed extens from *Palladio Londinensis*. But whatever the source, the carved brackets, turned balusters, and inlaid ings make the detailing of the stair among the richest American examples of the period. The four-hu acre Carter's Grove Plantation was purchased in 1964 by Sealantic Fund, Inc., and is now administer Colonial Williamsburg. PHOTOGRAPH, *courtesy* COLONIAL WILLIAMSBURG, WILLIAMSBURG, VA.

the early 18th century an even more striking American example is offered by "Stratford," where the most severe exterior of the period is made to enclose a hall of unusual richness and sophistication (*Plate 42*).

Plate 42. GREAT HALL, "STRATFORD," WESTMORELAND COUNTY, VIRGINIA. *Circa* 1730. By virtue of its scale, fine proportions, and highly developed architectural ornament, this may fairly be considered the largest and most important early paneled room in the colonies. Original throughout, the paneling has been restored to its early grey-blue color. PHOTOGRAPH, *courtesy* ROBERT E. LEE MEMORIAL FOUNDATION, STRATFORD, VA.

95

Prior to 1750, the other American colonies produced few houses that can be compared with the great mansions of Virginia, though something of the monumentality of "Stratford" and Sir John Vanbrugh appears as early as 1714 at "Mulberry" (*Plate 43*) in South Carolina. French, English, Dutch, and even Chinese, are but the most important of numerous influences sometimes cited to explain the four flared-eaved pavilions of this delightful house. But whatever the explanation of these nearly free-standing forms, "Mulberry" remains a welcome exception in a period generally noted for its architectural conformity, as well as a warning to the historian against the temptation to force his material into too rigid a pattern.

Plate 43. Mulberry Plantation, Berkeley County, South Carolina. 1714. Thomas Waterman would trace the plan of Mulberry to French Huguenot sources, specifically *Les plus excellents Bastiments de France*, brought out at Paris in 1576 and 1579 by Jacques du Cerceau the Elder (*circa* 1520–*circa* 1584). Certainly the four pavilions do suggest similar forms favored in the early Renaissance architecture of France, as elsewhere, and usually explained as a survival from the defensive towers of the late Middle Ages. PHOTOGRAPH BY WAYNE ANDREWS

Wealth from rice lay behind "Mulberry," just as tobacco lay behind the mansions of Virginia, but in New England the greatest fortunes were derived from the commerce that passed through the principal ports of the coastal regions. The fine granite house that the bookseller Thomas Hancock built on Beacon Hill in 1737 was demolished during the Civil War, but the early Georgian style of Boston is reflected in the changes Isaac Royall (d. 1739) made between 1733 and 1737 in the east façade of his house at Medford, Massachusetts (*Plate 44*). By sheathing an earlier brick building with the wooden forms favored in the North, Royall obtained, and at a minimum of expense, a wide variety of the classical details then coming into vogue. Indeed, the modillioned cornice, quoins, and panels beneath the windows recall similar features at Independence Hall of which the remodeled Royall House is an exact contemporary.

Plate 44. East Front, Royall House, Medford, Massachusetts. Remodeled 1733–1737. Included in Isaac Royall's plans for the enlargement of the simple brick house he purchased from John Usher in 1732 were a number of outbuildings. Of these one built of brick was intended for slaves' quarters, a rarity in New England. photograph by cervin robinson, *courtesy* historic american buildings survey and library of congress, washington, d.c.

Scarcely less ambitious than the great houses of the Boston area were those of Portsmouth, the only major seaport of neighboring New Hampshire. The brick residence that Captain Archibald Macpheadris began about 1716 may lack the opulence of the Hancock or Royall mansions, but it has few peers in the integrity of its details and the restrained dignity of its design (*Plate 45*). Of particular distinction is the doorway with its segmental pediment, the curve of which is echoed by similar shapes on alternating dormers, as well as by the arched lintels above the windows of the first floor. Here, too, should be mentioned the Portsmouth residence built by the wife of Mark Hunking Wentworth as a wedding present for her son Thomas, brother of John Wentworth, last of the royal governors. Despite its date of

Plate 45. MACPHEADRIS-WARNER HOUSE, PORTSMOUTH, NEW HAMPSHIRE. *Circa* 1716–1723. Originally the house was covered by two parallel gabled roofs. Later, the deep trough between was covered over—probably because it trapped too readily the heavy New England snows—thereby forming the present gambrel. On the west wall may still be seen the lightning rod installed in 1762, reputedly under the direction of Benjamin Franklin himself. PHOTOGRAPH BY WAYNE ANDREWS

1760 the Wentworth-Gardner House (*Plate 46*), as it is usually known, looks back to the Early Georgian period in the use of such features as the unbroken façade, swan's-neck pediment above the doorway, and quoins (rather than giant pilasters) at the corners. More characteristic of the

Plate 46. Wentworth-Gardner House, Portsmouth, New Hampshire. 1760. Since it was purchased by Major William Gardner in 1796, the house has had a succession of owners, including the Metropolitan Museum of Art, which at one time planned to move it to Central Park. Fortunately, that scheme was abandoned, and Thomas Wentworth's fine house was left facing its quiet bay. Beautifully restored by the Wentworth-Gardner and Tobias Lear Houses Association, it is now open to the public. Photograph by Wayne Andrews

99

second half of the 18th century are the low, hipped roof, pediments above the windows of the first floor, and the extraordinary richness of the interior, notable especially for the woodwork of the stair hall (*Plate 47*).

Plate 47.
STAIR HALL OF THE WENTWORTH GARDNER HOUSE, PORTSMOUTH, NEW HAMPSHIRE. Although the plan is customary for its time and place—four rooms with interior chimneys, center hall, and kitchen ell at the rear—the woodwork of the Wentworth-Gardner House is among the richest of the period. When one considers the complexity of the twisted balusters, elaborate cornices, and Ionic pilasters with full entablature, it is easy to believe the tradition that ship carvers labored fourteen months in their creation. PHOTOGRAPH BY SAMUEL CHAMBERLAIN

100

THE MIDDLE GEORGIAN PERIOD (*circa* 1750–*circa* 1790)

WELL before his death in 1754, even so confirmed an admirer of Wren as James Gibbs had found it desirable to forsake the inspiration of the baroque in favor of the stricter Palladianism championed by the current arbiter of taste, Richard Boyle, 3rd Earl of Burlington (1694–1753), and his principal protégés, Colin Campbell (d. 1729) and William Kent (d. 1748). It was not to be expected, of course, that this new turn of fashion would immediately be followed by large numbers of the English colonists, but by the middle of the 18th century, neo-Palladianism may be said to have gained the day in most of the major American towns and cities. Such baroque features as the broken (swan's-neck) pediment, which had been used with some frequency previously in the century, tended to disappear, and in their place a number of the earlier Renaissance motifs favored by Palladio were widely adopted. Of these the most important are the Venetian (Palladian) window, the giant and double porticos, the classical pediment in the center of the facade (frequently accompanied by a projecting central bay), and lower roofs with balustraded decks. Windows and windowpanes continued to expand in size, and exterior shutters were usually found on all but the simplest dwellings. Moreover, the common interest in the forms of Roman classicism, which during the Early Georgian period had begun to diminish the local differences characteristic of pre-Renaissance architecture, made for even greater uniformity as the century progressed. But to the last some regional preferences remained.

The stricter academic approach fostered by the Burlingtonians is illustrated by the Redwood Library of 1748 at Newport, Rhode Island (*Plate 48*). Its design follows closely those shown in several of the architectural books then popular, particularly Edward Hoppus' edition of Palladio, published in London in 1735 (*Plate 49*). The Redwood Library is one of the earliest colonial examples of the neo-Palladian style then at the height of its popularity in England, as well as the first American example of the Roman temple façade, complete with portico of free-standing Doric columns and entablature. It seems also to have been the earliest major architectural effort of its designer, Peter Harrison (1716–1763), an exceptionally talented young merchant whose trips to England could be counted upon to keep him abreast of the architectural mode currently in favor. If by modern standards the design of the Redwood Library may be said to suffer from too great a reliance on the copybook, this must have been one of the qualities that appealed most to Harrison's contemporaries. Even before the library was

Plate 48. REDWOOD LIBRARY, NEWPORT, RHODE ISLAND. 1748–1750. Designed by Peter Harrison. The library is named for Abraham Redwood, a member of the Philosophical Club who in 1747 gave £ 500 for the purchase of books. After being enlarged in 1858 and 1875, the library was restored in 1913 on the basis of the original detailed specifications. PHOTOGRAPH BY WAYNE ANDREWS

finished, its architect had been invited to submit plans for a new King's
Chapel soon to be built in Boston (*Plate 50*), a project for which work of
James Gibbs is believed to have supplied the stimulus. The tower of King's
Chapel was never finished, but its designer is known to have planned a
steeple of the lofty and elaborate variety not infrequently found in New

103

England and perhaps best exemplified by the First Baptist Meeting House at Providence, Rhode Island (*Plate 51*). However, Harrison scored his greatest success with the interiors of his buildings. In 18th century America, both

Plate 50.
King's Chapel, Boston
Massachusetts. 1749–
Designed by Peter Har
Although the original p
called for an Ionic porti
this was not executed u
1785–1787, and then in
wood instead of stone. ￼
walls of King's Chapel
of Quincy granite, how
one of the first docume
uses of that material.
PHOTOGRAPH
BY SAMUEL CHAMBERLAI

Plate 51. First Baptist Meeting House, Providence, Rhode Island. 1774–1775. **105**
Designed by Joseph Brown. A member of a prominent mercantile family, Joseph Brown's
interests were more scholarly than those of his brothers, John and Nicholas, for whom
he is presumed to have designed the two fine houses that still stand on the hill above
Benefit Street. As in the case of Peter Harrison, Joseph relied on English pattern books
for most of his architectural ideas; the interior of the First Baptist Meeting House resembles that of Marylebone Chapel in London and the tower follows very closely one of
the rejected schemes for St. Martin's-in-the-Fields. Gibbs had published both of these
designs in his *Book of Architecture,* a copy of which Brown is known to have owned.
The church was restored in 1957–1958. *Courtesy,* Rhode Island Historical Society,
Providence, R. I. Photograph by Norman S. Watson

King's Chapel (*Plate 52*) and Christ Church, Cambridge—despite the latter's modest size—are unsurpassed for spacious elegance, as is the Touro Synagogue (*Plate 53*) in the richness of its classical detail.

Plate 52. INTERIOR OF KING'S CHAPEL, BOSTON, MASSACHUSETTS. Designed by Peter Harrison. Probably few would dispute Hugh Morrison's characterization of the interior of King's Chapel as "the finest of Georgian church architecture in the Colonies." Founded in 1686 as one of the earliest important Anglican parishes in New England, in 1785 King's Chapel became the first Unitarian Church in the United States. Gradually, however, many of the furnishings associated with the Church of England have been restored. PHOTOGRAPH, *courtesy* OF KING'S CHAPEL, BOSTON

Plate 53. INTERIOR OF TOURO SYNAGOGUE, NEWPORT, RHODE ISLAND. 1759–1763. Designed by Peter Harrison. One of the few public buildings in Newport to have survived the Revolution undamaged, this oldest of extant American synagogues was named for Isaac de Touro, who had emigrated to the American colonies from Amsterdam. Books by William Kent, James Gibbs, and Batty Langley may have inspired the details, but the fine ensemble is Harrison's own. The 12 columns are symbolic of the 12 tribes of Israel. PHOTOGRAPH, *courtesy* HISTORIC AMERICAN BUILDINGS SURVEY AND LIBRARY OF CONGRESS, WASHINGTON, D.C.

For the last of his architectural designs, the Brick Market at Newport (*Plate 54*), Harrison chose giant pilasters on an arcaded base, a formula long popular with architects working in the tradition of the Italian Renaissance. Similar motifs also distinguish the most advanced domestic architecture produced in New England during what has here been called the Middle Georgian period. Thus as early as 1747 Isaac Royall, Jr., substituted giant pilasters at the corners of the new west façade of his house at Medford (*Plate 55*) in lieu of the quoins employed by his father ten years earlier during the remodeling of the east front (*Plate 44*). And similar forms were widely favored for other, but related, uses. Probably the engaged columns that enframe the central pavilion at the "Lindens" (*Plate 56*) were never common, but a similar effect might be achieved by the use of more easily executed pilasters, as in the case of the contemporary Lady Pepperrell House (*circa* 1760) at Kittery Point, Maine. In 1759 both the corners and center

Plate 54.
BRICK MARKET, NEWPORT, RHODE ISLAND. 1761–1772. Fiske Kimball has shown that Harrison based his design for the Newport market on Inigo Jones's Old Somerset House, as illustrated by Colin Campbell in *Vitruvius Britannicus* (1716). After serving variously as a theater (1793) and town hall (1842–1900), the Brick Market was carefully restored in 1928–1930 by the Newport Chamber of Commerce. PHOTOGRAPH BY WAYNE ANDREWS

Plate 55. West Façade of the Isaac Royall House, Medford, Massachusetts. 1747–1750. When he enlarged the house he inherited from his father, Isaac Royall, Jr., more than doubled its depth. From this second remodeling date the end walls (one brick and one frame) with their double chimneys, as well as the richest details of the interior woodwork. Since 1905 the house has been maintained and opened to the public under the auspices of the Royall House Association. photograph by wayne andrews

Plate 56.
"The Lindens," Danvers,
Massachusetts. *Circa* 1754.
Built as the "country-seat" of
Robert ("King") Hooper of Marblehead. This view shows the house before
it was moved to Washington, D. C.
in 1937. Although a skillful reproduction
now replaces the paneled drawing
room that was moved to the William
Rockhill Nelson Gallery in Kansas
City, the interior of the Lindens still
retains its three series of scenic
wallpapers and its remarkable stenciled
floors, the latter among the earliest
and best-preserved examples of this
form of decoration. photograph,
courtesy historic american buildings
survey and library of congress,
washington, d. c.

section of the Vassall-Longfellow mansion in Cambridge, Massachusetts (*Plate 57*), were defined in this way; indeed, so popular was the motif throughout New England that nearly a quarter of a century later the youthful Samuel McIntire (1757–1811) used it in Salem for one of his first

110 *Plate 57.* Vassall-Longfellow House, Cambridge, Massachusetts. 1759. The ample proportions of the central pavilion, double-hipped roof with balustrade, modillioned cornice, and four giant Ionic pilasters capped with sections of entablature combine to make Major John Vassall's house on Brattle Street the culmination of the Middle Georgian style in New England. Here Henry Wadsworth Longfellow made his home from 1837 until his death in 1882. photograph by wayne andrews

architectural designs (*Plate 58*). Despite the appearance of solid masonry, such important examples of American architecture as the "Lindens," the Redwood Library, the Royall House, or the Wentworth-Gardner House are in fact faced with wood, cut and finished to imitate stone. There was ample precedent in Palladio for the treatment of one material to resemble another, but with one or two notable exceptions (Washington's Mount Vernon being the best known), this particular form of imitation is most characteristic of New England, where wood had been the preferred building material since the founding of the English colonies.

Plate 58. Peirce-Nichols House, Salem, Massachusetts. 1782. Designed and built by Samuel McIntire. While still a young man in his middle twenties, McIntire built this great house for Jerathmeel Peirce, one of the most successful of the East India merchants of Salem. Batty Langley's *City and Country Builder's and Workman's Treasury of Designs* (1740) supplied the most important decorative details, a majority of which McIntire is believed to have carved himself. PHOTOGRAPH BY WAYNE ANDREWS

Greater wealth and a more cosmopolitan atmosphere may have provided such coastal cities as Boston and Newport with the most ambitious examples of New England architecture, but the prosperous inland towns were by no means untouched by the changes taking place in architectural taste. Numerous fine doorways throughout the Connecticut River Valley would still bear witness to this, even did we not have the house Samuel Cowles had built at Farmington, Connecticut, about 1780 (*Plate 59*). Now widely regarded as among the most beautiful of its day, the Cowles house conforms to Middle Georgian practice in its use of a Palladian window in the projecting central pavilion, though the Ionic columns that support the overhanging second story seem to be a motif contrived by the designer, the soldier-architect William Sprats.

Not the least interesting aspect of Peter Harrison's architectural designs is the use he made of large free-standing columns at the entrance

Plate 59. SAMUEL COWLES HOUSE, FARMINGTON, CONNECTICUT. 1780. At least the front portion of this attractive house is usually considered to be among the earliest known work of William Sprats, an officer in Burgoyne's army who had received some architectural training and who was paroled in Connecticut after the surrender of the British at Saratoga in 1777. The south wing was probably built about 1660, but that on the north is modern. PHOTOGRAPH BY WAYNE ANDREWS

portico. This Renaissance device was common enough in the neo-Palladian architecture of England, but the American colonies seem to have produced few examples prior to the War of Independence. Among extant public buildings, New England is represented principally by Harrison's Redwood Library (*Plate 48*) and King's Chapel (*Plate 50*), while in the South there remain only modest St. James' at Santee, South Carolina (1768), and stately St. Michael's at Charleston (*Plate 60*), the latter so like Peter Harrison's work as to suggest to some that he may, in fact, have been the designer. Philadelphia, usually a leader in matters of architectural taste,

ate 60.

MICHAEL'S, CHARLESTON, SOUTH
ROLINA. Begun 1752. The giant portico
St. Michael's has been likened to that of
Martin's-in-the-Fields, London, and the
hitecture of James Gibbs was probably
inspiration also for the tower and
erior of this most monumental of American
orgian churches. Samuel Cardy was the
lder and Zachariah Villepontoux supplied
superior quality brick for walls probably
ended from the first to be covered with
d stucco. PHOTOGRAPH
WAYNE ANDREWS

appears to have produced no examples of the giant portico during this period, and New York does not seem to have fared much better. St. Paul's Chapel in New York City dates from 1764, of course, but the elaborate spire and fine Ionic portico were not erected until 1794–96, whatever provision for them Thomas McBean may have included in his original plans. Also of doubtful date is the Doric portico of the Roger Morris (Jumel) mansion (*Plate 61*), said to be the only colonial house of importance still standing in

Plate 61. ROGER MORRIS (JUMEL) MANSION, NEW YORK CITY, NEW YORK. 1765. Since the doorway with its elliptical transom and sidelights must be considered a later addition, it is possible that the columns of the portico were added or renewed at that time. During the Revolution a room in the octagonal rear wing was used briefly as a study by General Washington, who earlier had served on Braddock's staff with Major Roger Morris, for whom the house was built.
PHOTOGRAPH BY WAYNE ANDREWS

114

Manhattan. Although early descriptions suggest that this feature belongs to the house as originally planned in 1765, the attenuated proportions of the present columns are more characteristic of houses erected after the Revolution than of those built a decade or so before it. This is readily apparent when the lightness of the portico at the Morris mansion is compared with the robust mass of that at Whitehall (*Plate 62*), the country retreat overlooking the Severn River opposite Annapolis, which was begun in 1764 for Governor Horatio Sharpe.

te 62. Whitehall, Anne Arundel County, Maryland. Begun 1764. Unusual among American houses aving the central block devoted to a single room carried the full height of the building, Whitehall seems ave been intended at first as a simple pavilion for entertaining guests on excursions across the river from apolis. Somewhat later, wings extended to the east and west provided additional space for kitchens and rooms. A second story added about 1793 was removed in 1957 as part of the painstaking restoration g carried out by the present owners, Mr. and Mrs. Charles E. Scarlett, Jr. *Courtesy,* historic annap-, inc., annapolis, md. photograph by m. e. warren

Whitehall offers the only extant pre-Revolutionary example of the giant order in the domestic architecture of the South, but builders of that area seem to have been more fond of another of Palladio's favorite devices—the double or two-story portico. If a date close to 1740 for Drayton Hall (*Plate 63*) is indeed correct, then this finest of South Carolina's plantation mansions offers not only the earliest surviving American example of the double portico, but also a variety of other architectural features that seem

Plate 63. WEST ("LAND") FAÇADE, DRAYTON HALL, CHARLESTON COUNTY, SOUTH CAROLINA. *Circa* 1738. Few other American houses equaled in size or elaboration of detail this mansion built for John Drayton member of the King's Council. A typical example of Palladio's use of the double (or two-level) portico illustrated by *Plate 25.* PHOTOGRAPH BY WAYNE ANDREWS

stylistically well in advance of contemporary houses elsewhere in the colonies. On the east side, for example (*Plate 64*), the roof is interrupted by a classical pediment to create a central axis for the composition, while, below, the main doorway of imported Portland stone is raised a full story above the ground and is approached by a double flight of steps—a motif repeated to good effect by the stairway of the front hall, immediately inside. The double

e 64.
т ("RIVER") FAÇADE OF
.YTON HALL, CHARLESTON
NTY, SOUTH CAROLINA. A
ice area is provided by the
 basement, and originally
ther side of the main
ie were symmetrically
:d dependencies of which
 the foundations survive.
OGRAPH, *courtesy* LIBRARY
ONGRESS, WASHINGTON, D. C.

portico again appeared in South Carolina at the Miles Brewton House (*Plate 65*) in Charleston about 1765, though even before its use there this characteristically Palladian form had begun to attract the attention of Virginia builders. "A portico . . . of two orders" that had been added in 1751–1753 to the west façade of the Capitol was one of the few architectural features of

Plate 65. MILES BREWTON HOUSE, CHARLESTON, SOUTH CAROLINA. 1765–1769. Ezra Waite, joiner carver. The finest city residence in South Carolina, and perhaps in any of the colonies, the Brewton H escaped destruction by being selected as headquarters for the British during the Revolution and fo Federal army during the Civil War. PHOTOGRAPH BY WAYNE ANDREWS

Williamsburg for which Thomas Jefferson could find words of praise. And this Middle Georgian addition must also have delighted his fellow Virginian, Charles Carter, sometime student at William and Mary, who built double porches about 1769 on both façades of "Shirley" (*Plate 66*), his estate in Charles City County. Nor should it be forgotten that Jefferson himself, matching opinions with action, had used a double portico at Monticello, as first erected between about 1770 and 1775.

Plate 66. SHIRLEY, CHARLES CITY COUNTY, VIRGINIA. *Circa* 1769. The four buildings that enclose the forecourt at Shirley were probably completed about 1740 and together form the most complete ensemble of this kind to survive from the colonial period. The interior of the house is noted for its fine paneling as well as for the "suspended" form of the carved walnut staircase, a type of construction occasionally employed in England but otherwise extremely rare in the colonies. The columns, entablature, and steps of the two porticoes were renewed during the first half of the 19th century. PHOTOGRAPH BY WAYNE ANDREWS

119

Later, under the impetus of his archaeological interest, Jefferson modified somewhat the earlier Palladian character of Monticello, and many of his other architectural designs, such as the Capitol at Richmond (conceived *circa* 1785; built 1789) and the University of Virginia at Charlottesville (1817–1826), belong more appropriately to a discussion of the classical revivals of the early 19th century than to a brief essay on the Georgian style. One important exception to this would be "Brandon" (*Plate 67*), begun about 1765 and traditionally ascribed to Jefferson, who was then a young man of only twenty-two and had that year served as groomsman at the wedding of the owner, Nathaniel Harrison. As in the case of most other important houses of the period, the plan of "Brandon" has been shown to have been patterned on English sources, specifically Robert Morris' *Select Architecture* (London, 1757), but its ultimate models were no less certainly Italian. In Virginia, especially, flanking dependencies had served the main house as offices and kitchens almost from the first, but it was not until the 1760's that it became customary to connect the "flankers" with the central block by means of open or closed passageways, thereby conforming more precisely to the form of "Roman Country House" illustrated by Palladio. "Brandon" is probably the purest example of this type of plan. Whitehall, as finally completed, may be considered an elaboration of it, however, and in various forms it is found in other contemporary Maryland mansions such as "Tulip Hill" and "Montpelier" (enlarged *circa* 1770), the former (*Plate 68*) in Anne Arundel County and the latter in Prince George's.

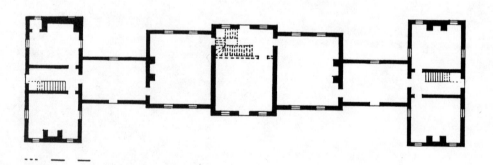

PLAN OF BRANDON

From Thomas T. Waterman, *The Mansions of Virginia, 1706–1776*, Chapel Hill, 1946. PHOTOGRAPH, *courtesy* THE UNIVERSITY OF NORTH CAROLINA PRESS

Plate 67. BRANDON, PRINCE GEORGE COUNTY, VIRGINIA. *Circa* 1765. Attributed to Thomas Jefferson. In the opinion of Waterman, the style of the interior paneling argues against assigning to Brandon a date after Jefferson's return from France in 1789. The present low porticoes were added in the 19th century when the window sash were also renewed. PHOTOGRAPH, *courtesy* VIRGINIA STATE CHAMBER OF COMMERCE, RICHMOND

Plate 68. TULIP HILL, ANNE ARUNDEL COUNTY, MARYLAND. 1756–1763. Representative of the smaller type of mid-Georgian mansion in Maryland, Tulip Hill belongs with such other notable examples as Bohemia (*circa* 1745) in Cecil County and Acton in Annapolis. The wings were not added until 1787, but a variety of details connect portions of the interior of the main block with the work of William Buckland. PHOTOGRAPH BY WAYNE ANDREWS

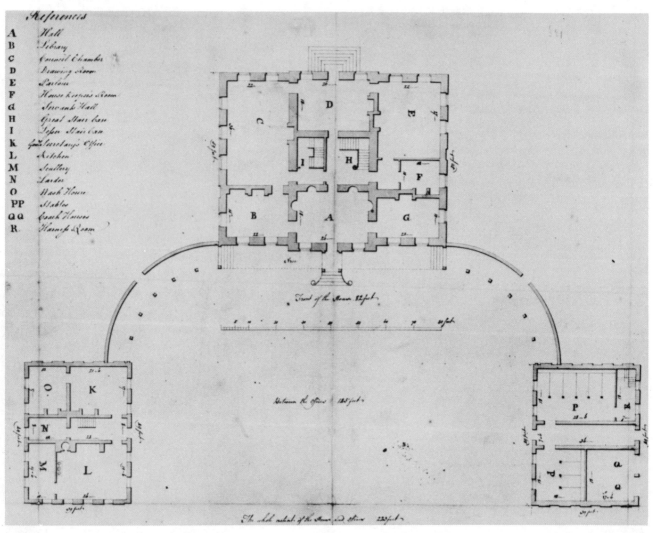

Plate 69. ORIGINAL PLAN FOR GOVERNOR TRYON'S PALACE, NEW BERN, NORTH CAROLINA. *Circa* 1767–1771. John Hawks, architect. Financed by the colonial treasury, Tryon's "palace" provided state apartments on the first floor and the governor's living quarters on the second. Hawks' preliminary design is in the New-York Historical Society, while this one in the British Public Record Office is presumably that promised by the governor "for his Majesty's approbation." *Courtesy,* PUBLIC RECORD OFFICE, LONDON. BRITISH CROWN COPYRIGHT; REPRODUCED BY PERMISSION OF THE CONTROLLER OF H. M. STATIONERY OFFICE

Even more impressive than the straight linking members of the forego-
ing examples are the curving colonnades used to connect the central structure with its dependencies at the palace begun in 1767 by Governor William
Tryon at New Bern, North Carolina. Now reconstructed from original
drawings, Tryon's palace (*Plates 69 and 70*) was designed by John Hawks,
a professional architect whom the governor had brought with him from
England to "superintend this work in all its branches." Though the palace at
New Bern was probably the most sumptuous American dwelling of its day,

*te 70. GOVERNOR TRYON'S PALACE, NEW BERN, NORTH CAROLINA. As reconstructed 1952–1959. Re-
ding began with the West Dependency, portions of which remained after the destruction of that on the
and of the Main Building, the latter by fire on the night of February 27, 1798. Now owned by the
e of North Carolina, Tryon Palace is open to the public. John Hawks, designer of the original palace,
one of the first professional architects to remain in America. PHOTOGRAPH, courtesy NORTH CAROLINA
ARTMENT OF CONSERVATION AND DEVELOPMENT, RALEIGH*

similar quadrant passageways were part of the five-part plans used for several of the later mansions of Virginia. Of these the best known is certainly George Washington's Mount Vernon (1756–1787), and the most distinguished John Tayloe's mansion in Richmond County, called Mount Airy (*Plate 71*). Throughout the several enlargements and remodelings of Mount Vernon, Washington is known to have taken a personal hand in adapting the designs of English builders' guides such as those by Abraham Swan and Batty Langley. Mount Airy, however, is believed to be the work of John Ariss (*circa* 1725–1799), a trained carpenter-architect whose name has been linked by attribution with more than a dozen houses of the period, at least half of them notable examples of the neo-Palladian style.

124   *Plate 71.* MOUNT AIRY, RICHMOND COUNTY, VIRGINIA. 1758–1762. Attributed to John Ariss. Despite the loss by fire of the original interiors in 1844, Mount Airy ranks among the finest neo-Palladian mansions in America and was one of the few in Virginia to be built of stone. The south façade follows closely a design by James Gibbs (*Plate 36*). PHOTOGRAPH BY WAYNE ANDREWS

Not only do the remarkably rich interiors of such Virginia mansions as Whitehall or Mount Airy attest to the high degree of skill attained by American craftsmen, but similar details shared by these and other houses have led historians to associate at least some portions of them with the hand or shop of one man. This is William Buckland (1734–1774), an English joiner who came to Virginia in 1755 and while still bound by indenture executed the elaborate interiors of George Mason's new house in Fairfax County (*Plate 72*), a few miles down the Potomac from Mount Vernon. Completed in 1758, Gunston Hall was undoubtedly Buckland's first work in

Plate 72. CHINESE CHIPPENDALE ROOM, GUNSTON HALL, FAIRFAX COUNTY, VIRGINIA. 1755–1758. William Buckland, joiner. Considerably more graceful than the heavier Palladian manner employed in the drawing room, the fanciful details of the dining room represent the earliest important example of *chinoiserie* in the American colonies. To judge from his extant work, Buckland never again made extensive use of Chinese motifs. PHOTOGRAPH, *courtesy* BOARD OF REGENTS, GUNSTON HALL

the colonies, and, if we may judge from the plan before him on the table in his portrait by Charles Willson Peale, the Hammond-Harwood House at Annapolis (*Plate 73*) was probably his last. Less certain is the rest of Buckland's career. At Annapolis he is known to have worked at the State House, and the papers of the Lloyd family show him to have been occupied intermittently during 1771–1772 on the woodwork of the unfinished mansion that Edward Lloyd had recently purchased from Samuel Chase (*Plate 74*). Begun in 1769 on a site directly across the street from that soon to be occupied by the new residence of Matthias Hammond, this most monumental of the colonial houses of Annapolis is especially remarkable for its three-story height and for the grandeur of a stairway lit at the landing by an

126   *Plate 73.* HAMMOND-HARWOOD HOUSE, ANNAPOLIS, MARYLAND. 1773–1774. William Buckland, architect and joiner. For most of the earlier houses with which his name has been associated, Buckland probably did no more than plan and execute the interior paneling and woodwork; only for Mathias Hammond does he seem to have taken charge of the entire fabric. Although the five-part plan is clearly better suited to the country estate than to the city residence, at the Hammond-Harwood House extensive ground at the rear must originally have permitted a comprehensive view of the architectural ensemble from the garden side. PHOTOGRAPH BY WAYNE ANDREWS

Plate 74.

CHASE-LLOYD HOUSE, ANNAPOLIS, MARYLAND. 1769–1774. William Buckland, joiner. To oversee the erection of his mansion on North-East Street, Samuel Chase had imported a builder from England. Presumably it was he who made the initial design and supervised at least the beginning of the exterior walls. Edward Lloyd's unusually complete records also show substantial payments to William Noke, who seems to have been in charge of construction after Buckland left in the fall of 1772. PHOTOGRAPH, *courtesy* HISTORIC AMERICAN BUILDINGS SURVEY AND LIBRARY OF CONGRESS, WASHINGTON, D. C.

exceptionally large Palladian window and separated from the entrance hall by paired Ionic columns with full entablature (*Plate 75*). Scarcely less remarkable is the entrance of the Chase-Lloyd House, which includes a central portion not unlike the doorway of the Hammond-Harwood House, and, in addition, small flanking windows or sidelights, a form rare in American architecture prior to the Revolution.

Plate 75.
ENTRANCE HALL OF THE CHASE-LLOYD HOUSE, ANNAPOLIS, MARYLAND. William Buckland, joiner. The central hall extends the entire depth of the house with the customary two rooms at either side. More unusual are the lateral passageways that separate the front and rear rooms and the division the entrance area from the stair hall b paired Ionic columns and pilasters, motifs repeated on the exterior of the entrance. PHOTOGRAPH, *courtesy* HISTORIC AMERICAN BUILDINGS SURVEY AND LIBRARY OF CONGRESS, WASHINGTON, D. C.

128

Although the classical pediment, with or without a projecting central pavilion, has been found to be the feature most characteristic of all American architecture of the mid-18th century, this motif did, in fact, appear much earlier in one or two isolated examples. Its use in South Carolina about 1740 was noted previously at Drayton Hall, and even earlier it is found in fully developed form at the College of William and Mary (*Plate 76*), established in 1693. Tradition has it that Wren himself designed this building for the

Plate 76. COLLEGE OF WILLIAM AND MARY, WILLIAMSBURG, VIRGINIA. First built 1695–1702; burned 1705 and rebuilt 1708–1716; burned 1859 and rebuilt the same year in an Italianate form designed by Eben Faxon of Baltimore; burned 1862 and rebuilt 1867–1869 after a more "Georgian" design of Alfred L. Rives. Despite three fires and the subsequent rebuildings, most of the original walls remained standing, and these were again used in 1928–1931 when the College was restored to its second form, that "nicely contrived, altered and adorned by the ingenious Direction of Governor Spotswood." Apparently it was the Governor who added the central pavilion in the course of the rebuilding of 1708–1716.
PHOTOGRAPH, *courtesy* COLONIAL WILLIAMSBURG, VA.

first of Virginia's colleges, and certainly it was stylistically in advance of most other colonial buildings of its time. Except for Massachusetts, where Harvard had been founded as early as 1636, the other colonies did not get around to providing for institutions of higher learning for a number of years, but then, more often than not, the new colleges were housed in buildings not unlike that of William and Mary. Dartmouth Hall (1784–1791), Univer-

A North-West Prospect of Nassau-Hall, with a Front View

sity Hall (1770–1772) at Brown, and Nassau Hall (*Plate 77*) at the College of New Jersey (now Princeton University) were all cast in this general mold.

The identity of the designer of Dartmouth Hall and University Hall at Brown is uncertain, but the building at Princeton is associated with the name of Robert Smith (*circa* 1722–1777), then the leading carpenter-

Presidents House in New Jersey

Plate 77. NASSAU HALL, PRINCETON, NEW JERSEY. From an old print. 1754–1757. Designed by Robert Smith with the assistance of Dr. William Shippen. A higher cupola was added by Benjamin Henry Latrobe, who served as architect for the repairs after the fire of 1802. The present stair towers at either end of the building are part of the Italianate additions made by John Notman (1810–1865), architect for the rebuilding after the fire of 1855. A full history of this influential building is given in *Nassau Hall, 1756–1956,* edited by Henry Lyttleton Savage (Princeton, 1956). *Courtesy,* NEW YORK PUBLIC LIBRARY

131

architect of Philadelphia. For Nassau Hall, as for the steeple of Christ Church (*Plate 35*) and the erection of St. Peter's (1758–1761) in Philadelphia, Smith may have served as master carpenter in the development and execution of the general designs of others. But by the 1770's he emerges as an architect in his own right; in that capacity he is credited with the designs of a number of important Philadelphia buildings, including the Walnut Street Prison (1773–1776), sometimes called the first penitentiary in the world, and Carpenters' Hall (*Plate 78*), headquarters of the powerful Carpenters' Company. The Prison was demolished in 1836, but the Hall, still serving the organization that built it, is today a part of the Independence National Historical Park.

The Palladian window that dominates the east end of Christ Church was unusual for a building begun in 1727, and the Middle Georgian period in Philadelphia may more appropriately be dated from Edmund Woolley's

Plate 78.
Carpenters' Hall, Philadelphia, Pennsylvania. 1770–1775. Robert Smith, architect. Basing its practice on English models, the Carpenters' Company was founded about 1724 "for the purpose of obtaining instruction in the science of architecture and assisting such of their members as should by accident be in need of support, or the widows and minor children of members. . . ." In his account of Carpenters' Hall that appeared in *Historic Philadelphia* (Vol. 43, Part 1, "Transactions of the American Philosophical Society," 1953), Charles E. Peterson has reproduced pages from the little-known *Rule Book* of the Carpenters' Company, as well as an important list of documents relating to the career of Robert Smith. photograph
by cortlandt v. d. hubbard, philadelphia

132

use of that and similar High Renaissance motifs in his design for the tower of the State House, begun in 1750. This was not immediately followed by other notable examples of the neo-Palladian revival in Philadelphia, but the decade of the 1760's saw the construction in that area of not a few of the finest residences in the colonies. The Metropolitan and Philadelphia museums have each installed a room from the house on Third Street erected in 1765 and known by the name of its second owner, Samuel Powel, while the handsome parlor of the Blackwell House (*Plate 79*) that once stood on Pine Street is among the treasures of the Henry Francis du Pont Winterthur Museum. And only in the South can be found country residences equal in

Plate 79. PARLOR OF THE BLACKWELL HOUSE. 1764. Originally at 224 Pine Street, Philadelphia, and now in the Henry Francis du Pont Winterthur Museum, Winterthur, Delaware. One of the outstanding examples of the High Georgian style in Philadelphia, this parlor now forms the setting for a superb collection of Chippendale furniture, also of Philadelphia origin. Abraham Swan's *Collection of Designs in Architecture* (1757) supplied the form of the overmantel (see *Frontispiece*), and doubtless other of the decorative details were taken from English pattern books as well. PHOTOGRAPH, *courtesy* HENRY FRANCIS DU PONT WINTERTHUR MUSEUM, WINTERTHUR, DEL.

grandeur to Mount Pleasant (*Plate 80*), once owned (but never occupied) by Benedict Arnold, or to Cliveden, the Germantown residence begun in 1764 for the distinguished jurist Benjamin Chew. Still in possession of the descendants of its first owner, Cliveden is perhaps best known for the beauty of its hall (*Plate 81*) where a pair of free-standing Doric columns brings to mind the similar arrangement of the Chase-Lloyd House at Annapolis (*Plate 75*), begun five years later.

Plate 80. MOUNT PLEASANT, FAIRMOUNT PARK, PHILADELPHIA, PENNSYLVANIA. 1761. Capt. John MacPherson (Macpherson), who made his fortune as a privateer in England's war with France and Spain, was the owner for whom was built this most sumptuous of the mansions in the Middle Colonies. No one has yet identified the architect, but Waterman has suggested that the design may owe something to the work of Daniel Marot. PHOTOGRAPH BY WAYNE ANDREWS

ENTRANCE HALL, CLIVEDEN, PHILADELPHIA (GERMANTOWN), PENNSYLVANIA. 1764. Drawings
d among the Chew papers in 1963 failed to identify the designer of Cliveden; perhaps like many another
tleman of that day Benjamin Chew served in large part as his own architect. On the right of the spacious
rance hall is the library and behind it a larger parlor; on the left is a small office and behind it (corre-
nding to the parlor on the other side) is the dining room. Space for the kitchens and other services is
vided by flanking dependencies in the rear. PHOTOGRAPH, *courtesy* HISTORICAL SOCIETY OF PENNSYLVANIA,
ADELPHIA

Though lacking some of the more elaborate features of those in Philadelphia, the Georgian houses of Delaware are also worthy of attention. Indeed, the absence of a Palladian window or central pediment can scarcely be considered a disadvantage in the design of William Corbit's house at Odessa (*Plate 82*). Completed on the eve of the Revolution, its simple but eminently satisfying lines are a tribute to the sensibilities of its Quaker owner and one of the finest expressions of the Georgian style in the domestic architecture of the state.

Plate 82. CORBIT HOUSE, ODESSA, DELAWARE. 1772–1774. Robert May, joiner-architect. The first floor the Corbit House is divided into the four rooms and central hall customarily found in houses of this type, b on the second floor a large drawing room has been created by including the width of the hall as part of t northeast room. In Philadelphia this feature is found at the Powel House, which also shares with its neighb at Odessa a number of distinctive details of interior woodwork. Now restored on its fine site overlooking t Appoquinimink Creek, the Corbit House is open to the public in the care of the Henry Francis du Po Winterthur Museum. PHOTOGRAPH BY WAYNE ANDREWS

EPILOGUE: THE LATE GEORGIAN STYLE

AFTER the conclusion of the War of Independence (1775–1783) and the emergence of the United States as a political entity, exception could easily be taken to the use of the term "colonial" in connection with American architecture. But it has been well said that since the American Revolution was fought by Englishmen against Englishmen, only Englishmen could win; by the severing of all political ties with the English Crown the American colonies achieved no corresponding independence in matters of architectural taste. Considering the success of his design for the residence of Samuel Cowles (Plate 59), it is understandable that William Sprats should have used the same projecting central bay and Palladian window when a decade later he remodeled Sheldon's Tavern (*Plate 83*) at nearby Litchfield. Little

Plate 83. SHELDON'S TAVERN, LITCHFIELD, CONNECTICUT. Remodeled *circa* 1790, reputedly by William Sprats. His favorite motif of a central pavilion containing a Palladian window flanked by Ionic pilasters and supported by four Ionic columns was again used by Sprats in 1790 for the house of Julius Deming that still stands across the street from Sheldon's Tavern. New light on the career of this interesting soldier-turned-architect—including the correct spelling of his name—has been supplied by the research of William L. Warren (*Old-Time New England*, January and April, 1954). PHOTOGRAPH BY WAYNE ANDREWS

but inherent conservatism, on the other hand, seems to explain the tenacity with which not a few 19th-century builders continued to cling to the architectural vocabulary of the Renaissance, especially for the country churches of New England (*Plate 84*).

Plate 84.
MEETING HOUSE, ACWORTH, SULLIVAN COUNTY, NEW HAMPSHIRE. 1821. Elias Carter, builder. Not a few of the churches in this area were apparently erected by Carter who seems to have used the books of Asher Benjamin (1773–1845) as the principal source for his designs. That at Acworth is among the best preserved of the larger meeting houses in the middle Connecticut Valley. PHOTOGRAPH, *courtesy* HISTORIC AMERICAN BUILDINGS SURVEY AND LIBRARY OF CONGRESS, WASHINGTON, D. C.

138

Nor was the use of the Georgian style after the Revolution confined at first to the more backward rural areas; even the largest cities appear to have surrendered their allegiance to Palladio with some reluctance. Except for a few details like the lower roof with balustrade at the eaves, there is little to distinguish from earlier Georgian work the building begun in 1795 to house the new Bank of the United States (*Plate 85*). Moreover, the designer of this impressive structure was 38-year-old Samuel Blodgett, Jr. (1757–1814), an entrepreneur of sorts who here emerges as another of the talented amateur architects in the tradition of Peter Harrison and Thomas Jefferson.

Plate 85. Bank of the United States, Philadelphia, Pennsylvania. 1795–1797. Designed by Samuel Blodgett, Jr. Although it still resembles a large Georgian house, Blodgett's bank was one of the first important structures in the United States to be designed specifically for a commercial purpose. Had the original specifications been followed, it might also have been the first American structure faced entirely with marble on the exterior; as it was, considerations of expense led to the substitution of brick on the sides and back. photograph, *courtesy* historic american buildings survey and library of congress, washington, d. c.

But in stressing the continuity of the Georgian tradition, recognition should also be given to the important ways in which the buildings of the new republic differed from their predecessors. A house like that begun about 1800 for Washington's nephew, Lawrence Lewis, continues the use of Renaissance forms (*Plate 86*), including the five-part Roman plan noted previously in connection with "Brandon," but with a greater regard for round and elliptical forms than had usually been apparent earlier. Especially when accompanied, as here, by simple moldings and plain walls, the possibilities of these and similar motifs might on occasion be exploited with

Plate 86. WOODLAWN PLANTATION, MOUNT VERNON, VIRGINIA. Begun *circa* 1800. Designed by Dr. William Thornton (1759–1828). In preparation to deeding 2000 acres of his land to his nephew, Washington himself ran the survey for this estate and selected "a most beautiful place for a Gentleman's Seat" overlooking Dogue Creek, the Potomac River, and his own mansion at Mount Vernon. In 1948 the Woodlawn Public Foundation purchased the house and nine years later turned it over to the National Trust for Historic Preservation, which after furnishing it suitably has opened it to the public. The Garden Club of Virginia restored the gardens. *Courtesy*, NATIONAL TRUST FOR HISTORIC PRESERVATION, WASHINGTON, D. C. PHOTOGRAPH BY MARLER

such distinction as to constitute the definite style to which historians have given the name "Federal" in recognition of its flowering during the first decades of the new federation of American states.

Either the design for the Library Company of Philadelphia with which Dr. William Thornton launched his architectural career in 1789, or the central pavilion of the Pennsylvania Hospital, begun five years later (*Plate 87*), offer conspicuous proof of the success with which the Late Georgian (or Federal) forms might be applied to public buildings. In general, however, the use of large windows with the slenderest of muntins, attenuated columns and pilasters, and flat surfaces gives to this style an elegance and grace perhaps more suited to the private residence than to larger civic

Plate 87. CENTER SECTION, PENNSYLVANIA HOSPITAL, PHILADELPHIA, PENNSYLVANIA. 1794–1805. As finally constructed, the skylight of a surgical amphitheater took the place of the central dome originally planned. Begun in 1755 as the first building of its kind in the colonies, the Hospital was designed by Samuel Rhoads, one of the original Board of Managers, who as a young man had been apprenticed as a carpenter but who was by then a prosperous builder. Benjamin Franklin composed the words still to be read on the cornerstone. PHOTOGRAPH BY WAYNE ANDREWS

141

structures. No doubt this helps to explain why it is in area of domestic architecture that the style appeared first and continued longest. In Philadelphia as early as 1788, the rich banker William Bingham built one of the most beautiful of Late Georgian town houses (*Plate 88*), patterned, it is said, upon the London house of the Duke of Manchester. Before it was turned into a hotel and later burned, the grandeur of the Bingham house on Third Street excited numerous remarks and probably no little envy. One of those to comment was Charles Bulfinch, who, in the course of a visit to Philadelphia in 1789, wrote his parents in Boston that he found the Binghams' town house "in a stile (*sic*) which would be esteemed splendid even in the most luxurious parts of Europe . . . a palace . . . far too rich for any man in this country."

That the final phase of the Georgian style should be characterized by a graceful and sophisticated elegance is not at all surprising inasmuch as a number of earlier epochs—the Greek and medieval among them—had witnessed a similar development. But what might have been normal stylistic evolution under any circumstances received added impetus in this case from the archaeological excavations that had been taking place at Pompeii and Herculaneum since about 1735. Now, instead of basing their knowledge of Roman architecture largely upon Palladio or other Renaissance authors, artists in all media were offered a fresh view of Roman art, itself a manifestation of the last period of antique culture. In this way it was discovered that for the interiors of their private villas the Romans of the mid-first century A.D. had employed a style characterized by light and fanciful forms—a fact known to Raphael and his contemporaries, to be sure, but one very largely overlooked by English architects in their admiration for Palladio.

Of course, most Americans could not study the ruins of Pompeii at first hand any more than they learned about the villas of Palladio by visiting Vicenza. As so often in the past, they found their sources in the work of British artists, specifically the brothers James (1703–1794) and Robert (1728–1792) Adam, who together were responsible for the tasteful adaptation of late Roman forms with which their name has subsequently been identified. Nor should we forget that the designer of the nation's capital was

French, and other of L'Enfant's countrymen active in the United States during the first years of the new republic come readily to mind. But since the brothers Adam are also thought to have been influenced by their French contemporaries, and they by them, this becomes much too complicated a question to unscramble here, even provided that a coherent statement of the problem is possible. For our purposes we may assume that it was such a model as the Adams' Kenwood (begun 1767) that William Hamilton had in

Plate 88. Town House of William Bingham, Philadelphia, Pennsylvania. *Circa* 1788. From an engraving, *circa* 1798, by William Birch (1755–1834) and published by him in *The City of Philadelphia, in the State of Pennsylvania North America; as it appeared in the Year 1800*. Although doorways with sidelights and elliptical transoms like that of the Bingham House are usually considered among the distinguishing features of the Federal Style, their origin in the previous phases of the Georgian Period is evidenced by such notable examples as the Chase-Lloyd House (*Plate 74*) and even the much earlier Stenton (*Plate 26*). Engraving from *The City of Philadelphia* by William Birch & Son, Philadelphia, 1800. *Courtesy*, NEW YORK PUBLIC LIBRARY

143

mind when about 1788 he altered the "Woodlands" (*Plate 89*), then a country estate and now a part of West Philadelphia. But whereas the large size of the typical English country house made the Adams' fragile, almost feminine, style most appropriate to the design of furnishings and interiors, the smaller scale of American buildings, especially at the residential level, readily permitted American architects to give local variants of the Adamesque a somewhat wider application.

Plate 89. NORTH FAÇADE OF THE WOODLANDS, WEST PHILADELPHIA, PENNSYLVANIA. Remodeled *circa* 1788. Built about 1742 as a summer home, the Woodlands was first owned by Andrew Hamilton II, son and namesake of the Andrew Hamilton (d. 1741) who is remembered for his contribution to the freedom of the press through the defense in New York of John Peter Zenger and as one of those charged with developing a design for the new State House (Independence Hall). During the Revolution, the second Andrew's son William (b. 1745) was obliged to live in England by reason of his Tory sympathies, and it was doubtless there that he developed a taste for the new Adamesque forms which on his return to America he incorporated in the remodeling of his country estate. In 1845 the Woodlands was converted into one of the "rural cemeteries" then in vogue, a function which it still serves. PHOTOGRAPH BY CORTLANDT V. D. HUBBARD, PHILADELPHIA

In the end, however, the significance of the new archaeology went far beyond specific discoveries or the art forms they inspired. For the first time, style was seen as the imprint on aesthetic form of a point of view, and with this realization was born the modern concept of history. Gradually it was recognized that Rome, instead of being the originator of the classical style, was itself the heir of Greece and that Egypt had been a flourishing kingdom for nearly three thousand years when Pericles planned the rebuilding of the Athenian Akropolis. Before the end of the 18th century Philadelphia had witnessed the construction of buildings that may fairly, if somewhat loosely, be termed "Greek" and "Gothic." A few years more and these would be followed by architectural essays in a variety of modes, of which the Egyptian, Chinese, and Moorish are only the best known and the most easily identified. Understandably, the excitement that came with the discovery of unfamiliar things, remote in time or place, proved to be both exhilarating and irresistible; in contrast, the familiar forms derived from English sources must have seemed dull indeed.

But in art, as in politics, what is thought advanced or retarded depends in large measure on the posture of the subject. If, from the vantage point of the 19th century, Late Georgian buildings inevitably seem somewhat out of place amid the Gothic spires and Greek temples of their contemporary surroundings, how differently they appear when viewed against the background of the preceding century. Far from being simply an engaging anachronism, the slender columns and graceful fanlights that characterize the architecture of the new republic appear to the historian of the 18th century as the final, logical, and in many ways most beautiful expression of the Renaissance classicism that had first emerged in the English colonies more than a century before. One might as easily hope to perform *Hamlet* without including the last act as to understand Georgian architecture in America without some reference to the serene and sophisticated style that represents its ultimate form.

PAINTING

by John W. McCoubrey

Busy with the practical necessities of establishing themselves in a new world, struggling to meet the basic needs for food and shelter, the earliest American colonists required little of the painter's art. From the beginning many colonial painters were forced to earn their livelihoods by working at a craft, as glaziers or painters of houses or signs. Many of these artists remain as anonymous as the humblest craftsmen, their pictures without documentation or signature and their travels through towns and villages recorded only by an occasional newspaper notice of their presence.

With the burgeoning of trade and the establishment of family fortunes, colonial houses and their furnishings became more and more elegant, but painting, whether done by a native born artist or by a newly arrived immigrant painter trained abroad and lured here by the new wealth, seems to have lagged behind the accomplishments of our builders, furniture makers and silversmiths. One reason for this lag is that architecture and the decorative arts, no matter how elegantly they were practiced, remained basically utilitarian. Even the work of the silversmith not only served a function at the table but provided a repository of wealth protected from loss or theft by the uniqueness of its design and by its identifying marks. The decorative arts were more closely bound than painting to a craft tradition which, for practical reasons, was kept alive in the colonies. A skilled joiner was more likely to produce a handsome and serviceable chair than was a house painter likely to produce a lifelike portrait. Furthermore, the illusionistic art of painting could less readily be transmitted to the colonies at second hand. A carpenter or mason armed with an English builder's book could more easily approach in wood or brick the English models he found therein than could a painter find guidance in an English black-and-white mezzotint to the intricacies of the oil medium, to the mysteries of chiaroscuro, to flesh tints or, least of all, to the art of producing a likeness.

149

But the painter labored under another limitation which had nothing to do with technical difficulties. The increasing prosperity of the colonies brought no significant extension in the range of his art. Although we can find in colonial portraiture some reflection of this new elegance in more and more elaborate settings for the figure, sometimes including fictitious parks and gardens, the painter was only rarely called upon for landscapes or still-lifes and almost never for the great themes of history, mythology or religion. There are a variety of reasons for this limitation. Colonial life did not provide the leisure for such tastes, nor were there many colonists learned enough to enjoy such themes. There were, furthermore, no royal patrons, no court and no public buildings which might have required such paintings. Finally, history painting and landscape did not flourish in the first half of the eighteenth century either in England or on the continent. Although these might be reasons enough, there remains the possibility that a strain of Puritanism in the colonies was responsible too for this limitation. Acknowledged only later by early writers on American art, Margaret Fuller and Horatio Greenough among them, it must have been a force in the colonial period as late as 1726, when Samuel Willard's sermons were published and the faithful could read that "for any to entertain or fancy any other image of God, but those reverend impressions of his glorious Perfections that are engraven upon his heart, is highly to dishonour him and provoke him to jealousy." The portraits which were ordered by such people served neither for decoration nor moral instruction but rather as outward signs of establishment and permanence in a growing and insecure environment.

The style of our colonial painting was a provincial reflection of the great styles of European painting transmitted here via England. It was based at first only on the memory of paintings seen in the homeland and later upon mezzotints after the fashionable portraits of London. Until immigrant artists trained abroad began to arrive in the colonies, it was almost impossible for an American to see an original European or English portrait of the first quality. There were no schools here, no collections to speak of, nor even that continuity of master-student relationships so necessary to the establishment even of a local tradition. The colonial artist desired only to paint as best he could in hopeful emulation of the successively fashionable styles from abroad. It is therefore pointless to speak of an

American style in colonial painting without extensive qualifications, some of which may emerge in the course of this essay. Generally we are to be concerned with English painting modified, particularly in the work of our native-born and therefore least trained artists, by the visual habits of the untutored provincial, habits which were common to such painters elsewhere cut off from the great sources of the European tradition. For the artists trained abroad there is almost nothing to say in defense of their being in any way American, and even less of their sharing in a common provincial vision. John Smibert, a London-trained painter who settled in Boston in 1730 where he painted Mrs. Edward Tyng (*Plate 90*), was therefore hardly more in-

Plate 90.
Mrs. Edward Tyng (Anne Waldo), *circa* 1742. Portrait by John Smibert. *Courtesy,* Yale University Art Gallery. Gift of the Yale University Art Gallery Associates

volved in the formation of a uniquely American style of painting than was Jacques Le Moyne, who recorded in 1565 Coligny's settlement in Florida (*Plate 91*) or John White, who illustrated in water color Raleigh's colonial venture in Virginia (*Plate 92*).

LAVDONNIERVS ET REX ATHORE ANTE COLVMNAM A PRAEFECTO PRIMA NAVIGATIONE LOCATAM QVAMQVE VENERANTVR FLORIEN

Jacobus Le Moyne dictus de Morgues ad vivum pinxit

Plate 91. SATURIBA, THE INDIAN CHIEF, AND RENÉ LAUDONNIÈRE AT RIBAUT'S COLUMN. A water colo Jacques Le Moyne, 1565. *Courtesy,* PRINTS DIVISION, NEW YORK PUBLIC LIBRARY. BEQUEST OF JAMES HAZEN HYDE

Plate 92. INDIANS FISHING, VIRGINIA, 1585. From original water color by John White. *Courtesy* OF THE TRUSTEES OF THE BRITISH MUSEUM, LONDON

We know very little of the painters active here before 1700. We cannot say with certainty which of the approximately four hundred surviving works of the 17th century were actually painted here, for undoubtedly many more than those of the Saltonstall family or of Governor Stuyvesant were brought here from overseas. Some colonials may have followed John Winthrop in having their portraits done abroad, during return visits to England or the Netherlands. The confusion becomes worse when we remember that painters were at work in small towns abroad who had no more proficiency than those who were active in the New World.

Plate 93.
MRS. FREAKE AND BABY MARY.
Portrait by an Unknown Artist, probably 1674. *Courtesy*, WORCESTER ART MUSEUM, WORCESTER, MASS.

154

One group of portraits, probably from the same hand, stands out among the surviving 17th-century New England portraits: those of Mr. Freake, of Mrs. Freake and Baby Mary (*Plate 93*) *circa* 1674, and three portraits of the Gibbs children, Margaret (*Plate 94*), Henry and Robert. Here, surprisingly, the artist ignored the sober style of the Commonwealth which might be expected in Puritan New England. Possibly still ignorant of it, the unknown limner recalls instead the elegant, embroidered style of Tudor England which he may have learned in some provincial corner before his departure or remembered, perhaps with the aid of a treasured engraving,

Plate 94.
Margaret Gibbs. Portrait by an unknown Artist, 1670–1675. *Courtesy,* Mrs. David M. Giltinan. photograph from the worcester art museum, worcester, mass.

165

after his arrival in America. In the Freake and Gibbs portraits he shows a sure grasp of two-dimensional, patterned design achieved by crisp edges or repeated diagonals. This is supported by a great delicacy in the treatment of surface, of laces and of fabric which lightens and overcomes the stiffness of the figures. It is a style which calls to mind the angular design of lozenge and diamond inlays on New England furniture and the linear surface patterns of New England houses with their board cladding and small-paned windows.

Other portraits from the Bay Colony, while painted with a similar flatness, lack the delicate charm of the Freake painter's work. John Foster (1648–1681) may have painted the Reverend John Davenport (*Plate 96*), and his woodcut of the Reverend Richard Mather (*Plate 97*) is a unique survival of work in that medium. The Rawson portraits (see portrait of Rebecca Rawson, *Plate 95*) and those of the Mason children are close to the

Plate 95.
Rebecca Rawson. Portrait by an Unknown Artist, *circa* 1674.
Courtesy, NEW ENGLAND HISTORIC GENEALOGICAL SOCIETY. PHOTOGRAP
BY GEORGE M. CUSHING

156

Plate 96.
REVEREND JOHN DAVENPORT. Portrait
attributed to John Foster, *circa* 1670.
Courtesy, YALE UNIVERSITY ART GALLERY

Mr. Richard Mather.

Plate 97.
REVEREND RICHARD MATHER. Woodcut by John
Foster. *Courtesy*, PRINCETON UNIVERSITY LIBRARY

157

Plate 98.
SELF-PORTRAIT BY THOMAS SMITH
(*circa* 1690). *Courtesy,*
WORCESTER. ART MUSEUM, WORCESTER,
MASS.

work of the Freake painter but, although they have been very badly
preserved, they seem to have been modeled on more recent works in the
Anglo-Dutch tradition. Captain Thomas Smith (active 1680–1690), a
mariner who came to New England in 1650, is known to have been paid by
Harvard for a portrait in 1680. Perhaps because of his travels his style
reflects a closer contact with English painting. His self-portrait (*Plate 98*)
and those of Captain George Curwen and Major Thomas Savage (*Plate 99*)
are more ambitious than those of the Freake painter. There is evidence of a
stronger attempt at characterization, somewhat more solid modeling and
looser brushwork, and Major Savage is portrayed in an imposing three-
quarter length pose of military grandeur. But despite Smith's apparent
willingness to abandon the unassuming manner of his contemporaries in
favor of more pompous likenesses, verses on his self-portrait which proclaim
the painter's farewell to a "World of Evils" strike a note of somber reflection

158

Plate 99. Major Thomas Savage. Portrait ascribed to Thomas Smith. *Courtesy,*
HENRY L. SHATTUCK, ESQ. PHOTOGRAPH FROM THE WORCESTER ART MUSEUM, WORCESTER, MASS.

and suggest that he was spiritually at home among the New England Calvinists.

In New Amsterdam the absence of a deep Puritan tradition may account for the presence of more imported paintings—landscapes are mentioned there at an early date—and for there being more early records of practising artists than in New England. Hendrick Couturier was a guild member in Leyden before coming here about 1660. He left for England in 1674, but during his brief stay he was probably the first and certainly the most completely trained artist working in the colonies. Seventeenth-century portraiture in New Amsterdam remained more closely linked to the Dutch tradition, and there one encounters none of the lingering medieval traditions which mark the work of the Freake painter. Portraits of Peter Stuyvesant (*Plate 100*), Nicholas William Stuyvesant and Jacobus Strycker have been attributed to Couturier without any certainty, but in such matters the surviving New Amsterdam pictures are and will remain as perplexing as those from New England. Those pictures mentioned, less idiosyncratic and perhaps less interesting than some of the New England paintings, suggest nevertheless that a generally higher level of traditional competence prevailed in New York than in and around Boston.

Lured by the increasing prosperity of the colonies—a prosperity elsewhere evident in the elegance that building began to acquire from Charleston to Portsmouth toward the middle of the 18th century—trained painters from abroad began to arrive in growing numbers and to paint with varying competence portraits which reflected either by genuine elegance or mere pretension the newly found colonial fortunes.

In 1705 Henrietta Johnston arrived at Charleston where she was active until her death (*circa* 1728-29). In 1739 the Swiss Jeremiah Theüs established a practice in Charleston which flourished there until 1774. Justus Engelhardt Kühn came from Germany to Annapolis in 1708 and painted there until his death in 1717. In 1714 John Watson (1684–1762), a Scot, settled at Perth Amboy in Jersey; in 1726 Peter Pelham, a mezzotint-engraver from England, came to Boston; and in 1735 Charles Bridges, a portraitist newly arrived from England, startled the planters of Virginia by riding to their estates in his own carriage. Although this first wave of

Plate 100. GOVERNOR PETER STUYVESANT. Portrait by an Unknown Artist. *Courtesy*, THE
NEW-YORK HISTORICAL SOCIETY, NEW YORK CITY

immigrant professionals brought a more generally acceptable version of the baroque portrait to these shores and one closer to current transatlantic style, none of them was in a position to alter profoundly the condition of painting in the colonies. Henrietta Johnston's work was limited to small pastel portraits (see portrait of Anne Broughton, *Plate 101*) little known beyond Charleston, and Theüs, apparently successful in the same city, turned out tidy, competent but rather shallow likenesses as in *Elizabeth Rothmaler* (*Plate 102*). Although Bridges was master of a more flamboyant style

Plate 101.
ANNE BROUGHTON. Portrait by Henrietta Johnston, 1720. *Courtesy*, YALE UNIVERSITY ART GALLERY, JOHN HILL MORGAN COLLECTION

162

than the Charleston painters (see portrait of Maria Taylor Byrd, *Plate 103*)
and was closer to the most recent decorative and aristocratic court portraiture of England, his stay in Virginia was a short one. Other portraits of
Virginia families in the same courtly style have survived but they are
probably the work of other visiting painters, for Bridges put down no roots.
Kühn, during his short career in Annapolis, produced portraits of considerable but naive charm in which figures (like that of Eleanor Darnall, *Plate
104*) are sometimes swallowed up by their backgrounds of pictorially un-
assimilated props which suggest a splendor his sitters probably never knew.

Plate 103. MARIA TAYLOR BYRD. Portrait by Charles Bridges, 1735–1740. *Courtesy,* THE METROPOLITAN MUSEUM OF ART, NEW YORK, FLETCHER FUND

Plate 104. ELEANOR DARNALL. Portrait by Justus Engelhardt Kühn *circa* 1710. *Courtesy,* **165**
MARYLAND HISTORICAL SOCIETY, BALTIMORE

Plate 105. TISHCOHAN. Portrait by Gustavus Hesselius. *Courtesy,* HISTORICAL SOCIETY OF PENNSYLVANIA, PHILADELPHIA

More significant than these artists of different origins and skills were two painters who settled in major cities and established, if not a continuing tradition for the art of painting, at least a concentration of artistic endeavor in which such a tradition might eventually take hold. Gustavus Hesselius (1682–1755) was born in Sweden. The place of his training is not known, but he arrived in America as a trained painter in 1711 and shortly thereafter settled in Philadelphia where he became the principal portraitist. A letter from James Logan described Hesselius as "no bad hand, who generally does justice to the men, especially to their blemishes," and it is true that Hesselius' portraits are noteworthy for their stubborn forthrightness rather than for any particular elegance or charm. But his importance lies less in the quality of his works than in the way he was able to extend his talents, in the liberal atmosphere of 18th century Philadelphia, to a wide range of subject matter new to the colonies. His portraits, painted for John Penn in 1735, of the Delaware Indians Tishcohan (*Plate 105*) and Lapowinsa, who had taken part in the notorious "walking purchase" of Indian lands, were the first objective—one is tempted to say sympathetic—pictorial record of American Indians. In 1721 Hesselius had already painted for the parishioners of Saint Barnabas Church in Prince George County, Maryland, a *Last Supper* (now lost) and later in his career a *Holy Family*. The only other religious painting of consequence in the colonies was done by John Valentin Haidt (1700–1780) who, after a career in Dresden, Venice, Rome, Paris and London, joined the Moravian Brotherhood and spent the last thirty years of his life painting religious pictures for the Moravian colony around Bethlehem, Pennsylvania. Religious painting was rigidly excluded in areas where Calvinist doctrines were strong and was never prevalent in the colonies even when the rigors of that doctrine began to soften. It should be mentioned, however, that in the 18th century religious painting in England and in France was already on the wane. More surprising were the scenes of classical mythology probably painted by Hesselius in the 1720's—a *Bacchus and Ariadne* (*Plate 106*) and a *Bacchanale*. These representations of classical nudity in the colonies are further evidence of the enlightened spirit of Philadelphia, a city which in mid-century launched the foreign career of

Plate 106. BACCHUS AND ARIADNE. Painting by Gustavus Hesselius. *Courtesy*, THE DETROIT INSTITUTE OF ART.

its native son, Benjamin West, and later fostered the inquiring spirit of Charles Willson Peale.

The second important painter of the early immigration was John Smibert (1688–1751), a contemporary of Hesselius, who arrived at Newport in the company assembled by George Berkeley to establish a college in Bermuda "for the Better Supplying Churches in our Foreign Plantations and for Converting the Savage Americans to Christianity."

Funds for the Dean's project never arrived, but the success of a Boston exhibition of Smibert's own work along with his copies of Raphael, Titian, Rubens, Van Dyck and Poussin brought the painter to that city in 1730. Smibert's arrival was celebrated in a poem by Mather Byles published in the London *Daily Courant* of 14 April, 1730. It claimed that, until Smibert's providential arrival,

> *Ages our Land a Barb'rous Desert stood,*
> *And Savage Nations howl'd in every Wood,*
>
> *No heav'nly Pencil the free Stroke could give,*
> *Nor the warm Canvas felt its Colors live.*

Some of Byles' enthusiasm and Smibert's eventual success may indeed be attributed to the "Barb'rous" state of painting in Boston where competition with Smibert's work could be found only in Pelham's uninspired mezzotints, in small portraits in black and white by Nathaniel Emmons (1704–1740), and in paintings by Joseph Badger (1708–1765; see *Plate 107*). Like Hesselius, Smibert brought to America a competent, unspectacular style based (in Smibert's case) on that of Kneller's English court portraiture. Dominant in England during the early 18th century, this style was the basis of Charles Bridges' work in Virginia and was behind the work of the unknown who painted Reverend James Pierpont (*Plate 108*) and his wife in 1711.

In Smibert's hands it is a straightforward, unflattering style, comparable in this regard to Hesselius'. His portraits of Mrs. Tyng (*Plate 90*) or Nathaniel Byfield (*Plate 109*) appear consistent with Walpole's description of his character, "a silent, modest man who abhorred the finesse of some of his profession." None of Smibert's later work can match, either in conception or execution, his 1729 group portrait of Bishop Berkeley and his entourage (*Plate 110*). In this, the most elaborate composition yet undertaken in the colonies, Smibert commemorated the venture with life-sized figures posed in attitudes of easy nonchalance which bespeak Smibert's familiarity with

Plate 107. Mrs. John Edwards. Portrait by Joseph Badger *circa* 1750. *Courtesy,* Museum
OF FINE ARTS, BOSTON

Plate 108. REVEREND JAMES PIERPONT. Portrait by an Unknown Artist, 1711. *Courtesy,*
YALE UNIVERSITY ART GALLERY

171

European masters and museums. His attempts to capture the full rhythms of baroque composition were perhaps inspired from some representation of the Holy Family. In addition to the modest proficiency he brought to the barren Boston art world, he provided the rudiments of a school in his painting rooms, where the already mentioned copies plus a few casts after the antique were shown, and in his print and color shop. To Smibert's tiny gallery came a series of younger painters—Copley, Peale and Trumbull among them—to absorb the lessons its modest collection could afford them.

Plate 109.
NATHANIEL BYFIELD. Portrait by John Smibert, 1730. *Courtesy,* THE METROPOLITAN MUSEUM OF ART, NEW YORK. BEQUEST OF CHARLES ALLEN MUNN, 1924

172

Plate 110. DEAN (LATER BISHOP) GEORGE BERKELEY WITH HIS FAMILY, AND FRIENDS. Painting by John Smibert, 1729. *Courtesy,* YALE UNIVERSITY ART GALLERY. GIFT OF ISAAC LOTHROP

With these new arrivals came some broadening of taste. Smibert once spoke of diverting himself "with some things in a landskip way," and landscapes are mentioned quite early in New York and in the estate inventories of Kühn and Theüs. No independent landscapes have survived, however, and they could not have been common. Several painted panels from interiors suggest that such painting was usually part of decorative schemes, like those from "Marmion" in Virginia (*Plate 111*) and the early panels (pre-1725) from the Clark-Frankland House in Boston. More common were topographical prints, a genre in which William Burgis was the first to specialize with engravings of Boston (*Plate 112*), New York, and Harvard College, dating from between 1715 and 1723. Events around the

Plate 111. Landscape Panel from "Marmion" in Virginia. Painting by an Unknown Artist. *Courtesy*, the Metropolitan Museum of Art, New York, Rogers Fund, 1916

e 112. VIEW OF BOSTON HARBOR. Engraving by William Burgis, *circa* 1722. *Courtesy*, THE NEW-YORK
ORICAL SOCIETY, NEW YORK CITY

struggle for independence produced a later flurry of activity including the
propagandistic *Boston Massacre*, 1770, engraved by Paul Revere after the
drawing of Henry Pelham. Bernard Romans' *An Exact View of the Late
Battle at Charlestown* (*Plate 113*), half view and half map, appeared
shortly after the event, and in 1775 Amos Doolittle engraved four scenes:
The Battle of Lexington; A View of the Town of Concord (*Plate 114*); *The
Engagement at the North Bridge;* and *A View of the South Part of
Lexington*.

Sculpture was the least developed of colonial arts. Woodcarvers were
busy on architectural decorations and figureheads early in the century, and
much of our sculpture, like landscape painting, was treated as a decorative
art. Such works include Shem Drowne's Indian weathervane of copper

175

Plate 113. AN EXACT VIEW OF THE LATE BATTLE AT CHARLESTOWN. Engraving by Bernard Rom
Courtesy, PRINTS DIVISION, NEW YORK PUBLIC LIBRARY

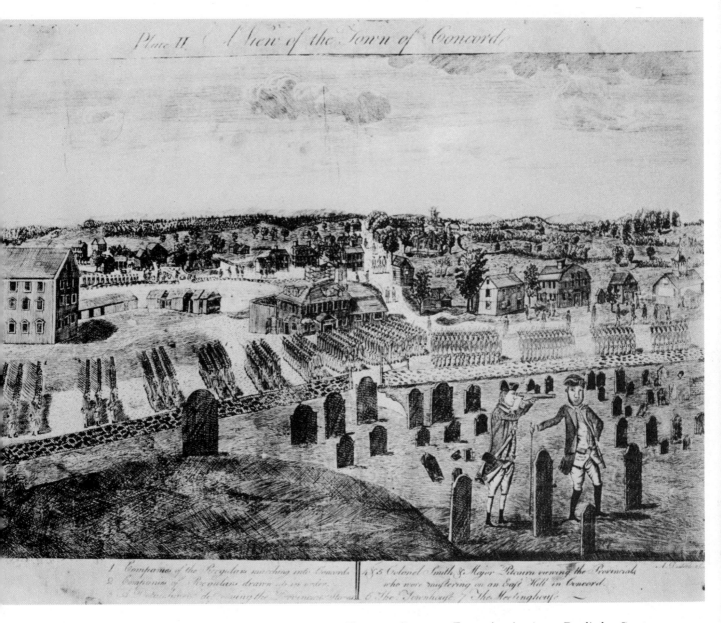

Plate 114. A VIEW OF THE TOWN OF CONCORD. Engraving by Amos Doolittle. *Courtesy,* STOKES COLLECTION, PRINTS DIVISION, NEW YORK PUBLIC LIBRARY

Plate 115.
Copper Weathervane. By
Shem Drowne, *circa* 1750. *Courtesy*,
MASSACHUSETTS HISTORICAL SOCIETY,
BOSTON. PHOTOGRAPH BY
GEORGE M. CUSHING

(*Plate 115*) which once threatened Boston with its enormous pointed arrow, and a wooden figure of Mercury by Simeon Skillin the elder (*Plate 116*), which surmounted Isaac Royall's summerhouse. There was almost no free standing figure sculpture. The wax effigies of Patience Wright are lost and the first truly monumental work in sculpture in America was by a foreigner —Houdon's standing figure of George Washington. One of the most fascinating arts of the colonial period was the carving on gravestones. Here the carvers, working in low relief, were able to call upon a rich and varied

Plate 116. FIGURE OF MERCURY. A figure of gilded pine by the elder Simeon Skillin; it is also attributed to John Skillin. From Index of American Design. *Courtesy,* NATIONAL GALLERY OF ART, WASHINGTON, D. C.

179

imagery derived from ancient symbolism. Many of the representations are chill reminders of the transience of human existence, like the gravestone of John Foster, 1681 (*Plate 117*). In later stones, crude likenesses of the departed gaze out like the flat images of early Christian mosaics. Others, like the stone of Benjamin Wyatt, 1767 (*Plate 118*), attributed to John Bull, reveal a surprising delicacy of curving line and a touch of moving, human compassion.

180   *Plate 117.* GRAVESTONE OF JOHN FOSTER. By an Unknown Artist, at Dorchester, Mass., 1681. PHOTO-GRAPH, *courtesy* OF ALAN LUDWIG

Plate 118. GRAVESTONE OF BENJAMIN WYATT, 1767. Attributed to John Bull. PHOTOGRAPH, *courtesy* OF ALAN LUDWIG

The Arts in America: The Colonial Period

While the current English fashion was being established in Boston and elsewhere by visiting or recently immigrated professionals, the increased demand for portraits also brought work for a number of native trained artists. To this group belong the patroon painters active between 1720 and 1740 in the Hudson Valley and, most notably, the mysterious Robert Feke who was active from 1740 until 1750. To all of these painters, most of them anonymous, were available as guides not only works of the new arrivals which brought a closer view of current English style, but also, apparently in considerable number, prints after Lely, Kneller and eventually after Hudson and Reynolds.

Plate 119.
MRS. ANTHONY VAN SCHAICK.
Portrait by an Unknown Artist, 1720.
Courtesy OF THE OWNERS, THE
ALBANY INSTITUTE OF HISTORY AND
ART, ALBANY, N. Y.

182

The achievement of the patroon painters was extremely uneven. Typical of their general mediocrity are the portraits of Mrs. Anthony van Schaick (*Plate 119*) and Johannes de Peyster (*Plate 120*), both by unknown hands. In the former, sharp angular ridges of highlights described on a stiff plane of drapery continue to reveal the awkwardness of the provincial and relatively untrained painter. The same is true of the de Peyster portrait which stems directly from a mezzotint after Kneller. Both of these untutored hands attempted more than they were competent to imitate, and the result of their impatient assault on contemporary English style was a compromise between provincial patterning and, for them, an unattainable illusionism. J. Cooper,

late 120.
OHANNES DE PEYSTER III. Portrait
y an Unknown Artist, 1718.
ourtesy, THE NEW-YORK HISTORICAL
OCIETY, NEW YORK CITY, WALDRON
HOENIX BELKNAP, JR., COLLECTION

who was active between 1714 and 1718 in New England, left similar portraits, less harshly modeled and somewhat more graceful (*Plate 121*). It would seem that the key distinction between painters like these and the man who painted Madelena Dow Gansevoort (*Plate 122*, "The Girl with the Red Shoes") lay in the latter's ability to recognize his limitations and to work, as best he could, entirely within them. He avoided the problems of reflected light and windblown drapery which were beyond him. In his picture, light glows from the intensity of the color itself, and his contours and boldly quilted pattern, reminiscent of the Freake painter's sensibility,

Plate 121.
UNKNOWN GENTLEMAN. Portrait by J. Cooper, 1714–1718. *Courtesy*, THE NEW-YORK HISTORICAL SOCIETY, NEW YORK CITY

184

185

Plate 122. MADELENA GANSEVOORT. Portrait by an Unknown Artist. *Courtesy,* HENRY FRANCIS DU PONT WINTERTHUR MUSEUM, WINTERTHUR, DEL. PHOTOGRAPH BY GILBERT ASK

Plate 123.
ADAM WINNE. Portrait by an Unknown
Artist, *circa* 1730. *Courtesy,* HENRY
FRANCIS DU PONT WINTERTHUR MUSEUM,
WINTERTHUR, DEL. PHOTOGRAPH BY
GILBERT ASK

create a forceful but orderly design. Another painter of similar persuasion painted Adam Winne's portrait (*Plate 123*), in which everything is simplified and flattened so that the accents of red and white and the curving contours of clothes and clouds are allowed to reveal the full extent of their refinement. The then prevalent use of mezzotints to furnish the details of pose, costume and background has been proven by the late Waldron Phoenix Belknap, but for these painters the practice brought apparently no temptation to overreach their wise restraint. With Smith's mezzotint after Kneller's *Lord Buckhurst and Lady Mary Sackville* (*Plate 124*) before

186

Plate 124. LORD BUCKHURST AND LADY MARY SACKVILLE. Mezzotint by John Smith, 1695, after Godfrey Kneller. *Courtesy*, HENRY FRANCIS DU PONT WINTERTHUR MUSEUM, WINTERTHUR, DEL.

Plate 125. JOHN VAN CORTLANDT. Portrait by an Unknown Artist, *circa* 1730. *Courtesy,*
THE BROOKLYN MUSEUM, BROOKLYN, N. Y.

him, the unknown painter of John Van Cortlandt (*Plate 125*) irreverently
simplified the architecture and brought the sitter's feet into tidy alignment
with the curving step and then echoed that line across the middle of his
landscape background. Buttons, buttonholes, leaves and drapery folded in
crisp patterns make his painting something quite different from its model.
His work must be judged on its own merits deriving from the painter's
instinctive ability to create a self-sufficient and internally consistent work.

The rough-hewn portrait of Anne Pollard (*Plate 126*), produced
in Massachusetts on the occasion of that lady's one hundredth birthday

189

in 1721, reveals that all our native painters were not as subtle as the Gansevoort painter. Indeed, such refinement was usually to be found among the otherwise mawkish New York painters. Their approach to painting was similar to that of the craftsman. For them an unfinished surface or a sketchy, untidy illusionism was no more possible than it was for the furniture-maker or silversmith. The special gifts of judicious exclusion and refinement evident in the Van Cortlandt painter's treatment of his source in Kneller will become more apparent when contrasted to the portrait of Eleanor Darnall (*Plate 104*). The two artists had much in common. Both of them were provincially and inadequately trained and probably for the most part self-taught, Kühn in Europe and the other in the colonies. Both display the same inclination to exclude atmospheric effects and the play of light and shadow, and both tend to compose in rather two-dimensional, orderly patterns. Despite these similarities, Kühn's painting has a proliferation of details in the balustrade, near and far, and in the ornate vase and flowers which detracts from the importance of the figure and offers no redeeming elegance of line or pattern. Furthermore, the background is not treated consistently with the figure; it remains with the perspective of the terrace a three-dimensional space which the flat, doll-like figure does not sufficiently occupy. The Van Cortlandt painter, as we have suggested, relies on play of elegant, curving lines, a consistent and uniform elimination of details, and even bends the foreground out of perspective in creating this unity. The continuation of the formal qualities exhibited by the Van Cortlandt or Gansevoort painters in the work of later colonial painters presents a sequence which has the look of an evolving and elaborating style, but it represents a peculiar kind of art history. The elements which customarily account for such a development—a local tradition, school or dominant master—simply were not present. The continuity exists rather in the gradual elaboration of a basically similar, even provincial, approach in the work of Robert Feke and John Singleton Copley.

The career of Robert Feke remains shadowy. He was born on Long Island, traveled, perhaps as a mariner, in his youth, returned to the sea in 1750 and died shortly thereafter. A document of 1767 refers to him simply as "mariner, deceased," but it has been claimed that his early "voyaging" was actually spent acquiring an education in painting abroad. In support of this notion are alleged the sudden demand for his pictures after 1740 in cities from Boston to Philadelphia; Dr. Hamilton's description of him as "a painter, the most extraordinary genius I ever knew"; and his first commission, one for an ambitious family group portrait given him in 1741 by Isaac Royall. But if Isaac Royall, a prospering Boston merchant with a splendid house outside the city, summoned Feke because of his European experience, there is nothing in the portrait he received (*Plate 127*) to suggest that the painter had profited much from the great galleries of Europe.

Plate 127. FAMILY OF ISAAC ROYALL. Painting by Robert Feke, 1741. *Courtesy,* THE HARVARD LAW SCHOOL, HARVARD UNIVERSITY

Feke may well have been challenged by Smibert's Bishop Berkeley group, but he made no attempt to imitate its baroque composition or flowing drapery. Standing at the right, Royall presides over his seated women. The edge of his coat falls with the stiff grace of a New England Queen Anne chair. A strong horizontal extends from its lower edge across the covering of the table and is paralleled above by the forearms of the women. These horizontals bind the staccato rhythm of the seated figures enforced by the repeated V-shaped necklines and bold contrast of their colored dresses. This boldness of pattern and reticent grace are qualities we have already observed in some of the work of the seventeen-twenties. They were entirely possible to a painter who learned his craft here and who was endowed with the sensitivity which seems to shine from the large eyes, long flowing hair and delicate features of Feke's first self-portrait (*Plate 128*)—a conception of an artistic personality quite out of place among the robust likenesses of his contemporaries in New England.

Some of Feke's compositions are built into substantial pyramids and capped with imposing, dominant features. Such is the masterful portrait of the Reverend Thomas Hiscox (*Plate 129*) whose face, crowned with silvery hair, is aloof and powerful despite the luminous brilliance and delicate brushwork. But Feke's most distinctive works are those in which the brush is more closely controlled, surfaces are disciplined, and line moves with simple,

Plate 129.
REVEREND THOMAS HISCOX. Portrait by Robert Feke, 1745. *Courtesy*, COUNTESS LÂSLÓ SZÉCHÉNYI. PHOTOGRAPH FROM FRICK ART REFERENCE LIBRARY, NEW YORK

Plate 130.
ISAAC WINSLOW. Portrait by Robert Feke, *circa* 1748. *Courtesy*, MUSEUM OF FINE ARTS, BOSTON

open grace—qualities evident in his portraits of Isaac Winslow (*Plate 130*) and James Bowdoin. These are based upon the style of Hudson which supplanted the earlier style based on prints after Kneller. Here the figures are more convincingly modeled than those of the Royall family and placed in a light-filled, outdoor setting. But Winslow's commanding presence is not derived from a description of his physical bulk, but stems more abstractly from the upthrust spear of his satin waistcoat, repeated in the sharply pointed touches at the cuff, and by the long, sweeping curves which lead swiftly upward to the face, revealing little of the figure underneath. Indeed the male costume with its clear edges was ideally suited to Feke's fondness for line. In his portraits of women he was less successful, and, although their garments gleam with the same radiance of silk and satin, their composition

is less clear and resolved. Whether he learned his art abroad or not, Feke is a link between men like the painters of Adam Winne or Johannes de Peyster and Copley. In his work their linear sensibility is present but has become more open and free; his surfaces remain like theirs tight and controlled (although more elaborate and polished) and continue to serve their elegant, linear boundaries; light still springs not from an illusion of atmosphere but glows principally from within the colors themselves.

The American portraits of John Singleton Copley (1738–1815) represent the culmination of this colonial style. Nearly all of them were painted in Boston where Copley lived until his departure just before the Revolution. Copley was fortunate in his mother's marriage to Peter Pelham, her second husband, who was one of the first trained professionals to arrive here from England. Pelham was a mezzotint engraver whose *Cotton Mather* of 1727 (*Plate 131*) was the first such print produced in America; he also ran a

195

school of "reading, writing, needlework, dancing, and the art of painting on glass." In this rather unusual Boston household Copley had his first training in the arts, but when he was only fourteen his stepfather died. Feke and Smibert had both recently been removed from the scene, so that at the moment when Copley was beginning to find his way the city was suddenly bereft of its best talent. At this opportune time, Joseph Blackburn arrived in Boston from England, bringing with him a lightsome, 18th-century style which supplanted the ponderous baroque of Smibert and Pelham. To the young Copley, Blackburn's flashy style, visible in the quick rhythms and glossy surfaces of his *Theodore Atkinson* (*Plate 132*), must have been a revelation.

Out of this varied background, and with the overshadowing presence of Blackburn always with him, Copley forged in a decade of activity his own splendid style. In this earliest phase of his work he drew frequently, as colonial artists before him had done, on a variety of mezzotint sources. In his portrait of Mrs. Joseph Mann of 1753 (*Plate 133*), he followed rather timidly a print after Wissing's painting of Princess Anne, subjecting his prototype to the familiar angular simplification of the provincial. His *Jonathan Belcher* stems from a print by Hudson and his *Mrs. Jerathmael Bowers* of 1767–1770 (*Plate 134*) from one after Reynolds. But the awkwardness of the Mann portrait has disappeared, and, though still somewhat simplified, the modeling of the figure is fuller (see portrait of Joshua Winslow, *Plate 135*) and the surfaces more polished than in his very early work. Much of this change must be credited to Blackburn's example and perhaps to Feke. Such borrowing did not last long in Copley's work, although in these early works—the gropings of a precocious talent—he can be seen learning, as artists have traditionally learned, as much from other artists as from nature.

But it was indeed "truth, nature and fact" that John Adams found so admirable in Copley's portraits. "You can scarcely help discoursing with them, asking and receiving answers," said Adams. It is this quality of factual observation, based upon patient examination and exhausting imitation, which brings Copley's sitters so close to the viewer and invites discourse with them. Copley never indulged in flattery in any form. He could

Plate 132. COLONEL THEODORE ATKINSON. Portrait by Joseph Blackburn. *Courtesy,*
WORCESTER ART MUSEUM, WORCESTER, MASS.

197

Plate 133. MRS. JOSEPH MANN. Portrait by John Singleton Copley, 1753. *Courtesy,*
MUSEUM OF FINE ARTS, BOSTON

Plate 134. Mrs. Jerathmael Bowers. Portrait by John Singleton Copley (1767–1770). *Courtesy*, THE
METROPOLITAN MUSEUM OF ART, NEW YORK, ROGERS FUND

Plate 135. Joshua Winslow. Portrait by John Singleton Copley, 1755. *Courtesy*, SANTA BARBARA (CALIFORNIA) MUSEUM OF ART, PRESTON MORTON COLLECTION. PHOTOGRAPH FROM M. KNOEDLER AND COMPANY, NEW YORK

present Mr. Jeremiah Lee of Marblehead in a regal setting full of expensive furniture and fabric (*Plate 136*), yet the sitter remains in the midst of his possessions, short, stout, and quite incapable of living up to them. Mrs.

ate 136.
REMIAH LEE. Portrait by
nn Singleton Copley, 1769. *Courtesy,*
DSWORTH ATHENEUM, HARTFORD, CONN.

Thomas Boylston is dressed in all her finery (*Plate 137*), yet she gazes at the viewer rather uncertainly, her small face dark and old, precisely, one feels, as it looked. The column and hanging drapery, vestiges of the baroque state portrait, cannot help her. But she is not painted without sympathy, for Copley, while recording what he saw, yet tempers his relentless vision with humanity and a respect for the sitter's individuality. He gave his sitters a kind of self-possessed integrity, touched sometimes with an expression of self-conscious, bemused tolerance as they went through the unfamiliar and agonizingly slow process of sitting to him.

Plate 137.
Mrs. Thomas Boylston. Portrait by John Singleton Copley, 1766. *Courtesy,* HARVARD UNIVERSITY

202

In many of Copley's portraits, however, the traditional props disappear, and the sitters present themselves as they were—their station, their trade and often, one suspects, even their personality projected in the whole composition or enhanced by a few simple, marvelously detailed accessories. Mrs. Ezekiel Goldthwait (*Plate 138*) sits informally at a table with a plate

Plate 138.
Mrs. Ezekiel Goldthwait.
Portrait by
John Singleton Copley, 1770–1771.
Courtesy, MUSEUM OF FINE ARTS,
BOSTON

of fruit she seems to enjoy. Nathaniel Hurd (*Plate 139*) and Paul Revere (*Plate 140*), silversmiths and engravers, are shown with objects connected with their trade. Presented in informal or working attire, both of them sit squarely before the viewer who, in the absence of deep illusionistic space, may imagine himself almost at the table opposite them. In these democratic, informal portraits, however, there is a prevailing atmosphere of stillness, a product perhaps of the immobility a realist cannot help conveying in his laborious recording of fact, but yet here one of an almost classical dignity and calm.

Plate 139.
NATHANIEL HURD. Portrait by John Singleton Copley, *c.* 1765. *Courtesy,* THE CLEVELAND MUSEUM OF ART, JOHN HUNTINGTON COLLECTION

Plate 140. Paul Revere. Portrait by John Singleton Copley, 1768–1770. *Courtesy,* museum of fine arts, boston

205

The two very different portraits of Epes Sargent (*Plate 141*) and Isaac Smith (*Plate 142*) are examples of Copley's ability to characterize his sitters both by the nature of the inanimate objects around them and by the disposition of the whole composition as well. The mood of the Sargent portrait, like those of Revere and Hurd, is one of weightiness and bulk. It is conveyed generally by the massive pyramid of figure and architecture, the heavy figure of the sitter unbroken by light contrasts or quick lines, and

Plate 141. Epes Sargent. Portrait by John Singleton Copley, 1759–1761. *Courtesy*, national gal‐ lery of art, washington, d. c. Gift of the avalon foundation

206

particularly from the heavy hand and stubby fingers pressed against the coat. This characterization of a grave and substantial citizen is also supported by the solid, sturdy adjunct of the rugged architectural fragment, a base without a column. The whole composition of Isaac Smith's portrait is, on the other hand, alive with crossing and diverging lines and nervous edges which never build toward a resolved, stable unity. Quick stabs of white scattered sharply throughout the picture, and the vibration of the subject's plum suit against the brilliant blue drapery behind it, further contribute to the impression that here is represented a merchant of ceaseless, restless energy.

Plate 142. Isaac Smith. Portrait by John Singleton Copley, 1769. *Courtesy,* Yale University Art Gallery, Maitland F. Griggs Collection

Yet in these astonishingly vivid portraits Copley masked the unavoidable gaps in his training. The brilliant color contrasts which seem at home in the Smith portrait would be unthinkable to a professionally trained painter. Since he had no opportunity in Boston to study the nude, Copley's figures were almost invariably "wrong." Arms emerge too short and heads too large from torsos which are unsubstantial, ill-constructed, hidden or almost nonexistent. Mrs. Goldthwait's bulk disappears somehow behind the edge of the gleaming table top, and Isaac Smith's legs are unconvincingly joined to the rest of his body. These defects pass unnoticed at first because Copley painted such arresting features and because, indulging himself in what he confessed to be "a certain luxury in seeing," he lavished his sensuous delight on still-life details which seize the willing eye—Paul Revere's teapot, Mrs. Goldthwait's fruit, and everywhere the shimmer of silk, satin and lace. Thus he found a way around his difficulties with the human figure. Just as Feke and others before him had masked their ignorance of figure painting with an elegance of line and surface, Copley further elaborated these elements and confirmed the reality of his sitters with foci of attention on their faces and convincingly present, three-dimensional accessories.

In most instances his inadequacies become the strength of his pictures. The cool somber colors of the Sargent portrait are as proper to its mood as is the untutored brilliance of color in the Smith portrait. When he painted Governor and Mrs. Thomas Mifflin of Philadelphia, one of the last master portraits of his American residence (*Plate 143*), Copley was apparently at a loss to fill the yawning space of the imposing setting he gave them. The informal, touchingly awkward couple, their hands piled up in the very center of the composition, and the husband's book negligently and precariously pointed at the wife's neck, simply ignore it. Yet the two exist in a plausible relationship, seemingly interrupted at home in a space for kings which they do not require.

For seven years before his departure Copley was restive in the provincial city of Boston. He felt "peculiarly unlucky in living in a place into which there has not been one portrait brought within my memory that is worthy to be called a picture," and complained that in Boston painting was esteemed "no more than any other useful trade, as they sometimes term it, like that of a

Plate 143. GOVERNOR AND MRS. THOMAS MIFFLIN. Portrait by John Singleton Copley, 1773. *Courtesy,* HISTORICAL SOCIETY OF PENNSYLVANIA, PHILADELPHIA

carpenter, tailor or shoemaker, not as one of the most noble arts in the world." In 1765 he sent a portrait of his young half-brother, Peter Pelham, to an exhibition of the Society of Artists in London. The portrait, the famous *Boy with a Squirrel* which, unfortunately, we have been refused permission to reproduce, was favorably received. Reynolds, the reigning luminary of English painting, let him know indirectly that, given the chance for study and instruction that only Europe could offer him, his future prospects might be unlimited, but added chillingly, "provided you could receive these aids before your manner and taste were corrupted by working in your little way in Boston." The criticisms of his picture were predictable. He heard indirectly that Reynolds, though enthusiastic in his praise, "observed a little hardness in the drawing, coldness in the shades, and over-minuteness, all which Example could correct." Benjamin West gently informed him (in his customary inventive spelling) that "the picture struck the eye as being too liney, which was judged to have arose from there being so much neetness in the lines .... great Correctness in ones out line ... is apt to Produce a Poverty in the look of ones work." His figure wanted the necessary subordination of parts to the whole, but it was good enough to win him election in 1766 to the Society of Artists of Great Britain and an invitation from West to stay with him in London.

In 1774 Copley sailed to Europe at last, leaving his wife and family temporarily behind him. He apparently shared his in-laws' view that the Boston patriots were mere troublemakers, but the brewing storm in Boston was a sufficient pretext for making a decision perhaps already too long deferred. He left a city in which he could no longer grow. Like West before him, he was an English colonial going where his ambition naturally took him. He was in no positive way conscious of being an American or even that an American school might come into existence. With the Revolution, colonial painting by definition ceased to be, and, although provincial painters continued to work in America long after the war was over, independence brought American painters not sudden isolation but rather closer ties with London and Europe.

There were, in addition to Blackburn, a few other visiting professionals in the colonies during Copley's time and one or two native painters who deserve mention. The Englishman, John Wollaston, painted until 1758 in the middle and southern colonies in the manner of Blackburn and enjoyed astonishing success, despite his reliance on stock types and standardized expressions. William Williams provided naive variations on the conversation piece during visits in Philadelphia through the middle decades of the century. Neither of them settled here permanently. Wollaston was eventually off to India, and Williams was apparently back and forth to the West Indies. John Greenwood, a New England painter who ended his days in London, painted his *Sea Captains Carousing in Surinam* (*Plate 144*) after residence in that South American port. Similarly fragmented were the careers of the first group of Americans who returned to the colonies after study in the studio of Benjamin West. These Americans, who had been attracted by West's growing reputation and his unfailing hospitality, were

144. SEA CAPTAINS CAROUSING IN SURINAM. Painting by John Greenwood, 1757–1758. *Courtesy*, CITY MUSEUM, ST. LOUIS, MISSOURI

documented in a painting *The American School* (*Plate 160*) by one of their number, Matthew Pratt. Of the early students of West—Pratt, Benbridge, Delanoy and Peale—only the last established himself successfully in his profession upon his return. The rest, upset in the troubled years of war, turned to other pursuits or fell into obscurity. One of West's later pupils, William Dunlap, painted for a while here after the war and then turned to playwriting and producing, but his chief legacy was his *A History of the Rise and Progress of the Arts of Design in the United States* which appeared in 1834.

Charles Willson Peale on his return from London in 1767 became the chief painter of Philadelphia and was the founder of a family of painters active far into the 19th century. Just as Hesselius had been able to try his hand at a variety of subjects in that city, so Peale eventually challenged the old limitations to portraiture. Even the early family portrait of 1773 (*Plate 145*) by this ingenious jack-of-all-trades reveals in its inclusiveness his own abundant sense of life. In it, the older and more rigid type of group portrait

Plate 145. PEALE FAMILY GROUP. Painting by Charles Willson Peale. *Courtesy*, NEW-YORK HISTORICAL
CIETY, NEW YORK CITY

with perfunctory background gives way to an informal setting suggesting, not a park or a palace, but some place breathing an atmosphere of family affection and of respect for humanistic learning and the arts. His portrait of *Washington After Trenton* (*Plate 146*) reveals these same informal qualities invading, rather disconcertingly, a formal portrait of a military hero.

Plate 146.
WASHINGTON AFTER TRENTON.
Painting by Charles Willson Peale.
Courtesy, THE METROPOLITAN MUSEUM OF ART, NEW YORK. GIFT OF COLLIS P. HUNTINGTON

Plate 147. Roger Sherman. Portrait by Ralph Earl. *Courtesy*, yale university art gallery. Gift of roger sherman white

The war made little difference to the itinerant portrait painters who continued to move from town to town in rural New England, painting in the familiar ways of their predecessors in orderly, strong patterns and bold colors. In much of their work there is an almost forbidding primness, despite their brilliant colors, which suggests not only an incapacity but also perhaps an unwillingness to indulge fully in the sensuous delights of the painter's art. This might be said generally of all our native-born colonial painters. Many of their figures have an iconic stiffness which is found as well in the figured headstones of New England graveyards, cut in shallow, flat relief by stonecutters who seemed to have their minds not on this world but on the next. Certainly the most forceful document in portraiture of this stern sensibility is Ralph Earl's portrait of Roger Sherman (*Plate 147*) painted about 1777. Earl, a loyalist, painted this distinguished patriot in somber tones of brown and black against a background of neutral, muted tones. The face is harshly lighted and the figure, clad in homespun and seated in a black Windsor chair, dominates the spare setting. Even though Earl painted William Carpenter in England, the portrait (*Plate 148*) reveals no change in his approach, and the few tricks he eventually learned in England—an ability to endow his figures with some grace and to put them in a more convincing, lighter atmosphere—fell away from him soon after his return to New England. Like Earl, Reuben Moulthrop, Winthrop Chandler (*Plate 150*), William Jennys and John Durand, the oldest of this group, continued to paint in this manner in the early decades of the Republic. Durand's portrait of the Rapalje Children (*Plate 149*), painted in 1768, represents this late provincial style. Such mannerisms continued to appear in work of 19th-century folk painters and even in self-taught primitives of the 20th century.

More immediately within the sphere of Copley's influence was the early work of John Trumbull. The figures of his family group (*Plate 151*) are set stiffly at a table and gaze fixedly at the viewer. The smoothly applied bright colors, the pale harshly modeled features with their dark, luminous eyes and the gleaming wooden table top suggest that Trumbull, as a student at Harvard, had certainly seen Copley's work. But Trumbull belongs to another generation. He was the first of that group of ambitious, college-educated

Plate 148. WILLIAM CARPENTER. Portrait by Ralph Earl, 1779. *Courtesy,* WORCESTER ART MUSEUM, WORCESTER, MASS.

216

Plate 149. THE RAPALJE CHILDREN. Painting by John Durand, *circa* 1768. *Courtesy,* THE NEW-YORK HISTORICAL SOCIETY, NEW YORK CITY

Plate 150. REVEREND EBENEZER DEVOTION. Portrait by Winthrop Chandler, 1770. *Courtesy*, BROOKLINE (MASSACHUSETTS) HISTORICAL SOCIETY. PHOTOGRAPH FROM THE WORCESTER ART MUSEUM, WORCESTER, MASS.

young men for whom painting was a high and noble calling. Like Allston and Morse who came later, he could no longer be content with the humble role of the face painter or the simple virtues of craftsmanship. The careers of these three men belong principally to the 19th century, but all of them turned first to Benjamin West (the first and most successful of our emigrés), who was the source of counsel and inspiration to generations of American painters.

Plate 151. Jonathan Trumbull, Jr., with Mrs. Trumbull and Faith Trumbull. Painting by John Trumbull, 1777. *Courtesy,* yale university art gallery. Gift of miss henrietta hubbard

Benjamin West was born near Philadelphia in 1738. His early portrait of Thomas Mifflin (*circa* 1758, *Plate 155*) reveals an attempt to work in the light, rococo manner of John Wollaston and William Williams (both of whom were active in and around Philadelphia) and in the style of the native-born John Hesselius, son of Gustavus. Taken together, Williams' *Deborah Hall* (*Plate 153*), Wollaston's *Mrs. William Walton* (1749, *Plate 152*) and Hesselius' *Charles Calvert* (1761, *Plate 154*) represent a fair selection of this new rococo manner. In Philadelphia, West had also acquired the rudiments of a classical education. Encouraged by William Smith, Provost at the College of Philadelphia, and by reading of European treatises on painting acquired through Williams, he produced a *Death of Socrates* while still in Philadelphia. An opportunity to fulfill his early ambitions to paint great historical pictures came when he was sent abroad to study. West went first to Italy, settled in London permanently in 1763, and there succeeded beyond his dreams. When he arrived in Rome, recent discoveries at Pompeii and Herculaneum were bringing the ancient world dramatically before contemporary eyes. Johann Jakob Winckelmann's *Thoughts on the Imitation of Greek Art in Painting and Sculpture*, which appeared only five years before West's arrival, proclaimed in exalted language the purity and harmony of Greek art. With his compatriot, Anton Raphael Mengs, Winckelmann helped to renew the traditional reverence for ancient art at a time when rococo painters had almost forgotten it. These writers insisted that artists must again strive for an ideal conception of beauty attainable through the study of antique marbles in which nature had already been purified, its finest aspects combined and harmonized in the noblest work of creation, the human figure.

Mengs and the Scotsman Gavin Hamilton were the first to carry these doctrines into practice, but certainly West was among the pioneers of this new classicism. He met the leading figures of the new movement, and his alleged comparison of the Apollo Belvedere to the Mohawk warriors he had seen in Pennsylvania may have shocked the Roman *cognoscenti*, but it suggests that he understood the ideal of noble simplicity his new Roman acquaintances were then advocating. An early example of West's neo-

Plate 152. MRS. WILLIAM WALTON. Portrait by John Wollaston. *Courtesy,* THE NEW-YORK HISTORICAL SOCIETY, NEW YORK CITY

Plate 153.
DEBORAH HALL. Portrait by
William Williams, 1766. *Courtesy,*
THE BROOKLYN MUSEUM, BROOKLYN, N.Y.

Plate 154. Charles Calvert. Portrait by John Hesselius, 1761. *Courtesy,* the baltimore museum of art, baltimore, md. Gift of alfred r. and henry g. riggs in memory of general lawrason riggs

223

224   *Plate 155.* THOMAS MIFFLIN. Portrait by Benjamin West, *circa* 1758. *Courtesy,* HISTORICAL
SOCIETY OF PENNSYLVANIA, PHILADELPHIA

classicism is his *Agrippina Landing at Brundisium with the Ashes of Germanicus (Plate 156)*, painted in London in 1768 when he had already acquired a reputation. The picture represents an act of family piety, an exemplary human act in a dignified and decorous setting, yet it reveals many of the limitations which plagued West throughout his whole career. The central group of Agrippina and her family may stem from the Roman reliefs of the Ara Pacis and the architectural setting is at least vaguely Roman, but the figures of the central group, despite their drapery, are not idealized Roman matrons at all. They are the thin, elegantly elongated figure types one encounters generally in 18th-century painting. The figures cluttered around them stem from a variety of sources and suggest that not only Winckelmann's reverence for the ancients but the broader eclecticism expounded by Mengs and later by Sir Joshua Reynolds was also on the painter's mind.

Plate 156. AGRIPPINA LANDING AT BRUNDISIUM WITH THE ASHES OF GERMANICUS. Painting by Benjamin West. *Courtesy,* YALE UNIVERSITY ART GALLERY. GIFT OF LOUIS M. RABINOWITZ

West's deficiencies, in view of his colonial origin and short experience with the grand manner, are less surprising than the success he won despite them. His quick adoption of the new style was perhaps made possible by his limited training in the rococo manner of his Philadelphia teachers and his high ambition. But this early neo-classicism, formed years before David gave it its most arresting and austere form, did not permanently fix the course of West's development.

Shortly after *Agrippina* came two subjects from modern history: *Penn's Treaty with the Indians* (1772) and *The Death of General Wolfe at Quebec* (1771). The former (*Plate 157*), painted on a commission from the Penn family, is a compromise between the high style of history painting and

Plate 157. WILLIAM PENN'S TREATY WITH THE INDIANS. Painting by Benjamin West. *Courtesy,* PENNSYLVANI. ACADEMY OF THE FINE ARTS, PHILADELPHIA

a straightforward representation of an important but pictorially unpromising event. It is dignified in its composition with a solemnity reminiscent of Massaccio's *Tribute Money* from which it could have been derived. The *Death of Wolfe* (*Plate 158*), on the other hand, is full of baroque ardor, sweeping diagonals, patches of light against menacing darks which have little stylistically to do with neo-classicism. Indeed the central group around the fallen general was perhaps based on a seventeenth-century *pietà*, and on the strength of this resemblance and of its subject matter, the painting has been called "the first *pietà* of nationalism." Its significance, however, lies not in its being the first painting of contemporary history—it was not—but rather in West's stubborn rejection of classical costume and his insistence on

Plate 158. DEATH OF GENERAL WOLFE. Painting by Benjamin West. *Courtesy*, THE NATIONAL GALLERY OF CANADA, OTTAWA

bringing to his subject, if not the style of neo-classicism, the sense of heroic grandeur, which, beyond specifics of style, the proponents of neo-classicism advocated. The picture grandly asserts that Wolfe's death was an event of comparable importance to that of a Greek or a Roman hero, and more generally that West's own time had its own place in the great fabric of history.

West soon began to favor more dramatic subjects. The Bible furnished the theme for *Saul and the Witch of Endor* (*Plate 159*) and, as he abandoned Hector, Regulus and Hannibal for scenes from medieval English history or from Shakespeare's plays, the restraint of his early compositions

Plate 159. SAUL AND THE WITCH OF ENDOR. Painting by Benjamin West, 1777. *Courtesy*, WADSWORTH ATHENEUM, HARTFORD, CONN.

gave way to the dramatic lighting and extravagant gestures required by his new "Gothick" subjects. Having no strong commitment to any given style, he worked in a variety of them; he was both a forerunner of neo-classicism and a prophet, like other of his English contemporaries, of 19th-century romanticism. Byron's caustic comment on "the dotard West, Europe's worst daub, poor England's best" may have had some justification as an objective evaluation of his enormous output. He was, as someone else has remarked, a bad painter but a good man. Were it not for this goodness, West's place in a history of American rather than English painting would be less important than it is, for his unfailing kindness and hospitality brought American painters year after year to his studio. The oldest of them, Matthew Pratt, whose *American School* of 1765 (*Plate 160*) records the high seriousness of

Plate 160. THE AMERICAN SCHOOL. Painting by Matthew Pratt, 1765. *Courtesy,* THE METROPOLITAN MUSEUM OF ART, NEW YORK. GIFT OF SAMUEL P. AVERY, 1897

the young Americans learning with him, was born in 1734; Samuel F. B. Morse, one of the last to seek counsel of the honored president of the Royal Academy, lived until 1872. West seems never to have forgotten his American background, was sympathetic to American independence, and continued throughout his life to guide painters of the young republic in their attempts to establish the great tradition of western painting in their homeland.

West's most distinguished early pupil, Gilbert Stuart (1755–1828), remained unmoved by his master's conception of history painting. In Newport, Rhode Island, Stuart began painting under the tutelage of Cosmo Alexander in a typically provincial style, evident in his portrait of William Redwood (*circa* 1774; *Plate 161*). On the eve of the American Revolution,

Plate 161.
WILLIAM REDWOOD. Portrait by Gilbert Stuart. *Courtesy,* REDWOOD LIBRARY AND ATHENAEUM, NEWPORT, R. I. PHOTOGRAPH FROM FRICK ART REFERENCE LIBRARY, NEW YORK

230

he went to London where his astonishing natural gifts and his ability to assimilate the style of leading English contemporaries brought him quick success. Whatever rewards this rapid rise may have brought him, financial troubles in 1787 forced his flight to Dublin. In 1793, again fleeing creditors, he left Dublin for America to paint George Washington and recoup his fortunes.

Stuart's development from a New England provincial to a stylish portraitist in London can be measured by comparison of any portrait he painted in the seventeen-eighties with his early Redwood portrait. While still in West's studio, he outstripped his master by study of Van Dyck and Rubens and by close scrutiny of Reynolds and Gainsborough. His swift, deft brushwork owed nothing to the bland, empty surfaces which deaden West's *Drummond Family* (1766; *Plate 163*). Although his portrait of Reynolds (1784; *Plate 162*), then president of the Royal Academy, was ridiculed for making the eminent sitter resemble "a cheesemonger," it reveals a keen understanding of Reynolds' own technique. His flickering brushstroke seems, however, to have stemmed principally from Reynolds' rival, Thomas Gainsborough. So close was the relationship in style that Stuart's *A Gentleman Skating* of 1781 appeared in an exhibition of 1878 erroneously attributed to Gainsborough. This picture, one of Stuart's rare full-length portraits, is a splendid combination of Gainsborough's light, brilliant style of painting with a strong solidity, especially in the head and shoulders, which endows the figure with a dignity and substance that the novel, potentially unstable pose might have taken from him. But Stuart's dazzling technique may have appeared somewhat less remarkable to his contemporaries in London who had its models in the work of Gainsborough close at hand. They remarked rather on his ability to probe the character of his sitters in terms which make his art appear more in keeping with what Copley had accomplished in Boston than with what Stuart in his assimilation of English technique had accomplished rapidly in London. An English critic, writing in the *London World* of 1787, had this to say of him: "In the most arduous and valuable achievements of portrait painting, *identity* and *duration*, Stuart takes the lead of every competitor. Those who wish to redress themselves of accident, and, independent of time and place as far as eyesight goes and eye

232   *Plate 162.* Sɪʀ Jᴏsʜᴜᴀ Rᴇʏɴᴏʟᴅs. Portrait by Gilbert Stuart, 1784. *Courtesy*, ɴᴀᴛɪᴏɴᴀʟ ɢᴀʟʟᴇʀʏ ᴏғ ᴀʀᴛ, ᴡᴀsʜɪɴɢᴛᴏɴ, ᴅ. ᴄ., ᴍᴇʟʟᴏɴ ᴄᴏʟʟᴇᴄᴛɪᴏɴ

service, to have before them the glowing fidelity of friendship or of love, may here secure the perpetual presence of the charm they wish. Not only skin deep, and skimming superficially over complexion and contour, Stuart dives deep—less deep only than Sir Joshua, more deep than every other pencil—Stuart dives deep into the *mind*, and brings up with him a conspicuous draught of character and characteristic thought—all as sensible of feeling and to sight as the most palpable projections in any feature of a face."

te 163. THE DRUMMOND FAMILY. Painting by Benjamin West, 1766. *Courtesy,* MINNEAPOLIS INSTITUTE OF ARTS

Stuart's resistance to West, his ridicule of West's technique and of his allegorizing, ran counter to the prevailing artistic currents of the time. Later on in America, where Stuart became a patriarchal figure and had his own following among young portrait painters, he achieved some of the timelessness ascribed to him in London in portraits which in their strict limitation to the head and features of his sitters show the influence of classicizing portraiture in marble; yet his treatment of features, always enlivened by his magic brush and glowing flesh tones, never lost the facility he so quickly acquired in London. He remained a face painter somewhat in the colonial tradition insofar as he kept a journeyman's concern for the likeness and the means of attaining it, and was apparently untouched by the ambition to become a history painter, a thinker or a moralist which fired so many of his contemporaries.

In 1768 John Durand placed an advertisement in the *New York Journal* on the art of historical painting which he hoped to teach. In this notice he described that art as follows:

To such gentlemen and ladies as have thought but little upon this subject and might only regard painting as a superfluous ornament, I would just observe, that history painting, besides being extremely ornamental, has many important uses. It presents to our view some of the most interesting scenes recorded in antient and modern history, gives us more lively and perfect ideas of the things represented, than we could receive from a historical account of them, and frequently recalls to our memory a long train of events, with which those representations were connected. They show us a proper expression of the passions excited by every event, and have an effect, the very same in kind (but stronger) than a fine historical description of the same passage would have upon a judicious reader. Men who have distinguished themselves for the good of their country and mankind may be set before our eyes as examples, and to give us their silent lessons—and besides, every judicious friend and visitor shares, with us in the advantage and improvement, and increases its value to ourselves.

This conception of the painter's role came slowly to the colonies. West was perhaps the first to feel it, and Hesselius' classical subjects prove that it was never quite dead. Copley painted two historical subjects, a *Venus, Mars*

234

and Vulcan in 1754 and a *Galatea* (*Plate 164*), both of them based on engraved sources. Peale painted William Pitt in a Roman toga (1768; *Plate 165*), and Trumbull in 1774 was already trying his hand with a *Death of Paulus Aemilius at the Battle of Cannae* (*Plate 166*), his "first attempt at composition." But history painting was never really established here, nor was a concerted effort made to do so until after the republic had been established.

Plate 164. GALATEA. Painting by John Singleton Copley, 1754. *Courtesy,* MUSEUM OF FINE ARTS, BOSTON

Plate 165. WILLIAM PITT AS A ROMAN SENATOR. Portrait by Charles Willson Peale.
Courtesy, THE GENTLEMEN OF WESTMORELAND COUNTY, MONTROSS, VA. PHOTOGRAPH FROM
FRICK ART REFERENCE LIBRARY, NEW YORK

Copley's earliest works abroad are marked by a sudden extension of his
subject matter but by no dramatic change in his technique. Shortly before
his departure from Boston, he painted Mr. and Mrs. Isaac Winslow (*Plate
167*) sitting quietly side by side in a spare, economical composition which
proclaims the couple's relationship not by subtly interwoven forms but by its

237

238

naturalness. The figures have the human calm of the husbands and wives carved side by side in Roman funeral reliefs. In Rome, and eager to absorb the latest Roman fashion, Copley painted Mr. and Mrs. Ralph Izard (*Plate 168*) in a welter of props: a flamboyant rococo settee, a heavy classicizing table, a column, drapery in elaborately curving folds, a classical statue, a classical vase, and, for good measure, the Colosseum. But Copley found no one in Rome to teach him how to bring all these elements together, and the sitters, painted in Copley's tight Boston way, are almost overwhelmed as they lean awkwardly toward each other.

Copley's famous *Watson and the Shark* (1778; *Plate 169*) was an attempt to undertake perhaps prematurely the complexities of a group of figures in action. Copley succeeded well enough by traditional standards within the figure group, and the contrasting pulls and thrusts of his figures sustain the excitement of the dreadful encounter in the water. The drama of the event, however, is projected more emphatically, although unwittingly, by the effective naiveté of the whole composition which negates the correctness of the figures on the boat. There is a sudden convergence of movement as the boathook is thrust up to the top edge of the picture and the oar disappears at the left. The figures, too, are brought up close to the viewer in a wild and fortuitous projection of sudden shock consistent with the event described.

Gradually Copley acquired an ability to produce conventionally correct compositions and to soften his sharp edges, to tone down his colors and break up his surfaces with light and shade. This new facility is evident in his portrait of the *Daughters of George III* (1785; *Plate 170*) in which he tried to link the figures by their playful gestures to each other and to a grape arbor, birds, flowers and three dogs. But the elaborate garland of figures and accessories he hoped to weave never quite hung together. Although more accomplished by European standards than the Izard portrait, this later work, for all its new niceties of touch, still falls victim to his old disjointed way of composing, and that wonderful feeling of optical concentration of features and still-life which characterized his less ambitiously conceived American portraits is lacking in it.

Plate 169. WATSON AND THE SHARK. Painting by John Singleton Copley, 1778. *Courtesy,* MUSEUM OF FI
ARTS, BOSTON

Plate 170. THE THREE PRINCESSES (DAUGHTERS OF GEORGE THE THIRD). Painting by John Singleton Copley, 1785. REPRODUCED BY PERMISSION OF THE LORD CHAMBERLAIN. COPYRIGHT RESERVED TO HER MAJESTY, THE QUEEN

The Arts in America: The Colonial Period

Upon his arrival in London Copley was at first rather cool to West and later openly antagonistic. Like Stuart he sought other models to liberate his slow, tight brushwork. Furthermore, he seems never to have been drawn to the themes of classical antiquity which West painted, and when he undertook subjects of contemporary history the results were less overtly essays in the grand style, as West's had been. His *Watson and the Shark* commemorated an event in the life of a private citizen and was marked less by the dignity of historical painting than by melodrama prophetic of much that was to come in romantic painting. In his *Death of Major Peirson* (1782–84; *Plate 171*), *Defeat of the Floating Batteries at Gibralter*, and *Death of Chatham in the House of Lords*, 1779–81, (*Plate 172*) he did treat themes of

242 *Plate 171.* DEATH OF MAJOR PEIRSON. Painting by John Singleton Copley, 1782–1784. *Courtesy*, THE T
TEES OF THE TATE GALLERY, LONDON

contemporary history. In these pictures, with their heroes and heroic deaths, Copley was undoubtedly influenced by West, and like West took liberties with the facts to heighten the dramatic effects of his pictures. But in them the figures are scaled down, subordinate anecdote is sometimes overly stressed, and, in general the grandeur of traditional history painting is diminished. The antagonism between the reportorial and heroic was not easily solved by painters of contemporary life, and if Copley exhibited a certain American pragmatism and perhaps a bit of opportunism in his selection of subjects, he made a real attempt to face the problem which Gericault, Courbet and Manet had to contend with later. Copley's success in England came early, but the bravura style he sought and to a degree

te 172. DEATH OF THE EARL OF CHATHAM IN THE HOUSE OF LORDS. Painting by John Singleton Copley, 9–1781. *Courtesy,* THE TRUSTEES OF THE TATE GALLERY, LONDON

Plate 173.
LORD HEATHFIELD. A portrait
study by John Singleton Copley
Courtesy, NATIONAL PORTRAIT
GALLERY, LONDON

achieved in the oil studies for Lord Heathfield (*Plate 173;* for his
Defeat of the Floating Batteries at Gibraltar) never came easily to him. His
working methods remained slow and gradually commissions dwindled. He
was the first of a long line of American painters who submerged their native
provincial characteristics—which, in Copley's case, were a source of
strength—in attempting to capture the look of a European style without its
substance.

John Trumbull's career paralleled Copley's, but unlike Copley he came
quickly under West's influence and painted a *Priam Returning with the*

Body of Hector in 1785 after only a year in West's studio. He then conceived, with the encouragement of West and Thomas Jefferson, a series on the Revolutionary War. For five years Trumbull worked on the twelve paintings for it, taking individual portraits of surviving participants, and planning and executing the small paintings which were to be the basis for engravings sold by subscription. *The Death of General Montgomery at Quebec* (1786; *Plate 174*) would appear to be quite close to West's *Death of General Wolfe* (*Plate 158*). But in most of the battle pictures, he tempered the sweep of baroque composition with subordinate incidents, and made each of the principals identifiable as Copley had done. As a result preliminary oil sketches, like that for the *Death of General Mercer at the Battle of*

174. DEATH OF GENERAL MONTGOMERY IN THE ATTACK ON QUEBEC. Painting by John Trumbull.
tesy, YALE UNIVERSITY ART GALLERY

Princeton (1787; *Plate 176*), often convey a greater effect of the violence of battle than do the finished versions (*Plate 175*) which tend to be overladen with specifics. Other scenes which he chose to protray—*The Surrender of Cornwallis at Yorktown, Washington Resigning his Commission*, and the *Declaration of Independence*—were less rich in dramatic possibilities. The *Declaration* (*Plate 177*), produced in a large version for the Rotunda of the Capitol in Washington, was attacked in Congress, and Trumbull was accused of favoring the delegation from his home state of Connecticut in his treatment of the scene. Subscriptions to the engravings after Trumbull's

246   *Plate 175*. DEATH OF GENERAL MERCER AT THE BATTLE OF PRINCETON, 3 JANUARY, 1777. Painting by Jo Trumbull. *Courtesy*, YALE UNIVERSITY ART GALLERY. GIFT OF THE ARTIST

paintings were not forthcoming and with this failure, since the subjects were of American history and painted by an American painter, came the first of many setbacks to hopes of founding a tradition of history painting in America.

In the colonial period and the early years of the republic, a genuinely American tradition in painting had yet to be born. However, certain habits of seeing and patterns of development had been established which have marked

e 176. Death of General Mercer at the Battle of Princeton. A preliminary study by John Trum-
, Courtesy, yale university art gallery. Gift of the artist

247

Plate 177. THE DECLARATION OF INDEPENDENCE, JULY 4, 1776. Painting by John Trumbull. *Courtesy,* UNIVERSITY ART GALLERY. GIFT OF THE ARTIST

the later history of our painting. First of all, the appeal of Europe—in the early period, of England—had already made itself felt. The history of our early painting can be told in part by the gradually narrowing gap between colonial and English painting, measurable in the change from copying prints, to the emulation here of second-rate English immigrant painters, and finally to the actual removal, for varying periods of time, of Americans to London and their assimilation of the English style.

Secondly, there is an obvious and consistent pragmatism evident in the stubborn likenesses which seem, in the best of our portraitists, to shine through the borrowed formulae at a time when even English painters like

Wollaston or Blackburn were recording the features of their sitters with perfunctory and superficial expressions. This matter-of-factness is also evident in the frequent rejection of the most elaborate courtly formulae, culminating in the varied and telling characterizations of Copley which derive from the whole treatment of his sitters, pose and general composition, as well as face. This pragmatism may account too for the fondness of West, Copley and Trumbull for scenes of modern history, and for the way they painted them.

Thirdly, in this period was established perhaps the beginnings of a consistent American modification of whatever was borrowed. This is in part, as we have suggested, the transformation of the untrained provincial from round to flat—from illusionism to the patient, enumerative technique of the untrained artist who prefers to paint what he *knows* to be there rather than what the eye records. This approach is akin to that of the craftsman in its fondness for the finished, well-made thing. In the best of our colonial paintings this vision is marked by a particular elegance of design. Aided by the lessons of modern art, our fondness for the simple and direct, and our national reverence for what is taken to be indubitably American, we have continued to cherish the chaste products of such a vision from the Freake painter to Grandma Moses.

Most fascinating is the coincidence in America of this spare style, which rejects the overtly sensuous aspects of painting, and a lingering American distrust of that art's most elegant blandishments. From the 17th century down through the paintings of Feke, Copley and Earl, there is a continuous development of this kind of vision which, even in Copley's work, seems to ignore the underlying presence of a human figure or the delights of a free and delicate brushwork. There are perfectly good reasons why, given the limited opportunities for learning here, this should be so. But there yet remains an insistent rightness in the paintings of our earliest residents, as they are presented rigidly and forcefully on canvasses from which the fat of the baroque has been burned away. From what we know of their industry and of their faith, it would be difficult to imagine them painted in any other way.

THE DECORATIVE ARTS

by Robert C. Smith

AMERICAN craftsmen designed and executed some of the finest furniture and silver made anywhere in the 18th century. This was our greatest achievement in the field of the decorative arts and in the opinion of many critics it represents the major American artistic accomplishment of the period. More limited in scope, though scarcely less distinguished in quality, is the work of our best pewterers and the master craftsmen who wrought in brass and iron in Boston, Philadelphia and New York. American glass was less highly developed and the few impressive pieces that exist came late in the 18th century. They were made by Germans, the colonists who were also responsible for our most ambitiously decorated earthenware. True porcelain, although attempted on several occasions, was never successfully manufactured here in the colonial period, because of the high cost of production and because colonial Americans were accustomed to acquiring their china abroad. This is true also of the making of fine textiles, but wool embroidery flourished as an attractive art for amateurs. The essay which follows is principally concerned with colonial furniture and silver, although brief reference is made to certain masterpieces in other divisions of the decorative arts.

FURNITURE

THE SEVENTEENTH-CENTURY STYLE

THE earliest preserved American furniture was made in New England in the second half of the 17th century, mainly by anonymous craftsmen. Massively rectilinear, it belongs to an aspect of the northern European Renaissance which can be called an Anglo-Flemish style. This is because the basic forms were evolved in Belgium under French and Italian influences in the mid-16th century and then, in Elizabethan and Jacobean England, were modified to British taste.

In America these forms were further altered by a process of simplification. For example, a Connecticut oak draw table (*Plate 179*) clearly shows the bulbous supports and triglyph ornaments of a model in the pattern book of Paul Vredeman de Vries, son of Hans, the Dutch-born founder of the style (*Plate 178*). Yet in the American piece both elements have been flattened and the rest of the ornament eliminated without however sacrificing the essential form of the Flemish table. There results a new harmony of fine line and plain surface which was to become a commonplace, not only of American furniture but of all aspects of our colonial art in relation to its European sources.

In New England, as in the mother country, oak household chests were decorated with low relief carving that combines Renaissance with medieval themes. Those closest to the courtly Anglo-Flemish models are associated with the "joyner" Thomas Dennis (ca. 1638–1706), who settled at Ipswich, Mass., in 1668. The ornament of this Essex County furniture (*Plates 180 and 184*) includes interlace (guilloche) and strapwork derived via Flanders from the Italian architect Sebastiano Serlio, long leaf motifs from the French engraver Jacques Androuet du Cerceau, lozenges, spirals and intersecting lunettes, frequently mixed with English Tudor whorls.

254 *Plate 178.* Design for a Table (Flemish). From Paul Vredeman de Vries, *Verscheyden Schrynwerck als Portalen, Kleerkassen,* etc. Antwerp, 1630. *Courtesy,* the metropolitan museum of art, new york. Flemish Renaissance patterns profoundly influenced English furniture of the Elizabethan and Jacobean periods.

Other 17th-century chests made in the Connecticut River Valley have stylized leaves and flowers as their chief decoration and include one or more drawers at the base. One group, thought to be the work of Peter Blin of Wethersfield, Conn. (active *circa* 1675–1725), displays stiff tulip and "sunflower" designs (*Plate 181*), taken it would appear from contemporary English folk ornament. The ebonized split spindles applied to the façade and the "turtle-back" drawer pulls of these "sunflower" chests are typical Anglo-Flemish forms. A flatter style of carving, attributed to John Allis and Samuel Belding, was practiced in the Massachusetts towns of Hadley and Hatfield, further up the Connecticut River, between about 1675 and 1740. In over one hundred typical Hadley chests, which bear the initials of girls for whom they were made, the whole front surface is covered with stylized leaves and tulips. In one group these motifs are held together by serpentine

179. DRAW TABLE, OAK, NEW ENGLAND, LATE 17TH CENTURY. Indirectly inspired ...e Vredeman de Vries illustration, this table is derived from English Jacobean models, ...h were the principal influence on American 17th-century furniture. *Courtesy*, THE CON-...ICUT HISTORICAL SOCIETY, HARTFORD, CONN.

Plate 180.
CHEST, OAK, MASSACHUSETTS, *cir*
1675. The low relief carving,
attributed to Thomas Dennis,
represents varied borrowing from
academic European sources. *Cour*
THE METROPOLITAN
MUSEUM OF ART, NEW YORK. GIFT O
MRS. J. INSLEY BLAIR, 1948

Plate 181.
BLANKET CHEST, OAK, CONNECTICUT,
1680–1710. "Tulip and sunflower"
chests, from around Wethersfield,
Conn., were the product of carvers
trained in British folk-art forms.
Courtesy, YALE UNIVERSITY ART
GALLERY, MABEL BRADY GARVAN
COLLECTION

256

vine forms. In another they break forth in a riot of diagonal movement suggesting the early medieval linear decoration of northern Europe.

Much of this furniture was originally painted black (in imitation of ebony), red or green. Upon this surface some chests have painted decorations of flowers, scrolls and geometric patterns, possibly in imitation of brightly colored inlay. In the earliest examples, like the Staniford family chest of drawers, dated 1678, this is discreetly limited to a drawer front or decorative panel (*Plate 182*). Later, especially in coastal New England, crude paintings cover the whole surface of a chest or chest of drawers, as with the pieces decorated at Guilford or Saybrook, Conn., or in Taunton, Mass., where Robert Crosman did this kind of work as late as the second quarter of the 18th century.

Plate 182.
CHEST OF DRAWERS, PAINTED OAK, MASSACHUSETTS, 1678. The ancestor of much 18th-century New England painted furniture, this piece, owned by the Staniford family of Ipswich, Mass., combines tendril motifs painted probably in imitation of wood inlay with applied turned ornament. *Courtesy*, HENRY FRANCIS DU PONT WINTERTHUR MUSEUM, WINTERTHUR, DEL.

Plate 183. Court Cupboard, Oak, Massachusetts, 1684. This Foster family piece is representative of the geometric ornament that seems to have dominated the furniture of the Massachusetts coast at the end of the 17th century. *Courtesy,* HENRY FRANCIS DU PONT WINTERTHUR MUSEUM, WINTERTHUR, DEL.

The most monumental expression of the Anglo-Flemish style is the grand Elizabethan and Jacobean carved and inlaid beds and the cupboards or presses which frequently have open areas for the display of plate, pottery or textiles. No great beds are known to have been made here, but there are a number of oak and pine "court" cupboards or presses, most of which come from the region around Boston. This massive furniture has in common the use of split spindles for ornament and, mostly in the upper section, bulbous "melon" supports, horizontally incised in one or more places. Most of the lower sections have drawers with wooden pulls, like those of the Prince-Howes cupboard (*circa* 1650–1670); others have doors, as in the Vine family example, thought to have been made in Virginia before 1700. A few have an open shelf, seen in the Parmenter family piece of *circa* 1650–1660, which contains, in addition to simplified architectural detail like the Connecticut table (*Plate 179*), the uncommon feature of strips of wood inlay, or in the Foster family example, which is dated 1684 (*Plate 183*). This handsome "court" cupboard is typical of the majority in its use of geometric decoration, especially crossetted panels (with square angle projections), which seem to have superseded the old figurative carving in the last years of the 17th century.

Several types of armchair were made in this period and all are of medieval derivation. The most impressive is the oak wainscot with solid back and scrolled arms carried on turned supports, which like the front legs belong to the category of bulbous ornament. Two fine examples with carved backs, at the Essex Institute (*Plate 184*) and Bowdoin College respectively, display the kind of ornament associated with Thomas Dennis and Essex County. In the Bowdoin example this is grouped about a huge carnation of the sort seen in contemporary English and later American wool embroidery. The backs of both chairs have lateral profiles of masks and scrolls that come from Italian Renaissance title pages and occasionally mantels. Other plainer pieces have the undecorated back panel which will characterize belated examples made by the Pennsylvania Germans in the 18th century.

Another type is the "stick-back" armchair, derived from 17th-century English pieces that can be traced as far back as Byzantine prototypes. Assembled in a cage-like construction from as many as seventy-five turned

Plate 184.
WAINSCOT CHAIR, OAK, MASSACHUSETTS,
1670–1685. An important chair, attributed to
Thomas Dennis of Ipswich, Mass., which
displays Renaissance mask and scroll carving
characteristic of the furniture of Essex County.
Courtesy, ESSEX INSTITUTE, SALEM, MASS.

elements, including decorative spindles, the English chairs are prodigy pieces. American chairs of the Brewster variety, made of oak and ash with rush seats, have half as many parts, distributed in one or two tiers, in the back, below the arms and around the front and side stretchers (*Plate 185*). In the decidedly simpler Carver version there is a row of spindles only in the back. This type of construction served as a point of departure for 18th-century "stick" furniture, the notable windsor chairs, and settees (*Plate*

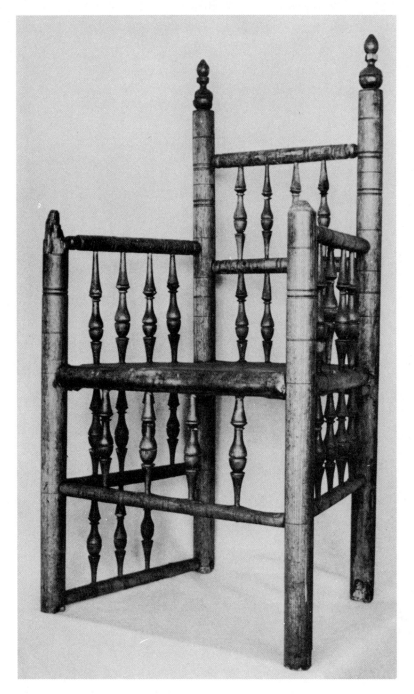

186). These were made, in a variety of woods generally painted, of more
delicately proportioned elements often necessitating additional support
which was provided in a projection at the rear of the wooden seat, following
a practice developed in ancient Egypt.

261

Plate 186.
WINDSOR ARMCHAIR, PAINTED HICKORY AND
OTHER WOODS, NEW ENGLAND, *circa* 1780. The
ultimate refinement of "stick" furniture,
extensively used in public buildings during the
colonial period. *Courtesy*, KENNETH HAMMITT,
WOODBURY, CONN.

A third type of rush-seated 17th-century armchair is the slatback form,
which also has turned upright and horizontal members, often terminating in
very handsome finials, and arms that are flat like the four splats of the back,
which in a few outstanding examples have elaborate shapes (*Plate 187*).

263

Plate 187. SLAT-BACK ARMCHAIR, MAPLE AND ASH, PROBABLY NEW YORK, *circa* 1700. A great example of a transitional category with unusually fine turned supports and finials and superlatively shaped slats. *Courtesy,* HENRY FRANCIS DU PONT WINTERTHUR MUSEUM, WINTERTHUR, DEL.

Plate 188.
GRADUATED SLAT-BACK ARMCHAIR,
MAPLE, DELAWARE RIVER VALLEY,
circa 1725. Refined from earlier
forms, chairs of this sort were made
in Pennsylvania and New Jersey
until well into the 19th century. The
best pieces have baroque turning in
stretchers and arm supports.
Courtesy, THE HENRY FORD MUSEUM,
DEARBORN, MICH.

264

The style continued in the 18th century, when as with windsors the parts became more delicate, the turning more refined. The best of the resulting "ladder-back" chairs, made in the Delaware River Valley about 1725 (*Plate 188*), have six arched slats graduated in size and handsome front stretchers of ball and reel turning characteristic of the baroque style of William and Mary, which by this time had largely run its course.

THE WILLIAM AND MARY STYLE

IN ENGLAND, following the Stuart Restoration of 1660, the Anglo-Flemish style was rapidly replaced at the court by a luxurious baroque mode inspired by Italy, the France of Louis XIV, and especially by Holland. Indeed, so strong did Dutch influence become that by the 1690's, with a Dutch sovereign on the British throne, we can speak of an Anglo-Dutch style, in furniture as well as in architecture. The style emphasized the dynamic and dramatic aims common to all aspects of baroque art and these were achieved by a new kind of "explosive" turning, by large unified shapes, by predominant curves, as well as by vigorous contrasts of color and the "color" evoked by high relief carving. From the East came the exotic practices of caning and japanning, or imitating lacquer, while the English made their own great contribution in the form of chests of drawers and desks with neat flat surfaces and architectural trim. These simple but deeply satisfying "architectural" forms were destined to remain for more than a century the basis of Anglo-American case furniture.

In the colonies a modest reflection of the new baroque style was felt at the beginning of the century, and its appearance coincided with the introduction of academic architecture and the spread of comfort throughout the home. The new types of turning, which often suggest oriental vase forms (then just entering the European market) were used at the same time in stair rails and in the legs of chairs and leaf tables. These include both the sumptuous gateleg and the more flamboyant butterfly variety, so called because of the scrolled profile of the supporting brackets, perhaps the most strikingly baroque invention of American colonial furniture makers. A similarly dynamic, though borrowed, form is the tapering scroll foot used

Plate 189.
ARMCHAIR UPHOLSTERED IN LEATHER, MAPLE,
NEW ENGLAND, 1700–1725. So many chairs of
this sort were exported from Boston that the
type came to be known as the Boston chair.
This piece has exceptionally fine baroque arms
and outstanding Portuguese paintbrush feet,
all characteristic of the William and Mary style.
Courtesy, HENRY FRANCIS DU PONT
WINTERTHUR MUSEUM, WINTERTHUR, DEL.

with many of the tables and stately chairs of the period, which has long been
misnamed the Spanish foot. In reality it was a Portuguese invention, said to
have been brought to England in the reign of Charles II, who married a
princess of that nation. In Portugal it is called a "paintbrush" foot, on the
basis of resemblance, and this term should be applied to its Anglo-American
counterparts.

A typical William and Mary chair with this kind of foot, block-and-
vase turned legs and often a scalloped skirt will have a high narrow back
encasing a single long panel, sometimes caned but more frequently covered
with leather (*Plate 189*). The form seems to have been inspired by Chinese
chairs (*Plate 190*), which were to have a great influence on English and
American chair backs. The moldings of the frame are convex, like the
bolections of contemporary wainscot. The various curved elements of the
cresting were developed from the patterns of Daniel Marot, a French

Plate 190.
ARMCHAIR, ROSEWOOD, CHINESE, 16TH CENTURY.
Traditional Chinese chairs appear to have influenced
the Anglo-American 18th-century chair, first in the
form of the splat, then in the lines of the cresting.
Courtesy, DAVID STOCKWELL, WILMINGTON, DEL.

267

Huguenot designer employed by William and Mary, and were further evolved by John Gaines (1704–1743) of Portsmouth, New Hampshire, one of the few craftsmen of the period whose work or style can be identified. This period also saw the introduction of the first entirely upholstered armchairs with high backs and rolled arms, whose curving forms are repeated in every part of the body of the chair, from the serpentine lines of the skirt to the arched crests of the back and the wings (*Plate 191*). Covered in bright

Plate 191.
EASY CHAIR, MAPLE, NEW ENGLAND 1700–1725. The baroque use of curve reached full expression in the rolled arms and grandiose wings of William and Mary style upholstered chairs li this one, which has an extraordinari fine crest and a rare scrolled skirt th suggests bed canopies of the period. *Courtesy*, HENRY FRANCIS DU PONT WINTERTHUR MUSEUM, WINTERTHUR,

268

textiles contrasting dramatically with the walnut or maple of the frame, these "easy chairs" are splendid symbols of the baroque urge to expansive forms suggestive of movement. They also epitomize the new luxury which the flourishing colonial economy was by now making possible.

Most of these characteristics are reflected in William and Mary case furniture, which developed around the severely designed five-drawer chest, as handsome in its well-balanced simplicity as the comely façades of the contemporary Anglo-Dutch brick houses of Williamsburg or Philadelphia. Outstanding are the high chests of drawers (highboys) borne on four or six legs of cup or trumpet turning, dramatic novelties of the Dutch baroque, with arched or undulant outlines in their skirts and stretchers (*Plate 192*). These are repeated in the three-drawer dressing and mixing tables, almost identical with the lower sections of the high chests of drawers. In New England pieces they are frequently emphasized by tapering pendants or bellying finials reminiscent of the house architecture of that region. This furniture generally has ball or bun feet, characteristic of the 17th century, which mark the transitional character of the style. Their façades are not infrequently covered with materials producing the strong contrasts of pattern and color required by the new esthetic. Sometimes this was gained by setting walnut crotch veneers against other woods, sometimes by japanning the surface with birds and animals, Chinese figures and long oriental scrolls, according to the illustrations of Stalker and Parker's *Treatise of Japanning*, published in London in 1688. Occasionally these high chests were given pyramidal tops for the display of oriental porcelains and Delft faïence, a practice which heightens these colorful contrasts.

The most architectural of the William and Mary case pieces are the massive fall-front desks because of their full entablatures with cushion friezes, built on English models long before these elements entered American wainscot. A walnut desk of this type marked "Edward Evans 1707" is thought to be the earliest signed and dated piece of Philadelphia furniture (*Plate 193*). An almost identical piece, the Brinckerhoff New York cedarwood desk, is one of the earliest known American examples of Anglo-Dutch scroll-and-flower inlay, which in simpler form was to be employed in Chester Co., Pennsylvania, throughout the 18th century (*Plate 194*).

Plate 192. HIGH CHEST OF DRAWERS, JAPANNED MAPLE AND PINE, BOSTON, *circa* 1700. The chief innovation in early 18th-century case furniture, the high chest of drawers, was destined to reflect until the Revolution successive changes in style. The William and Mary phase brought Dutch trumpet-turned legs and frequently involved japanning, or painted imitation of oriental lacquer. *Courtesy,* THE METROPOLITAN MUSEUM OF ART, NEW YORK. JOSEPH PULITZER BEQUEST

Plate 193. FALL-FRONT DESK, WALNUT, PENNSYLVANIA, 1707. Signed and dated by Edward Evans, this is the earliest documented piece of furniture that emphasizes architectural effects in the moldings and entablature, recalling contemporary room paneling. *Courtesy,* COLONIAL WILLIAMSBURG, WILLIAMSBURG, VA.

Plate 194. Fall-front Desk, Inlaid Cedarwood, New York, 1700–1725. A Dutch
version of the type, originally owned by the Brinckerhoff family. The size of feet and moldings is characteristically exaggerated. *Courtesy*, THE MUSEUM OF THE CITY OF NEW YORK

In New York also the Dutch *kas*, or wardrobe, the showpiece of
northern European 17th-century furniture (*Plate 195*), demonstrated the
baroque trend to dynamic unity in the compactness of its form and the
dramatic quality of its single pair of doors. Instead of the elaborate carving
that distinguishes the best Dutch and North German examples, however,
some of the *kases* of New York have all-over monochrome paintings of swags
of pomegranates (symbols of fertility) which reflect the fruit and flower

273

woodcarving with which the Anglo-Dutch sculptor Grinling Gibbons and his followers transformed British chimney breasts in the late 17th century.

With the transitional style of William and Mary, American furniture ceased to be a product of carpenter joiners and turners and entered the domain of fine cabinetmaking, where it was to be further refined and enriched in the subsequent styles of the 18th century.

THE QUEEN ANNE STYLE

EARLY in the 18th century there occurred a fundamental change in the composition of American furniture of all types, thanks to the introduction of the gracefully curved cabriole leg. In France the appearance of this slender scroll-like element about 1700 had led to a new style called rococo, which for half a century forced all forms of art into a framework of elegantly interlocking curves. In England the cabriole leg enjoyed a similar vogue from *circa* 1710–1760, but the accompanying curved surfaces and fantastic ornament of pure rococo furniture were at first largely rejected because of the prestige of architectural pieces, which grew increasingly scholarly in their use of classical moldings, pediments and other academic elements, under the aegis of neo-Palladian building. The result was a strange dichotomy, first seen in the reign of Queen Anne (1702–1714), which was to continue until the middle of the century, when a second, fuller rococo mode developed.

This first style of incipient or arrested rococo appeared in the colonies about 1725 and continued for over a quarter of a century. It coincided with the growth of strong regional characteristics in the use of materials (cherry, maple and walnut in New England, as against the almost exclusive use of walnut and eventually mahogany in New York and Philadelphia) and in the choice of forms.

In England, Queen Anne chairs were made with two kinds of backs. One was a further development from the Chinese chair with now an almost level cresting in two rounded forms. The other represents the application of the cabriole outline to the stiles, with some sort of baroque ornament in the center of the hooplike cresting. Both forms have single splats shaped like

274

Chinese vases. In England, hoof-and-pad feet were used at first but these were soon replaced by the claw-and-ball variety, which was last employed in medieval silver.

In New England, the first type of back became associated with Connecticut and Massachusetts, the second with Newport (Rhode Island) furniture. Thus a Connecticut Queen Anne chair will have a high, thin "oriental" back with a narrow splat of vase form like that of the transitional chair already noted, the seat will be square and an attenuated linear effect will pervade the entire piece (*Plate 196*). The Newport chair, on the contrary, shows the

Plate 196.
SIDE CHAIR, PAINTED MAPLE, CONNECTICUT, 1725–1740. Typical of the New England Queen Anne chair are the stretchers, the lean proportions of the back and the splat in the form of a gracefully tapering Chinese vase. *Courtesy,* HENRY FRANCIS DU PONT WINTERTHUR MUSEUM, WINTERTHUR, DEL.

second or "fiddle" type of back with the local motif of a stylized shell set at the summit of the cresting (*Plate 197*). In the finest examples the decided curves of the stiles are reflected in the curves of the compass-shaped seat and the splat is sometimes pierced in a simple design, again on English precedent. The feet, in contrast to the pads of the Connecticut chair, are often claw-and-ball, with the claws assuming a position distinct from those of other localities. Throughout New England, stretchers, surviving from the William and Mary style, were generally kept so as to strengthen the cabriole legs, but in New York and Philadelphia they virtually disappeared. In New York alone the English rear feet of pad shape were used, together with claw-and-ball front feet larger than those of other centers, thus producing a slightly ungainly effect.

Plate 197.
SIDE CHAIR, WALNUT, NEWPORT, RHODE ISLAND, 1740–1750. Peculiarities of Newport fashion can be seen in the shaping of the back, the stylized shell of the cresting and the form of the claw-and-ball feet. *Courtesy,* HENRY FRANCIS DU PONT WINTERTHUR MUSEUM, WINTERTHUR, DEL.

276

Philadelphia chair makers were the only ones who employed three-part "trifid" feet and "stump" or chamfered rear legs. They also followed the second or "fiddle" type of back, emphasizing the swinging curves which they repeated in the intricate outlines of their "horseshoe" seats (*Plate 198*). These are sometimes recessed in the center of the front to hold a naturalistically carved seashell that occurs again at the apex of the back and, in flatter form, on the knees. Another Philadelphia feature are the pairs of tight volutes that appear at strategic intervals in the backs of these handsome chairs as though to direct the eye as it follows the carefully contained movement of the essentially baroque design. This, when the splat is pierced, attains a richness found nowhere else in the colonies, especially through the use of opulently carved acanthus and other leaves.

Plate 198.
Side Chair, Walnut, Philadelphia, *circa* 1750.
Generously proportioned, the Philadelphia Queen Anne chair is distinguished by its paired volutes and naturalistic shell decoration. *Courtesy*,
henry francis du pont winterthur museum, winterthur, del.

These characteristics are reflected, though weakly, in the backs of New York chairs, which are, however, constructed according to New England custom. Their seats are composed of vertical boards with the corners formed by the legs, which in Philadelphia chairs are doweled to the frame.

Developing regional taste can also be seen in Queen Anne case furniture, where cabriole legs were now substituted for the straight turned variety of the William and Mary style. The resulting transformation was as

Plate 199.
HIGH CHEST OF DRAWERS, MAHOGANY, DELAWARE RIVER VALLEY, *circa* 1750. The canon of generous proportion applies as well to Philadelphia case furniture of the Queen Anne style. Typical also are the trifid feet and the high-rising skirt. *Courtesy,* PHILADELPHIA MUSEUM OF ART

278

great as that produced by the passage from casement to sash windows in the architecture of the period. Pennsylvania legs are relatively short and stocky but carved with a masterful sweep (*Plate 199*); those of New England are long and thin by comparison, narrower and more rounded at the knee (*Plate 200*). The high chests of drawers of this region are generally crowned by lofty segmental or scroll forms that sometimes reflect a local type of doorway.

Plate 200.
HIGH CHEST OF DRAWERS, INLAID WHITE WALNUT OR BUTTERNUT, MASSACHUSETTS, 1725–1740. Linear effects play a great part in the more delicately proportioned attenuated case pieces of New England. *Courtesy*, HENRY FRANCIS DU PONT WINTERTHUR MUSEUM, WINTERTHUR, DEL.

Another feature of New England high chests of drawers is the presence of a lunette-shaped ornament on a central drawer at both extremities of the piece. This is repeated in the center drawer of many dressing tables made as mates to high chests, following an American custom. In the predominantly cherry and maple furniture of the Connecticut Valley the lunette ornament is a discreet flat fan or pinwheel composed of shallow, parallel incision, sometimes filled with brilliant inlay. At Newport this ornament took the form of the local stylized intaglio shell, probably inspired by those used in silver, which along with the Newport practice of undercutting the claws of

Plate 201.
HIGH CHEST OF DRAWERS, MAHOGANY, NEWPORT, RHODE ISLAND, 1750–1760. Undercut claws and intaglio shells characterize fine Queen Anne style case furniture like this piece associated with the work of Job Townsend. *Courtesy,* MUSEUM OF FINE ARTS, BOSTON, M. AND M. KAROLIK COLLECTION

280

the feet gave a peculiar sharpness to the early furniture (*Plate 201*). In Boston the motif became a baroque architectural shell, frequently gilt and sometimes accompanied by garlands. These are seen in their fullest and most handsome expression in the great japanned high chests of drawers made by John Pimm (active *circa* 1736–1773), where the outline of the skirt is a baroque design associated with the Boston area (*Plate 202*). In New England old-fashioned pendants, like chair stretchers, lingered in case

te 202.
H Chest of Drawers, Japanned Maple and Pine,
ston, 1730–1750. Made by John Pimm for Joshua
ing and probably painted by Thomas Johnson, this is
of the foremost examples of baroque and oriental
oration joined on a rococo Queen Anne frame.
rtesy, henry francis du pont winterthur museum,
iterthur, del.

pieces of this category. They were abolished in the middle colonies in favor of a skirt of bounding curves that often penetrates high into the case, as with the Philadelphia high chest and certain Delaware Valley dressing tables whose cabriole legs are habitually squared and banded with small moldings called "wristers" just above their old-fashioned paintbrush feet, a detail especially typical of New Jersey.

In this period slope-front desks, first used in the William and Mary style, were combined with two-door bookcases to create a type of furniture called a secretary that was later to become in coastal New England the supreme expression of colonial cabinet-making, as the high chest of drawers was to be in Philadelphia. A Boston example of about 1730, built of walnut with bracket feet, conventional for this kind of furniture in England, has the narrow proportions fashionable in London secretaries of the start of the century and inlay of rosewood and satinwood in the form of stars, a device imported via England from Holland (*Plate 203*). Inlays of all sorts became rare in this period, when as in England, cabinet-makers preferred to leave the surfaces of lustrous walnut and mahogany without enrichment of other woods.

In Connecticut, desks and secretaries were frequently set upon frames carried by tiny bandy cabriole legs with pad feet, a mannerism that imparts a strong local flavor. This is intensified in a secretary at the Henry Ford Museum (*Plate 204*) because in addition to the conventional flat carved fan of the skirt and the narrow corkscrew-like flames of the finial urns, the bookcase section has long incised leaves and scrolls as well as sun and star motifs that appear on doorways in such Connecticut River towns as Wethersfield, Suffield, Hadley and Deerfield.

These two pieces represent metropolitan and provincial extremes in the architectural furniture of New England. Another important example, this time from Philadelphia, is the case for an air pump made by John Harrison for the Library Company in 1739 (*Plate 205*). Closely related in both proportion and design to the pedimented doorcases and chimney breasts of the city, the "press" as it was called in a contemporary description, is decorated with fluted Doric pilasters, a full entablature and the earliest known egg and dart and acanthus moldings of the Palladian school. Their

Plate 203.
SECRETARY DESK, INLAID WALNUT, BOSTON, 1720–1730. Although based on London patterns, this distinguished slant-front desk has the vertical quality of most Massachusetts furniture. *Courtesy*, MUSEUM OF FINE ARTS, BOSTON, M. AND M. KAROLIK COLLECTION

283

Plate 204.
SECRETARY DESK, CHERRY,
CONNECTICUT, 1730–1750. A
provincial version of the Bo
desk, showing the
diminutive feet, scrolled
skirting and stylized carving
associated with the Connect
River Valley. *Courtesy*, THE
HENRY FORD MUSEUM,
DEARBORN, MICH.

Plate 205.
CASE FOR AN AIR PUMP, PAINTED PINE,
PHILADELPHIA, 1739. Made by John
Harrison, a carpenter who worked on
Independence Hall, this is the earliest and
one of the richest surviving examples of the
use of neo-Palladian architectural decoration
in American furniture. *Courtesy,* THE
LIBRARY COMPANY OF PHILADELPHIA

285

presence here and in the splats of a few Philadelphia Queen Anne chairs is of interest because of the popularity of such academic decoration in the Chippendale furniture of the Quaker city.

The incipient rococo character of the Queen Anne style is better expressed in tables, where the flowing curves of the cabriole legs met with less resistance from the static body than in the various chests of drawers. Of the leaf tables now made in varying sizes, those of the Delaware River area are outstanding for the authoritative lines of their legs with trifid feet and the handsome shaping of the angles of the leaves, repeated in the frame, which is related to the arching of the skirts of dressing tables of this region.

In the Queen Anne period new table types, imported from England, were developed here, especially in New England. One of these is the extendible card table with rounded projecting angles called turrets intended

286

Plate 206. CARD TABLE, WALNUT, MASSACHUSETTS, 1740–1750. *Courtesy,* BAYOU BEND COLLECTION, HOUSTON, TEXAS

for candlesticks. A few of the finest Boston examples, like the Peter Faneuil table, have their original needlepoint covers (*Plate 206*). Small tables with dished tops and attenuated cabriole legs were made for serving tea, the new beverage that had so wide an influence on contemporary silver. Massachusetts pieces with especially thin legs sometimes have skirts shaped like those of the local Queen Anne style case furniture (*Plate 207*). Another category of tables with "slab" tops of marble to protect against the spilling of alcohol was made in the form of serving buffets, center tables and smaller mixing tables, which replaced those with octagonal tops inset with slate of the William and Mary period.

Finally, the frames of looking glasses eloquently declare the contrasting aspects of the Queen Anne style. On the one hand, a japanned frame made for Jon Johannes Bleeker of New York ripples continuously with the

287

Plate 207. TEA TABLE, WALNUT, MASSACHUSETTS, 1740–1750. *Courtesy,* HENRY FRANCIS DU PONT WINTERTHUR MUSEUM, WINTERTHUR, DEL. Tables like these exemplify the rococo lightness of the Queen Anne style and the New England fondness for plain surfaces expressing flowing line.

Plate 208.
LOOKING GLASS, JAPANNED PINE, PROBABLY NEW
YORK, 1740–1750. The frame is one of the finest
Queen Anne style designs based almost entirely on
rippling curves. *Courtesy*, HENRY FRANCIS DU PONT
WINTERTHUR MUSEUM, WINTERTHUR, DEL.

Plate 209.
LOOKING GLASS, MAHOGANY AND GILT, PHILADELPHIA,
1753–1761. This frame, labeled by John Elliott, Sr., emphasi
the academic moldings used in contemporary woodwork. The
finial bird and scroll pediments are transitional to the
Chippendale style. *Courtesy*, HENRY FRANCIS DU PONT WINTERT
MUSEUM, WINTERTHUR, DEL.

many small interlocking curves that are the essence of rococo design (*Plate 208*). On the other hand, American makers like John Elliott Sr. of Philadelphia produced frames in which the architectural features of crossettes, conventional leaf moldings and scroll pediments predominate, as in much of the case furniture of the period (*Plate 209*). Even here, however, the two strains sometimes intermingle, for in the fine Elliott looking glass at Winterthur the asymmetrically posed phoenix on the center plinth is a foretaste of the full rococo fantasy that will play so large a part in the ornament of the last period of colonial furniture-making—the era of the Chippendale style.

THE CHIPPENDALE STYLE

DURING the third and fourth decades of the 18th century the standard English chair was gradually modified from its Queen Anne form. The back was substantially lowered and a new type of cresting board was applied. This bow-shaped form seems to have come from the "pagoda roof" line that terminates the back of a typical Chinese chair, thus continuing a process of derivation begun in the age of William and Mary. In this period the square seat returned to favor and eventually the straight leg as well. Both of these changes may also have been made in imitation of the Chinese chair. The new type of cresting was accompanied by more elaborate piercing of the single splat so that a complex network of curving lines developed.

At the same time English woodcarvers introduced into wainscot and furniture a new vocabulary of curvilinear ornament taken from the fully developed repertory of the French rococo, which they combined with the traditional classical moldings of Palladian architecture. The new ornament featured curvaceous openings surrounded by ruffled foliate forms combined with extravagantly shaped bosses called cabochons, diaper work, minute flowers and tiny volutes, the latter set against one another in intricate rhythms and often asymmetrical patterns. By 1750 this Anglo-French rococo decoration was being further enriched by pseudo-Gothic and Chinese motifs. The resulting hybrid style of decoration formed the basis for several hundred illustrations of furniture in *The Gentleman and Cabinet-maker's*

Director, which Thomas Chippendale, a London furniture-maker, published in 1754. This book, which soon became the principal source for propagating the new rococo style of the reign of George II (1727–1760) in Europe and throughout the British colonies of North America, has been responsible for the use of the author's name as a popular way of designating Anglo-French rococo furniture.

The new style seems to have reached America in the late seventeen-fifties; it flourished in the sixties and seventies and waned in the eighties. Throughout this period the basic Queen Anne forms, dominated by the cabriole leg, continued to be used with very little change. Except in some provincial areas, mahogany and the claw-and-ball foot were almost universally employed, while, as in England, veneering and inlay were largely laid aside in favor of ornamental carving. In the great centers of Philadelphia, Newport, and Boston, Chippendale furniture was distinguished from that of Queen Anne by more commanding proportions, by superb craftsmanship and by the rich and varied ornament that the rococo age produced. In this period also, thanks to occasional labels, bills and other documents, a larger number of pieces of furniture can be identified with known makers. Much less is known, however, about these craftsmen than about contemporary silversmiths.

PENNSYLVANIA FURNITURE

WHILE rural Pennsylvania was the scene of the richest flowering of folk art in the colonies, Philadelphia in the third quarter of the 18th century was the second largest city in the British Empire and its furniture represented the closest American approach to the elaborate cabinet work of London and Dublin. Thomas Affleck (1740–1795), the major London cabinet-maker known to have emigrated to the colonies, worked in Philadelphia from 1763 until his death, and the trade card of Benjamin Randolph (active *circa* 1760–1790) of about 1770 shows that he was prepared to make furniture directly from the plates of Chippendale's *Director* and other English pattern books.

The style begins in Pennsylvania with the solid-splat transitional chairs associated with William Savery (1721–1788), which already show a bow-

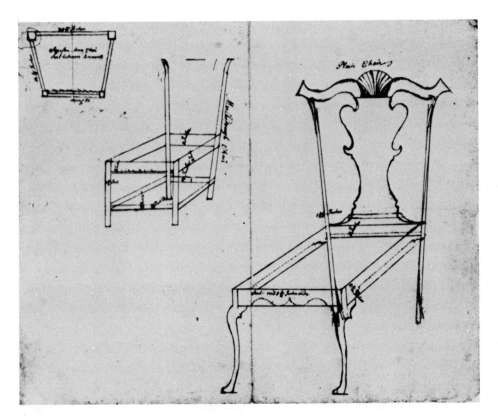

Plate 210. DESIGN FOR SIDE CHAIRS. DRAWING IN A DESIGN BOOK BY SAMUEL MICKLE, 1765. This drawing represents a transitional type of chair characteristic of Philadelphia, in which the solid Queen Anne style splat is combined with the new feature of the bow-shaped cresting derived from Chinese chairs. *Courtesy*, PHILADELPHIA MUSEUM OF ART, PHOTOGRAPH BY A. J. WYATT, STAFF PHOTOGRAPHER

shaped cresting board (*Plate 210*). Characteristically Philadelphian are the generous proportions of both stiles and rails, the firm carving of the widely projecting "ears" at the top of the stiles and the long tenons for extra security of construction, a survival of Queen Anne practice, which can be seen at the back of these chairs. All of these traits identify the Philadelphia adaptations of Chippendale models (plates X, XII and XIII of the *Director* were especially popular) as well as certain free arrangements developed by local cabinet-makers. Among the richest is the design of the Lambert family chairs, where every inch of the gracefully curved back is carved with lively realistic ornament (*Plate 211*). In the stiles and cresting there are rococo flowers, acanthus "grasses" and a classical leaf molding appears in the splat. The cresting board is crowned by an asymmetrical ruffled shell. Another appears above the scalloped skirt, enmeshed with volutes and a pierced ribbon, scintillatingly carved, while flowers and cabochons decorate the knees, flanked by volutes which turn into acanthus leaves.

The line of the cresting board occasionally varies. Chairs associated with James Gillingham (1736–1781), whose work is identified by a trefoil piercing of the splat, have sometimes a depressed yoke in the center, while those of Benjamin Randolph often curve inward at their extremities. The latter form, used also in England, is seen in one (*Plate 212*) of six sumptuous "sample chairs" made by that master, where the splat is intricately divided into arched muntin-like forms and quatrefoil openings reminiscent of Batty Langley's illustrated text on the Gothic Revival. These are combined with roses in characteristic rococo fantasy. The grandly carved legs end in French volute feet, a form preferred by Chippendale but seldom attempted in America. Another rare foot, the hairy paw variety, appears in Randolph's great easy chair (*Plate 213*), a rococo version of an upholstered form first seen in America with the baroque of William and Mary. This chair is of especial interest not only because of its fine carving but also because of the almost unique use, on English precedent, of carved rear feet.

Gothic backs of intersecting arched motifs, like those of the best contemporary dormers, became a specialty of Philadelphia. John Folwell combined in the speaker's chair at the State House of Pennsylvania (1779) the Gothic splat with pseudo-Chinese carving in the straight legs. Inspired by the *Director*, these "Marlborough legs," often accompanied by a pedestal foot (*Plate 214*), were probably introduced to Philadelphia by Thomas Affleck, who used them in his upholstered side chairs and sofa for Governor Penn as well as in a number of attributed armchairs and tea, card and serving tables. The "Marlborough leg" in its fully developed form also

Plate 211. SIDE CHAIR, MAHOGANY, PHILADELPHIA, 1760–1775. One of a famous set of Lambert family chairs showing the fully developed Philadelphia Chippendale formula, in which almost the entire surface is covered with naturalistic carving.

Courtesy, HENRY FRANCIS DU PONT WINTERTHUR MUSEUM, WINTERTHUR, DEL.

Plate 212. SIDE CHAIR, MAHOGANY, PHILADELPHIA, 1760–1775. *Courtesy,* PHILADELPHIA
MUSEUM OF ART. PHOTOGRAPH BY A. J. WYATT, STAFF PHOTOGRAPHER

Plate 213. EASY CHAIR, MAHOGANY, PHILADELPHIA, 1760–1775. *Courtesy,* PHILADELPHIA MUSEUM OF ART. PHOTOGRAPH BY A. J. WYATT, STAFF PHOTOGRAPHER. This piece and the chair shown on the facing page are two of the "sample" chairs attributed to Benjamin Randolph, which emphasize the plastic quality of much fine Chippendale furniture, thanks to the elaborate carving of naturalistic Anglo-French rococo motifs.

Plate 214. ARMCHAIR, MAHOGANY, PHILADELPHIA, 1765–1775. One of a few great upholstered chairs associated with the style of Thomas Affleck, who introduced the straight Marlborough leg to Philadelphia along with rippled cresting. *Courtesy*, HENRY FRANCIS DU PONT
WINTERTHUR MUSEUM, WINTERTHUR, DEL.

appears on certain majestic canopied Philadelphia beds like one at Winterthur whose graceful pillars already show the transition around 1790 to neo-classical forms, for their fine leaf carving is inspired by Plate 106 of George Hepplewhite's *Cabinet Maker's Guide*, published in London in 1788, a prime source for the classicizing style which succeeded the rococo. Plain straight legs were used throughout the colonies, as in Great Britain, with all types of Chippendale furniture.

Philadelphia case furniture of this period has the substantial proportions of the city's late colonial architecture. Its chests, carried on bracket feet of rococo ogee profile, are distinguished by fluted quarter columns at the angles. These are always of the Doric order, for no Ionic or Corinthian, so popular in Boston, were admitted in the local furniture and scarcely ever appear in Philadelphia wainscot or exterior architecture. Quarter columns, sometimes enriched with vines, were also used on dressing tables and matching high chests of drawers, whose surfaces display the supreme expression of rococo carving in Philadelphia.

These high chests (*Plate 215*) are surmounted by baroque scroll forms (borrowed like Queen Anne examples from English architectural books of the first half of the 18th century) which end in minutely carved acanthus leaves or flowers. The undulant skirt, at the other extremity, is generally edged with interlocking volutes from which emerge sprigs of foliage, following a custom probably introduced in the woodwork of the Pennsylvania State House in the 1750's. Just above this there is an ornamented drawer containing most often a naturalistic shell embellished with a flower from which scroll-like "grasses" rise on either side. This composition might be considered the most typical Philadelphia Chippendale motif. Sometimes the drawer has a relief from Aesop's fables, asymmetrically framed by volutes, as in a mantel from the Samuel Powel house now at the Philadelphia Museum. In the upper section of the chest there is carving above the drawers. Often this takes the form of a shell with foliage, repeating the formula of the drawer below. Occasionally, however, the grasses surround a multi-curved volute composition ruffled with foliage, a favorite Anglo-French rococo motif. This kind of carving is generally accompanied by a central finial cartouche of irregular outline derived, it appears, from French engravings of pierced ornament. In a second type of top this motif is replaced by a basket or vase of flowers, the scrolls rise from a cornice with carved frieze and are backed by a delicate rococo lattice. The frieze of the second type is decorated with pseudo-Chinese patterns like those used in wainscot.

Plate 215.
HIGH CHEST OF DRAWERS, MAHOGANY, PHILADELPHIA, 1760–1775. Philadelphia Chippendale case furniture, amply proportioned like that of the Queen Anne style, is decorated with naturalistic "grasses," shells, frilled openings and asymmetrical volutes and leaf finials evolved from French and English rococo designs. *Courtesy* MUSEUM OF FINE ARTS, BOSTON, M. AND M. KAROLIK COLLECTION

298

These two terminal designs, one sculptural, the other architectural, were also applied to the rare double chests (*Plate 216*) and secretaries made in Philadelphia. A hybrid version of the architectural form appears on high chests of drawers and desks attributed to Eliphalet Chapin, who after four

Plate 216.
DOUBLE CHEST OF DRAWERS, MAHOGANY, PHILADELPHIA, 1760–1775. For this type of Philadelphia furniture ogee bracket feet were mandatory, and the top section generally ends in a fretwork frieze and scroll pediments flanking lattice work. *Courtesy,* PHILADELPHIA MUSEUM OF ART

years of training in Philadelphia returned to his native East Windsor, Connecticut, in 1771 and there mingled Philadelphia motifs with cherry wood, lighter proportions and the flat linear ornament characteristic of the Connecticut Valley.

Some Chippendale tables of Philadelphia have an almost plastic quality, so vigorously are they modeled and so generously are they carved. Card and serving tables with Marlborough legs were frequently enriched with fretwork of vaguely Chinese look, taken like so many other elements from the *Director*. Both these and the tables with cabriole legs have in common the use of gadrooning at the lower base of the frame. The finest tables of the latter category, like those made by Affleck for Governor Penn, have turret angles with diaper carving and bold, sweeping "grasses." These relate them to certain marble-topped side tables with all-over carving of voluted forms, the surfaces of which become a cascade of swirling lines, like the gold and white looking glasses composed entirely of flowers and rococo scrolls. James Reynolds advertised frames like this in 1768 and a few years later made one, now at the Winterthur Museum, for John Cadwalader. They are the closest American approximation to the woodcarving designs of Lock and Copland in the 1740's which launched the full phase of the rococo style in England.

The specific characteristics of Philadelphia furniture of this period are perhaps best stated by a different type of table, the pedestal form for the serving of tea (*Plate 217*), which had already appeared in the Queen Anne era. In the finest examples superbly carved claw-and-ball feet are attached to powerfully shaped cabriole legs framed by ruffled volutes and covered with long grasses, like the legs of chairs, dressing tables and high chests of drawers. From this rich base gracefully rises the pedestal in which the upper part of a characteristic fluted Doric column is fused with a vase form of Chinese derivation, thus emphasizing that blending of classic and exotic elements essential to the style. Finally, the sensitive undulations of the scalloped circular top, which can be tilted when not in use against the "birdcage" base, recall the similar edges of the trays and salvers made by contemporary Philadelphia silversmiths, the acknowledged masters in that craft of the full rococo style.

Plate 217. PEDESTAL TABLE, MAHOGANY, PHILADELPHIA, 1760–1775. A masterpiece of the Chippendale style in which, with neo-Palladian license, classical and rococo forms are united. *Courtesy,* MUSEUM OF FINE ARTS, BOSTON, M. AND M. KAROLIK COLLECTION

Contemporaneously with this activity in Philadelphia and its reflection in the work of the Swiss cabinet-maker John Bachman (1746–1829) of Lancaster, the German people of Pennsylvania were making furniture based on the traditions of their homeland. Natives for the most part of the Rhineland and western Switzerland who had come in great numbers to the province during the first half of the 18th century, they kept alive here certain furniture forms that go back to the Middle Ages.

In addition to wainscot chairs, which sometimes preserve late Gothic coffer seats, they made sawbuck trestle tables and South German chests on prominent frames with dovetailed fronts like those seen in early 16th century prints by Albrecht Dürer. These dower chests, made of tulipwood and pine, were often painted in vivid colors with stylized tulips, confronted distelfinck birds, and prancing unicorns, symbolizing virginity (*Plate 218*). Marbleized effects were produced by rubbing wet paint with a corncob. One major painter, Christian Seltzer (1749–1831) of Jonestown, Pennsylvania, is known to have decorated chests between 1771 and 1796, and a number of his signed pieces have survived. The style was carried by emigrant Germans through the Valley of Virginia to the Moravian settlement at Winston-Salem, North Carolina. Chairs with raking "stick" legs, canted wooden seats and heart-pierced scroll backs were made on German and Swiss 17th-century patterns and are the only American colonial chair form that owes nothing to British fashions.

In Pennsylvania there occurred some fusion between these Germanic types and the academic Anglo-American style. Chests were given ogee bracket feet and were sometimes decorated with crossetted panels like those of the "tabernacles" of Philadelphia and Lancaster chimney pieces. Two-door wardrobes, sometimes painted and sometimes inlaid with wax, possibly in imitation of ivory, have cornices with dentils and key moldings. The one made for Georg Hüber, dated 1779, has the fully carved mutules of the Doric entablatures used at the State House of Pennsylvania and in a few great Philadelphia houses of the time (*Plate 219*).

The vivid florid painting applied to Pennsylvania German furniture is found again in pottery and glass. The Germans brought with them the sgrafitto earthenware technique, whereby designs were scratched upon redware plates and jars through a thin layer of yellow slip, the piece being then glazed and fired. The work of certain regional masters of the late 18th century is known. In 1786 George Hubener of Montgomery County signed a dated plate inscribed to Catharine Raeder which bears his characteristic symbol of loving union, a pair of doves with bodies joined to form a single heart (*Plate 220*). The stiff crisp lines of this ancient design contrast with the looser and more realistic style of David Spinner of Bucks County, who about 1800 decorated pie plates with figures of men and women, often on horseback, and rather nostalgic soldiers of the Continental Army, sometimes playing flutes and drums (*Plate 221*).

218. Marriage Chest of Margaret Kernan, Painted Tulipwood, Pennsylvania German, 1788.
ylvania German painted chests are a direct link with medieval manuscripts through their iconography,
ng and calligraphy. The flowers on this chest are like those of contemporary crewel embroidery. *Cour-*
enry Francis du Pont Winterthur Museum, Winterthur, Del.

Plate 219. WARDROBE, OR *Schrank*, INLAID WALNUT, PENNSYLVANIA GERMAN, 1779. On a traditional Germanic frame, German folk decoration is joined with Palladian architectural details. Made for Georg Hüber of Lancaster County. *Courtesy,* PHILADELPHIA MUSEUM OF ART.
PHOTOGRAPH BY A. J. WYATT, STAFF PHOTOGRAPHER

Plate 221.
EARTHENWARE PLATE WITH REVOLUTIONARY
SOLDIERS, SGRAFITTO TECHNIQUE,
PENNSYLVANIA GERMAN, *circa* 1800. *Courtesy,*
PHILADELPHIA MUSEUM OF ART. The most
important group of decorated earthenware
plates made before 1800 is the work of
German settlers in Pennsylvania. The plate
above is inscribed "Catharine Raeder, her
plate. Out of the earth with understanding the
potter makes everything." The plate at the left
is in the style of David Spinner of Bucks
County.

305

This folk art pottery in red, yellow, green and black, without parallel in North America, has a counterpart in the enameled and engraved glass made by Germans who alone defied the British prohibition against glass blowing in the colonies. Caspar Wistar at Wistarburg, New Jersey (1739–1780), William Henry "Baron" Stiegel at Mannheim, Pennsylvania (1769–1774), and John Frederick Amelung at New Bremen in Maryland (1785–1794), all used doves, swans and other symbolic birds (*Plate 222*), either as blown finials for covered bowls or in combination with wreaths and sprays of stylized flowers gaudily painted or more soberly engraved on the surfaces of flip glasses, flasks, perfume bottles, bowls or, in the case of Amelung (*Plate 223*), giant vessels for drinking called "pokals."

Plate 222.
FLIP GLASS, ENAMELED, PENNSYLVANIA GERMAN, *circa* 1774. In the style of William Henry "Baron" Stiegel, who made the first decorated table glass in this country, this piece has a blue-and-white enameled love bird and the inscription in English "We too will be true." *Courtesy*, HENRY FRANCIS DU PONT WINTERTHUR MUSEUM, WINTERTHUR, DEL.

306

Plate 223.
COVERED FLIP GLASS, ENGRAVED, 1788.
An outstanding example of early copper
wheel engraving made at the New
Bremen (Maryland) glass works of
John Frederick Amelung, it is inscribed
"Floreat Commercium—Charles
Ghequiere—New Bremen Glass
Manufactory the 20th of June 1788."
Courtesy, HENRY FRANCIS DU PONT
WINTERTHUR MUSEUM, WINTHERTHUR, DEL.

NEW YORK FURNITURE

THE Chippendale furniture of New York owes nothing to the Dutch traditions of the city, which were still strongly felt in the William and Mary style and in the fine local silver of the first half of the 18th century. On the contrary, in the making of chairs, New York craftsmen adhered closely to the models of Chippendale without, however, achieving the distinguished results of their colleagues in Philadelphia. One reason for this was their canon of proportion, which emphasized heaviness of forms, especially in the large balls of the front feet that create an awkward contrast with the

Plate 224.
SIDE CHAIR OWNED BY SIR WILLIAM JOHNSON, MAHOGANY, NEW YORK, 1760–1775. *Courtesy*, HENRY FRANCIS DU PONT WINTERTHUR MUSEUM, WINTERTHUR, DEL.

308

diminutive pads of the rear ones. Another reason was the flat dispirited carving which reduced the naturalistic motifs of Philadelphia to lifeless diagrams surrounded by mechanical cross-hatching. A final reason was the disconcerting New York tendency to mix old elements with new.

The Queen Anne horseshoe seat was retained in many of the Chippendale chairs of New York. It appears in a famous set made for Sir William Johnson, Indian Agent in New York State, possibly by Gilbert Ash, a chairmaker "in Wall St. near the City Hall" (*Plate 224*). Characteristic also of New York is the flared *chinoiserie* lozenge which seems to float upon the

e 225.

Chair, Mahogany,
York, 1760–1775.
tesy, the metropolitan
um of art, new york. gift
rs. george sands bryan,
emory of her husband.
York Chippendale chairs
large front feet with
dency to squareness, rear
mp" feet and very flat carving.

thick volutes of the splat. This design from the *Director* was extremely popular in New York, where it appears also in the pierced handles of silver porringers by Myer Myers, the city's greatest silversmith. Equally typical are the ruffed lunette over diagonal hatching of the cresting and the leaves in the "ears" of the chair. Other *retardataire* traits of New York chair-makers are the use of a heavy tassel and ruffle taken from British furniture of *circa* 1740 set in an aperture on the splat framed by scrolls covered with "grasses" and heavy gadrooning between the front legs (*Plate 225*). This last element is also found on New York "slab" tables, which bear the same relationship to those of Philadelphia as do the chairs.

The slope-front secretaries of Samuel Prince (d. 1778), who advertised from 1772 to 1776, suggest, however, a Boston influence in the use of very heavy claw feet with sculptured brackets and of broken triangular pediments. The same division of influences is indicated by the small quantity of late colonial furniture surviving from Charleston, South Carolina, where the London-trained cabinet-maker Thomas Elfe Sr. was at work from about 1747 until his death in 1775.

NEW ENGLAND FURNITURE

PENNSYLVANIA and New England were the foremost areas of late colonial furniture-making, but unlike Pennsylvania, dominated by Philadelphia, New England possessed in Boston and Newport two local centers of comparable importance where a regional style was expressed in distinctly different fashions.

Throughout New England the light forms and lean carving of local Queen Anne taste lingered in chairs, especially those of Massachusetts (*Plate 226*). In a chair with back taken from a favorite design (*Plate 227*) in a pattern book by Robert Manwaring (London, 1765), all the proportions are slighter than those of Philadelphia or New York, the profiles of the cabriole legs have a linear sharpness peculiar to New England, while the seat upholstered to the frame is a unique variant of the slip seat practiced elsewhere.

In this period other differences developed between Pennsylvania and New England. In the northern area, dressing tables and high chests of

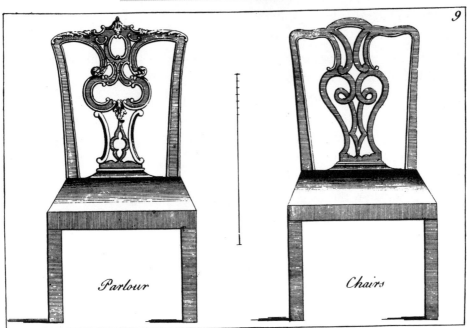

Plate 227. DESIGNS FOR PARLOR CHAIRS. Plate 9, from Robert Manwaring, *Cabinet and Chairmaker's Real Friend and Companion*, London, 1765. *Courtesy,* NEW YORK PUBLIC LIBRARY. Chippendale chairs made in Boston frequently follow a rococo design from Manwaring's book. Local characteristics are the thin forms of the back, the seat upholstered over the frame and the retracted claws of the front feet.

drawers gave place to double chests and secretaries as the showpieces of high fashion, while in Boston and Newport the kneehole desk, unknown in Philadelphia, was added to their company. New England case furniture is distinguished by the use of pilasters on the fronts rather than quarter columns at the angles of the upper section and by the block front treatment of the lower parts. This technique, which provides three rounded projections, the center one slightly recessed, first practiced in some Parisian chests of drawers of *circa* 1700, but never favored in England, became the most highly developed innovation of American colonial furniture. It appears not only in New England but also in New York and occasionally in the South. Used as early as 1738 by Job Coit of Boston in a signed and dated secretary at Winterthur, the block front is especially associated with Newport, along with shell ornament. The latter, however, is typical of all New England in this period, where the various linear stylizations through which it passed offer a final contrast with the plastic naturalism of Philadelphia shells.

In Massachusetts the fronts of desks and chests of drawers were given a number of new shapes through blocking and other technical procedures. When blocking was used, the convex projections sometimes extend like piers from the top to the bottom of the case. More frequently the top of the blocking is rounded to resemble an elliptical dome (*Plate 228*). This treatment is found in a number of fine secretary desks which end in broken pediments carried on fluted pilasters. Another local treatment especially associated with Boston and Benjamin Frothingham of Charlestown (active 1756–1809) was the oxbow or serpentine front, recalling Gostelow's work in Philadelphia, in which convex projections often appear in the topmost drawer to recall the blocking procedure.

Still another regional practice, and one of the greatest importance, was the partial application of the serpentine profile in the vertical sense so as to give a chest of drawers or desk a bombé or kettle shape. This process, derived from Holland, was greatly refined in Boston, where each drawer was nicely shaped to the undulant contours of the frame, producing a much more subtle effect than the usual European design, in which drawers of equal shape were the arbitrary rule (*Plate 229*). The central skirt ornament and

Plate 228.

SECRETARY DESK, MAHOGANY, 1760–1780. The finest Chippendale style secretary desks of Massachusetts were made with either blocked or bombé lower sections. This distinguished blocked example, owned by the Curwen family of Salem, has a typical upper section decorated with fluted pilasters, a broken pediment and a finial urn with a New England "corkscrew" flame. *Courtesy,* ESSEX INSTITUTE, SALEM, MASS.

Plate 229.

SECRETARY DESK, MAHOGANY, BOSTON, 1765–1775. A paramount example of the bombé shaped desk in combination with a rococo carved upper section, attributed to John Cogswell. *Courtesy,* HENRY FRANCIS DU PONT WINTERTHUR MUSEUM, WINTERTHUR, DEL. PHOTOGRAPH BY GILBERT ASK

heavy claw-and-ball feet used in place of the ogee bracket type, universally employed in Philadelphia for this kind of furniture, are further marks of Boston cabinet-making. Some of the best of this work was done by John Cogswell (active 1769; died 1818), whose skilful rococo leaf and scroll carving emphasizes the impression of restless movement that the forms evoke.

In Boston and the port towns to the north the regional urge to feats of technique produced Chippendale tea tables notable for their audacious construction and delicate proportions. In the cabriole leg variety, skirts were occasionally blocked to produce as many as fourteen turret-like scallops or "buttresses" to hold cups of tea (*Plate 230*). This *tour de force* is balanced in the straight leg group by several tables believed to have been made in Portsmouth, New Hampshire, ornamented with low galleries and frets of surpassingly delicate piercing, and by arched stretchers formed of interlocking volutes leading to an undercut "steeple" finial, which is the last survival of a 17th century ornamental form.

The Newport version of Chippendale style was invented by Job Townsend (1699–1765) and perfected by his son-in-law John Goddard (1723–1785) and nephews John and Edmund Townsend. Together they developed the blocking principle into a consummate blending of line and form that draws together in a single rhythm all the elements of a piece of furniture.

This is seen in Edmund Townsend's labeled kneehole desk in the Karolik Collection, where the rhythm begins in the convex voluted overlay of the ogee feet, which looks like a refined expression of the typical Connecticut Queen Anne base, suspended above the floor (*Plate 231*). Upon this rises the blocked area, defined with masterful outlines to terminate, on each side of the kneehole aperture, in a characteristic shell which had been the chief ornament of the Newport cabinet-makers since the days of the Queen Anne style. It is carved in a series of gracefully curving lines sweeping inward to interlocking volutes after the rococo principle already observed in Philadelphia. The principle is the same but the result is entirely different, for the Newport shell is the quintessence of linear convention according to New England tradition in which no suggestion of the playful

Plate 230.
TEA TABLE, MAHOGANY, NEW ENGLAND, 1750–1775. Another form of blocking is the convex "buttress" used to emphasize rim scallops designed to hold cups of tea. *Courtesy,* MUSEUM OF FINE ARTS, BOSTON, M. AND M. KAROLIK COLLECTION

Plate 231. BUREAU TABLE, MAHOGANY, RHODE ISLAND, 1765–1775. A great kneehole desk, called "bureau table" in the 18th century, labeled by Edmund Townsend, which shows characteristic Newport blocking ending in shells. Also typical of the finest Newport work is the subtle scroll form of the feet. *Courtesy,* MUSEUM OF FINE ARTS, BOSTON, M. AND M. KAROLIK COLLECTION

naturalism of the rococo is permitted. The rhythm of the Newport desk continues in the serrated edges of the three shells set across the top of the front and is emphasized by the alternation of convex and concave forms, in relief and intaglio carving, with which the shells are defined.

The same linear scheme appears with minor variations in other types of case furniture made by the Goddard-Townsend group. In double chests blocking was applied to the upper section and, as with secretaries, the number of shells was increased from three or four to six or even nine. Fluted Doric half columns ornament the angles of the bookcase portions of secretaries (*Plate 233*) and reappear in the cases of tall clocks, where the door panels are designed in austere block front forms surmounted by voluted shells like those of the case furniture. Similarly, some great Philadelphia tall clock cases are topped by scrolls with lattices and baskets of flowers which relate them to local secretaries, high chests and double chests of drawers.

The influence of Newport work can be seen on desks and chests of drawers made in coastal Connecticut, where blocking was practiced by Benjamin Burnham of Colchester, who like Chapin was trained in Philadelphia. Some pieces are especially rich in carving; a chest at Winterthur offers no less than nine shells on its drawers (*Plate 232*). Yet the way in which

Plate 232.
CHEST OF DRAWERS, CHERRY WOOD, COASTAL CONNECTICUT, 1765–1775. Deeply influenced by nearby Rhode Island in the use of shells and in the design of the feet, this chest of drawers asserts its Connecticut personality in the pattern of its skirting. *Courtesy,* HENRY FRANCIS DU PONT WINTERTHUR MUSEUM, WINTERTHUR, DEL.

316

they are crowded, stifling the Newport rhythm, their inferior carving which loses the pure line and distinctive form of Newport shells, as well as their use with the diminutive skirt scrolls of Connecticut, reveal the imitation.

Plate 233.
SECRETARY DESK, MAHOGANY, NEWPORT, RHODE ISLAND, 1760-1775. The Chippendale style of Newport culminated in towering showpieces like this one, attributed to John Goddard, with blocking and shells in both upper and lower divisions. *Courtesy,* YALE UNIVERSITY ART GALLERY, MABEL BRADY GARVAN COLLECTION

In other more distant areas incongruous effects were sometimes created, as with the maple furniture made by Samuel Dunlap II of Chester and Salisbury, New Hampshire, in the period *circa* 1775–1790. He applied crude and sometimes truncated versions of the Newport shell to old-fashioned high chests of drawers (*Plate 234*) and to strange high-back chairs with splats pierced in scroll patterns like those of the skirts of the chests, where the shell dictated the arched form of the cresting. This furniture is the closest New England counterpart to the hybrid provincial style of the Pennsylvania Germans.

Plate 234.
HIGH CHEST OF DRAWERS, MAPLE, NEW HAMPSHIRE. A provincial anachronism, this Queen Anne style case, attributed to Samuel Dunlap II, has shells like those of Newport combined with the flat linear variety used all over New England in the 18th century. *Courtesy*, YALE UNIVERSITY ART GALLERY, MABEL BRADY GARVAN COLLECTION

318

SILVER

ALTHOUGH there were silversmiths in Virginia as early as 1608, our oldest surviving silver, like the earliest furniture, was made in New England. The first silversmith whose work is known is Robert Sanderson (1608–1693), who arrived in 1638 from London and later formed a partnership with John Hull (1624–1683), another Englishman, in Boston. There they officially minted coin and transformed foreign money into flat and hollow silverware, a colonial form of banking. Together they trained Jeremiah Dummer (1645–1718), Timothy Dwight (1654–1691/2) and probably John Coney (1656–1722), under whom New England silver-making flourished at the end of the 17th and the beginning of the 18th centuries. These men and their successors called themselves goldsmiths, although they rarely worked in that metal. They followed the apprentice system and set personal marks on their silver, but they did not employ the hallmarks which make it possible to identify the date and place of origin of contemporary British silver.

American silver of the late 17th century has the same heavy decoration taken from Renaissance sources as the furniture, which, however, it seems to have preceded in the use of certain baroque motifs. For example, a standing cup (*Plate 235*) made for church use in 1674 by Hull and Sanderson has a stem that suggests the "explosive" forms of turning used in William and Mary furniture of the first decades of the 18th century. Similarly, Dwight's salver at the Boston Museum has as its only ornamentation an engraved frieze of flowers embracing a lion and other animals that anticipate the work of Boston japanners of a later date (*Plate 236*). This is the earliest known American attempt at *chinoiserie* decoration.

Relief ornament of embossed or *repoussé* technique, inspired by English Restoration work, is the principal link between this early New England silver and the great European Renaissance tradition. It appears in simple form on Robert Sanderson's large two-handled caudle cup of *circa* 1656 at Winterthur, made for drinking mulled wine, where the section above the base, bellying in a shape that goes back to ancient Egypt, has an embossed American turkey set in conventionalized foliage. In a later piece of similar form by John Coney, a cherub like those on early New England tombstones

Plate 235.
SILVER COMMUNION CUP BY JOHN HULL AND
ROBERT SANDERSON, BOSTON, 1674. Made for
the church at Rehoboth, Mass., by the first
American silversmiths whose work is preserved,
this Boston standing cup has the handsome
plain forms that are mainly responsible for the
beauty of early American silver. *Courtesy*,
YALE UNIVERSITY ART GALLERY,
MABEL BRADY GARVAN COLLECTION

Plate 236.
DETAIL OF A SILVER SALVER
BY TIMOTHY DWIGHT, BOSTON,
LATE 17TH CENTURY.
Courtesy, MUSEUM OF FINE
ARTS, BOSTON

wanders among carnations and other flowers that suggest the patterns used in crewel embroidery (*Plate 237*). These motifs also appear on a silver plate by Coney at the Boston Museum (*Plate 238*). Both cups have cast scroll "caryatid" handles, featuring female busts, a favorite device of this period descended from the northern European Renaissance.

Plate 237. AMERICAN CREWEL BED HANGINGS, 18TH CENTURY. Wool embroidery called crewel, one of the principal forms of colonial needlework, employed as a favorite motif a form of stylized flower which appears also in American silver and Pennsylvania German painted furniture. These complete bed hangings, made by Mary Bulman, are thought to be unique. *Courtesy*, THE OLD GAOL MUSEUM, YORK, MAINE.
PHOTOGRAPH BY DOUGLAS ARMSDEN

Plate 238. DETAIL OF A SILVER PLATE BY JOHN CONEY, BOSTON, EARLY 18TH CENTURY. *Courtesy,* MUSEUM OF FINE ARTS, BOSTON. Some early Boston silver was made lively by engraved patterns of flowers, animals and human figures like those used by contemporary embroiderers and japanners of furniture.

Similar flat-chased flowers and vines are spread over the surface of Jeremiah Dummer's punch bowl dated 1692 (*Plate 239*), the rim of which is decorated with large *repoussé* scallops, a Carolean convention like the "paintbrush foot" (see *Plate 189*). The elaborately scrolled handles end in the heads of serpents, another naturalistic motif of the period which appears on the lid of the greatest example of *repoussé* silver of this time, John Coney's sugar box of *circa* 1680–1690 (*Plate 240*). The small oval receptacle, made for the ritual of drinking hot mulled wine, is covered with elliptical bosses joined by fluting to form a Renaissance chain motif that goes back to the 16th century pattern book of Sebastiano Serlio. On the slightly domical top, against a matted front, appear acanthus leaves that will not be seen in American furniture until the style of Queen Anne, and then in considerably less florid form.

In New York City, which began making its own silver in the late 17th century, certain Dutch preferences for forms and ornament prevailed into the 18th century. One of the chief characteristics of New York silver of this period is a cut-leaf band, recalling contemporary typographical decoration, used to ornament a base. Typical, also, are the cast cherub heads combined with swags of fruit that suggest the monochrome painting of New York wardrobes and which appear on the handles of tankards and the Dutch coins set in their lids. Pictorial engraving, abundant in early New York silver, frequently represents bunches of fruit, caryatid forms, birds, and especially allegorical figures on handsomely shaped beakers made for family and

Plate 239. SILVER PUNCH BOWL BY JEREMIAH DUMMER, BOSTON, 1692. In addition to engraving, early Boston silversmiths decorated their best work with cast handles in complicated curved forms and with *repoussé* scallops that give movement to the surfaces. *Courtesy*, YALE UNIVERSITY ART GALLERY, MABEL BRADY GARVAN COLLECTION

Plate 240. SILVER SUGAR BOX BY JOHN CONEY, BOSTON, 1680–1690. One of nine known similar receptacles, this opulent work of the outstanding Boston master of the early period contains naturalistic relief ornament that precedes similar work by furniture carvers by more than a quarter of a century. *Courtesy*, MUSEUM OF FINE ARTS, BOSTON

church use. These were created by such silversmiths as the Master I. B., Cornelius van der Burgh (1653–1699) and the celebrated Cornelius Kierstede (1675–1757), whose fantastically shaped snuffer stand and columnar candlestick (*Plate 241*) made for the Schuyler family around 1705 are decorated with dancing figures in the capricious dress popularized by the prints of Jean Bérain. Figurative engraving of this sort soon passed out of favor to reappear in the commemorative silver gorgets and medals given by the government to Indian chieftains toward the end of the 18th century.

Plate 241. SILVER CANDLESTICK MADE FOR THE SCHUYLER FAMILY BY CORNELIUS KIERSTEDE, NEW YORK, *circa* 1705. The classical column was a popular form for 18th-century candlesticks. This great example combines the motif with fantastically dressed engraved figures and decorative birds used by Dutch silversmiths in New York City. *Courtesy*, THE METROPOLITAN MUSEUM OF ART, NEW YORK. GIFT OF ROBERT L. CAMMANN, 1957.

324

New York counterparts of the great *repoussé* pieces made in Boston in the late 17th century are the rich covered caudle cups by Gerrit Onckelbag (1670–1732) and the Master I. B., identified as either Jacob Boelen (*circa* 1657–1729) or Jurian Blanck (active *circa* 1668). Both have acanthus leaves on the lid beneath the three knops that serve as feet when the lid is used as a dish. These leaves are repeated on the section above the base in an opulent vertical design used in 17th-century Dutch and occasionally English silver which can be traced back to a pattern book by Hans Vredeman de Vries of 1563. On the Onckelbag cup (*Plate 242*) is engraved the Bayard family coat of arms with a shield and armorial foliage whose forms are characteristic of the florid taste of the late 17th century.

Plate 242. SILVER COVERED CAUDLE CUP BY GERRIT ONCKELBAG, NEW YORK, 1696. The New York caudle cups for drinking mulled wine differ from those of Boston in their use of applied decoration and by having lids equipped with tiny feet to serve as dishes, when removed from the cups. *Courtesy*, YALE UNIVERSITY ART GALLERY, MABEL BRADY GARVAN COLLECTION

The most original products of the contemporary silversmiths of New York seem to have been the low bowls with twisted wire or beaded caryatid handles made in a variety of sizes. The finest have six deeply outlined panels of roughly heart shape with paired scrolls at their lower extremities, a design only occasionally used in Dutch silver. These panels are sometimes decorated with a boldly executed fleur-de-lys, as in bowls by Kierstede's probable master, Jesse Kip (1660–1722), one of which, dated 1699 and now at the Henry Ford Museum, is the earliest known American racing trophy. Luxuriant *repoussé* flowers with surrounds of prick and punch work ornament the punch bowls of Cornelius Kierstede (*Plate 243*) of 1698, Bartholomew Le Roux (active 1689–1713) and Benjamin Wynkoop (1675–1751), as well as a slightly simpler example by Jacob Ten Eyck (1704–1793) made about 1730.

A number of events occurring around 1700 deeply affected the development of American silver. One was the late emergence of Philadelphia with the Huguenot goldsmiths Caesar Ghiselin (1670–1734) and John Nys (1671–1734) to be one of the three great colonial centers of silver-making.

Plate 243. SILVER BOWL ENGRAVED WITH THE INITIALS OF THEUNIS AND VROUTJE QUICK BY CORNELIUS KIERSTEDE, NEW YORK, 1698–1725. Luxurious bowls of this sort are as typical of New York as are the sugar boxes of New England. The great *repoussé* carnations suggest the engraved ones of Boston, but the shape of the panels and the geometric band on the base typify the silver of New York. *Courtesy,* THE METROPOLITAN MUSEUM OF ART, NEW YORK, SAMUEL D. LEE FUND, 1938

Another event was the appearance of teapots and other utensils of silver for use in drinking the oriental beverage recently introduced from Europe. A third was the employment of gadrooning (parallel vertical convex ornament) under English influence as a principal form of decoration.

Thought to have been launched first in Boston by Jeremiah Dummer in such masterpieces as the standing cup of 1700, owned by the First Parish Church of Dorchester, Massachusetts, gadrooning was expertly used by his pupil Edward Winslow (1669–1753), either to enhance an already lavishly embossed object like his sugar boxes of *circa* 1702 or as the chief adornment of the piece. The latter treatment is seen at its best in Winslow's great chocolate pot (*Plate 244*) made for Thomas Hutchinson where gadrooned decoration is used at various strategic places in effective contrast with plain surfaces. The lid is also decorated with cut-card work, a form of ornament suggesting textile patterns much employed in early Boston silver.

Plate 244.
SILVER CHOCOLATE POT BY EDWARD WINSLOW, BOSTON, *circa* 1700. Convex parallel ornament called "gadrooning" was the first great innovation in American silver of the 18th century. In this Boston example it is used at strategic intervals to create a rhythmic contrast with plain surfaces. *Courtesy*, THE METROPOLITAN MUSEUM OF ART, NEW YORK. BEQUEST OF A. T. CLEARWATER, 1933

The same diverse uses of gadrooning appear in the work of John Coney, the greatest of the early goldsmiths. In his Colman family monteith (a large bowl with scalloped rim from which glasses were hung by their feet to be cooled), in the Mabel Brady Garvan Collection at Yale, gadrooning on the base is combined with shallow fluting below baroque compositions of vases, scrolls and flowers, suggesting Augsburg patterns, surmounted by the cherub head characteristic of this master. On the other hand, in the superbly proportioned grace or loving cup presented to Harvard College by Governor Stoughton in 1701 (*Plate 245*), Coney used gadrooning and the closely related device of reeding as a unifying decoration which performs the same function of dramatizing plain surfaces that the cup and trumpet turning provides for the furniture of the style of William and Mary.

Plate 245.
SILVER GRACE CUP BY JOHN CONEY, BOSTON, 1700–1720. A covered cup for drinking toasts, decorated in the William and Mary gadroon style. It has "caryatid" handles like the New York punch bowls and bears the engraved arms of the Stoughton family of Boston. *Courtesy,* HARVARD UNIVERSITY

In the next phase of American silver, which corresponds roughly to the period of the Queen Anne style, smooth surfaces became the norm. This change was produced in part by an English law of 1697 raising the content of pure silver which made the metal softer and less suitable for ornate forms. It is also related to the taste for smooth, gracefully curving surfaces in contemporary furniture symbolized by the unadorned cabriole leg. Accordingly, *repoussé* work and gadrooning were replaced by banding and applied ornament which strengthened the surfaces of objects whose outlines take on a new beauty of interrelated shapes. Characteristic is the plain banded body of Benjamin Pickman's grace cup of 1749, made by William Swan (1716–1774) of Boston and Worcester, Massachusetts (*Plate 246*), whose paneled handles have assumed a new and vital relationship to the base, body and lid.

Plate 246.
Silver Grace Cup by William Swan, Boston, 1749. Presented to Benjamin Pickman by the Province of Massachusetts, this fine loving cup shows the plain taste of the second quarter of the 18th century, which, as Queen Anne furniture reveals, esteemed beauty of form over surface decoration. *Courtesy,* Essex Institute, Salem, Mass.

The same esthetic can be seen in the banded pear-shaped body of the domed teapots (*Plate 247*) made by such New York silversmiths as Peter Van Dyck (1684–1750/1), Adrian Bancker (1703–1772) and Jacob Gerittse Lansing (1681–1767) who worked in Albany. Wooden scroll handles of similar design were used with the apple or globular-shaped teapots taken from a form popular in Chinese porcelain and especially associated with John Burt (1692/3–1745) and Jacob Hurd (1702/3–1758; see *Plate 248*), John Coney's true successor in fame and talent in Boston. One of Hurd's teapots is dated 1737, another 1745, while a third which belonged to Sir William Pepperell shows the more loosely composed armorial foliage of this period crowned by a shell with volute forms similar to those carved on Newport furniture after about 1745.

Oriental influence was as pervasive in tea silver as in the baroque and rococo Anglo-American chair. It included the use of a bail handle and a "duck neck" spout in many teapots and kettles and found a more complete

Plate 247. SILVER TEAPOT BY PETER VAN DYCK, NEW Y[ORK] 1725–1750.
Teapots were another 18th-cen[tury] innovation. The earliest New York examples join domed lid[s] with scrolled "Queen Anne" handles. The "duck neck" spo[ut] was derived from Chinese porcelain teapots, while its octagonal surface reflects Engl[ish] taste of the William and Mary period. *Courtesy*, YALE UNIVERSITY ART GALLERY, MABEL BRADY GARVAN COLLEC[TION]

330

expression in a number of Queen Anne silver sugar bowls based on the typical Chinese rice bowls with reel-shaped handles and feet, the lids of which are shallower bowls. Examples by John Coburn (1725–1803) of

Plate 248. SILVER TEAPOT BY JACOB HURD, BOSTON, 1725–1750. Some of the earliest silver teapots have a shape suggesting an apple, which was also imitated from Chinese porcelain pieces. *Courtesy*, YALE UNIVERSITY ART GALLERY, MABEL BRADY GARVAN COLLECTION

Boston, Simeon Soumain (*circa* 1685–*circa* 1750) of New York (*Plate 249*) and John Leacock of Philadelphia, who advertised 1751–1759, are enhanced by the finest engraving, including their owners' initials rendered in orientalized patterns from the plates of Samuel Sympson's *New Book of Cyphers* (London, 1726). These graceful pieces replaced the high sugar casters of the William and Mary period, whose smooth banded surfaces were often designed in octagonal shape, like certain teapots, pepper pots and open salts and the bases of a number of candlesticks.

Creampots, an English addition to the oriental paraphernalia for serving tea, which were perhaps first made here by John Edwards (1671–1746) of Boston, were fashioned in pear shapes rising from a molded, splayed foot.

Plate 249.
SILVER COVERED SUGAR
BOWL BY SIMEON SOUMAIN,
NEW YORK, 1725–1750.
Still further oriental borrowing
is seen in this great New York
container for sugar, made in
imitation of two Chinese rice
bowls of outstanding
proportions. *Courtesy*, YALE
UNIVERSITY ART GALLERY,
MABEL BRADY GARVAN
COLLECTION

Gradually the rims assumed undulant shapes like those of contemporary sauceboats, repeating forms common in contemporary English porcelain, which also were imitated in the factory which Gouse Bonnin and George Anthony Morris established in Philadelphia in 1771 for the making of porcelain (*Plate 250*). This enterprise, one of several attempted in the colonies, soon failed, but not before at least one piece of true porcelain had been produced there.

e 250. GLAZED EARTHENWARE SAUCEBOAT BY BONNIN AND MORRIS, PHILADELPHIA, 1771–1772. *Courtesy,* BROOKLYN MUSEUM, BROOKLYN, N. Y.

Some silver creampots and sauceboats, unlike their porcelain counterparts, were made to stand on three curved feet, which with their hoof, pad and claw terminations suggest the cabriole legs of Queen Anne style furniture. This resemblance is increased by the use of high double scroll handles, among the most notable of which are those of a fine sauceboat (*Plate 251*) of Elias Boudinot (1706–1770), a goldsmith of Philadelphia and New Jersey, that end in the head of an eagle, a motif abundantly used in English furniture of the first half of the 18th century, as were, also, the diminutive hoofs of the sauceboat's feet. Small chafing dishes were made, usually in pairs, by silversmiths in various cities with pierced leaf and scroll designs beneath the rim and claw feet on insulating balls of wood. A pair by John Burt of Boston (*Plate 252*) have the massive claws which came to be associated with Boston desks and chests of drawers in the Chippendale style.

The rococo ornament inseparable from that style began to appear in American silver in the 1740's. Before he died in 1745, Charles Le Roux (1689–1745) of New York had made a pair of salt dishes for John Schuyler

334 *Plate 251.* SILVER SAUCEBOAT BY ELIAS BOUDINOT, NEW JERSEY, *circa* 1760. *Courtesy,* PHILADELPHIA MUSEUM OF ART. PHOTOGRAPH BY A. J. WYATT, STAFF PHOTOGRAPHER. The Bonnin and Morris sauceboat (*Plate 250*), product of an ill-fated attempt to make porcelain in Philadelphia, has a rococo form similar to Boudinot's masterful silver piece, with its reminiscences of Queen Anne furniture.

carried on feet in the form of dolphins embellished with rose garlands and *espagnolette* masks (*Plate 253*). By 1750 Thomas Edwards (1701/2–1755) of Boston had used the scalloped edges of European rococo silver on a salver engraved with a running border of diaper work and

Plate 252. PAIR OF SILVER CHAFING DISHES BY JOHN BURT, BOSTON, 1725–1745. These beautiful small objects, notable for their pierced surfaces, utilize a type of foot that goes back to medieval silver and which anticipated by at least a decade a form of claw-and-ball foot that became popular with Boston cabinet-makers. *Courtesy,* PHILIP H. HAMMERSLOUGH, HARTFORD, CONN.

Plate 253.
PAIR OF SILVER SALTCELLARS BY CHARLES LE ROUX, NEW YORK, 1740–1745. Strikingly different from the English and oriental themes is the use of applied ornament by a New York silversmith who drew upon French Regency sources in anticipation of the rococo vogue of the 1750's and 1760's. *Courtesy,* THE METROPOLITAN MUSEUM OF ART, NEW YORK, DODGE FUND, 1935

asymmetrical shells (*Plate 254*), while Jacob Hurd had imitated the rippled molding of French rococo silver in a pair of small candlesticks (*Plate 255*) which recall English work of the 1730's by Paul de Lamerie and James Gould.

Plate 254. Silver Tray by Thomas Edwards, Boston, 1740–1750. *Courtesy*, henry francis du pont winterthur museum, winterthur, del.

Plate 255. SILVER CANDLESTICKS BY JACOB HURD, BOSTON, 1740–1750. *Courtesy,* THE METROPOLITAN MUSEUM OF ART, NEW YORK. BEQUEST OF A. T. CLEARWATER, 1933. Rococo ornament appeared on American silver before it became popular with cabinet-makers.

From these beginnings developed the rococo phase of colonial silver, which reached its height, along with wainscot, in the 1760's. The style shows two outstanding characteristics. The first is the revival of embossed ornament in rococo designs; the second is a new form for hollow ware known as the "inverted pear" or "double belly" shape. The form is based upon a double convex curve which provides the same complexity of design and

337

impression of movement found in the bombé furniture of Boston. The basic difference between this and earlier work, such as the teapot of Jacob Hurd, lies in the new enrichment of the shape through the undulant tapering of the bowl, but there is also a new curvaceous movement in the ornament at the spout and handle, in the naturalistic bud finial of the lid and in the characteristic rococo garland of flowers and volutes embossed on the shoulder.

Plate 256.
SILVER TEA KETTLE ON STAND BY JOSEPH RICHARDSON, SR., PHILADELPHIA, 1750.
Originally owned by Clement Plumstead, mayor of Philadelphia, whose arms it displays, this is an extreme example of the exaggerated use of rococo ornament which, under London influence, sometimes occurred in Philadelphia. *Courtesy,* YALE UNIVERSITY ART GALLERY, MABEL BRADY GARVAN COLLECTION

338

All of these features are exaggerated in the richest silver of Philadelphia where, under London influence, *repoussé* work was used for the same plastic effects as was woodcarving. In extreme examples like the celebrated tea kettle and stand (*Plate 256*) made before 1760 by Joseph Richardson Sr. (1711–1784), the ornament has become so insistent that it dominates the form and the various kinds of ruffling and the scroll volutes seem the counterparts in silver of those on Benjamin Randolph's chairs (*Plates 212 and 213*).

In the work of Myer Myers (1723–1795) of New York, one of the greatest American silversmiths, a happy compromise was struck between predominant ornament and basic form. In the relative plainness of their lovely shapes, Myers' coffee pot, creamer and sugar bowl (*Plate 257*) at

Plate 257.
Sugar Bowl, Cream Pot and Coffee Pot by Myer Myers, New York, 1750–1770. Typical of the work of Myers, one of the supreme New York silversmiths, is the restrained effect of the rococo ornament and the elegant design of the coffee-pot handle. *Courtesy*, HENRY FRANCIS DU PONT WINTERTHUR MUSEUM, WINTERTHUR, DEL.

Winterthur offer the greatest contrast with Philadelphia pieces by Richardson, Edmund Milne (active 1757), Philip Hulbreat (died 1764) and George Christopher Dowig (1724–1807), heavily embossed with roses, daisies and scrolls, although all have the "inverted pear" shape in common. The characteristic coffee pots by Myers allow the new shape unhampered expression with *repoussé* leaf and shell ornament concentrated on the spout and about the handsome handle. The use of gadrooning at the base and rim, which also occurs in Myers' Jewish ritual silver, is a link with New York cabinet-makers, who constantly employed gadrooning in the skirts of chairs and tables.

A different aspect of rococo silver is found in the smooth surfaces of pieces made in imitation of oriental porcelain exported from England to this country. Myers and Halstead made a silver tea caddy based on the same vase form with flaring shoulder and base that was chosen in 1752 by the Philadelphia goldsmith Philip Syng Jr. 1703–1789) for the three receptacles of his inkstand for the Pennsylvania Assembly; it was subsequently used in signing the Declaration of Independence and is now on display in the State House in Philadelphia. Two Chinese porcelain bowls of slightly differing form provided the models for the silver bowls made by John Heath (active 1760–1763) of New York in 1760, and the patriot Paul Revere (1735–1818) of Boston in 1768 (*Plate 258*). The former is engraved with the Van Cortlandt arms in typical rococo style and the latter with the Sons of Liberty inscription in honor of the Massachusetts House of Representatives' defiance of the British Crown in refusing to rescind a seditious letter.

In the 1760's the Scottish architect and decorator Robert Adam revolutionized British taste by substituting classical archeology for rococo caprice. In English silver, undulant vase forms with asymmetrical ornament were superseded by a whole new vocabulary of tall thin forms based on the Graeco-Roman urn. That these new forms were used by Philadelphia silversmiths as early as 1774 is proved by the coffee or tea urn (*Plate 259*) made by Richard Humphreys which was presented in that year by the Continental Congress to its secretary, Charles Thomson. The inscription was engraved by James Smither in the same rococo style he had used a few years earlier on the cartouches of Benjamin Randolph's trade card. But the

Plate 258. SILVER BOWL BY PAUL REVERE (1735–1818), BOSTON, 1768. One of the most famous pieces of American silver, this punch bowl reflects the form of Chinese porcelain bowls imported from England. *Courtesy*, MUSEUM OF FINE ARTS, BOSTON

Plate 259. SILVER URN BY RICHARD HUMPHREYS, PHILADELPHIA, 1774. Presented by the Continental Congress to Charles Thomson, this historic piece of silver is the earliest dated example of the use in America of the classicizing decoration invented by the English architect Robert Adam. *Courtesy*, CHARLES T. CHAMBERLAIN. PHOTOGRAPH BY PHILADELPHIA MUSEUM OF ART

341

other ornament applied to the urn is entirely neo-classic and of the specific variety recommended by Adam, including beading, fluting in alternation with decorative disks, and the long water leaves that appear on a London sugar bowl made by Mary Makemeid in the same year of 1774. This ornament seems to have preceded by more than a decade any similar documented motifs in American architecture, wainscot or furniture.

Plate 260. SILVER TEA AND COFFEE SERVICE BY JOSEPH RICHARDSON, JR., PHILADELPHIA, 1780–1790.　new English urn and drum shapes seen here were first introduced in Philadelphia, where they were give special local flavor through the use of beading and pierced galleries. *Courtesy,* HENRY FRANCIS DU P WINTERTHUR MUSEUM, WINTERTHUR, DEL.

Nor is there any other American silver in this style which can now be dated so early. It is reasonable, however, to suppose that some of the tea sets of matching pieces in the classicizing manner of the Federal period (*circa* 1785–1810) were made within a few years of the Thomson urn. In Philadelphia, on English precedent, the urn shape was applied to coffee pots, cream pots, sugar and waste bowls, which assumed an architectural appearance, resembling finials on a balustrade. Reacting against the *repoussé* vogue of the rococo era, Philadelphia silversmiths, like the eminent Joseph Richardson Jr. (1752–1831), limited their ornament to discreet beading of edges, sometimes in combination with pierced galleries, a device used only in the silver of this area (*Plate 260*), which seems to have come from London trays of the 1770's. The popular English elliptical or drum shape with straight spout appears first to have been given to teapots in Philadelphia, where their handles continued to be made in the C-scroll form of the early 18th century. These teapots were sometimes given fluted sides, under the influence perhaps of the fan decoration which Robert Adam revived from Roman mosaics and frescoes. In 1792, Paul Revere (1735–1818) with the greatest skill applied this form of ornament to an entire tea set for John and Mehitabel Templeman of Boston, one of the acknowledged masterpieces of this Adamesque style (*Plate 261*).

Plate 261.
SILVER TEA SET BY PAUL REVERE (1735–1818), BOSTON, 1792–1793. Patriot, engraver and metal worker, Revere employed in this Templeman tea silver the delicate Adamesque decoration that Charles Bulfinch and Samuel McIntire were giving to Massachusetts architecture and woodcarving in the early Federal period. *Courtesy,* MINNEAPOLIS INSTITUTE OF ARTS. GIFT OF MR. AND MRS. JAMES FORD BELL

With the classicizing silver went a new form of gouged ornament called "bright cut" because of the sharp effect of its dots and dashes, not unlike that of the contemporary punched and gouged woodwork of the Delaware River Valley. "Bright cut" work was especially used for the beribboned and garlanded frames of inscriptions or engraved scenes like the one of the Charles River Bridge in Boston on the tankard of Richard Devens, made by Paul Revere's principal rival, Benjamin Burt, about 1786 (*Plate 262*). Like most other pieces of silver of the period, this late 18th century tankard is taller and thinner than its predecessors of the early 1700's, but unlike the later tankards of Philadelphia and New York, those of Boston have domed covers carrying a finial urn from which rises a spiral "blaze," as on the cornices of some of the great case furniture of the late colonial period.

Plate 262.
SILVER TANKARD BY BENJAMIN BURT, BOSTON, *circa* 1786. Presented to Richard Devens by the proprietors of the Charles River Bridge, this piece has the finialed lid and "bright cut" decoration characteristic of Boston tankards in the late 18th century. *Courtesy*, MUSEUM OF FINE ARTS, BOSTON, M. AND M. KAROLIK COLLECTION

344

The same motif appears as a finial on a pair of brass andirons by Revere (*Plate 263*), one of a number of colonial silversmiths who also worked in brass. The material was used relatively little by American craftsmen in this period, being employed principally for button-making, an industry which can be traced back to the German Caspar Wistar, who settled in Philadelphia in 1717. Although most of the brass hardware for furniture was imported from England, some drawer pulls and keyplates appear to have been made here. The handsomest and most elaborate brass products of the colonial period are without question certain sets of andirons produced just before the Revolution.

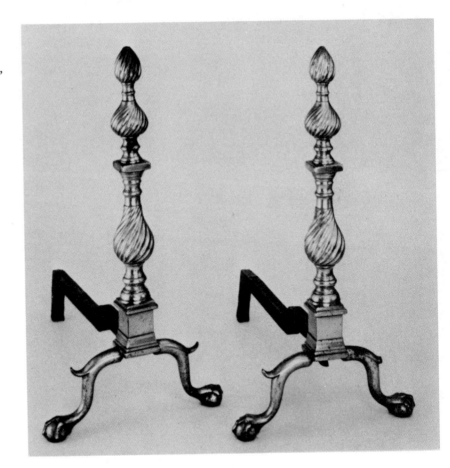

Plate 263.
BRASS ANDIRONS BY REVERE AND SONS, BOSTON, LATE 18TH CENTURY. The superbly designed shafts repeat the flamelike form of the finial found on Boston silver tankards of the time. *Courtesy,* THE METROPOLITAN MUSEUM OF ART, NEW YORK, THE SYLMARIS COLLECTION. GIFT OF GEORGE COE GRAVES, 1930

Outstanding among these are the Revere pieces, in which a bellying swirled form is repeated three times in slightly different expression, first as a baluster between academic base and capital, then as a base and finally as a finial flame. The legs represent a version of the cabriole form seen on Chippendale style pedestal tea tables, and the claw-and-ball feet have the flattened bottoms characteristic of this type of table. A similar leg appears on andirons marked by Daniel King, Philadelphia's paramount brass worker during the period 1760–1790 (*Plate 264*). Here, however, the shafts like those of certain Philadelphia silver candlesticks of the time were made in the form of stately Doric columns, always a favorite decorative device of the city. The finials are small baroque covered urns that repeat the typically English contrast between Palladian elements and fanciful ornamental details found so often in Philadelphia woodwork as well as in the background of Benjamin Randolph's richly engraved trade card of *circa* 1770.

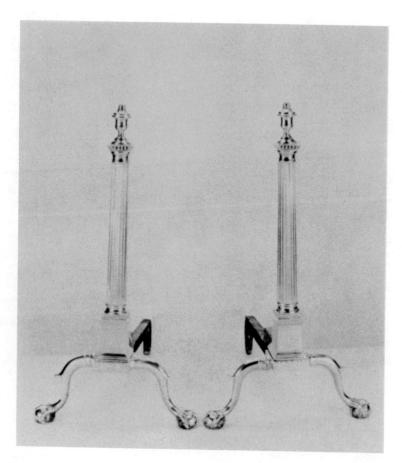

Plate 264.
BRASS ANDIRONS BY DANIEL KING, PHILADELPHIA, 1760–1790. The contrast between the rococo spurred legs and the classical Doric column of the shaft is typical of Philadelphia's neo-Palladian taste. *Courtesy,* HENRY FRANCIS DU PONT WINTERTHUR MUSEUM, WINTERTHUR, DEL.

Pewter wares like brass were made in limited quantities. This was chiefly because of the cost of tin, the essential ingredient, which had to be imported from England and was subject to duty while pewter of British manufacture entered the colonies without tax. As a result, large quantities of the latter were imported and comparatively few men before the Revolution undertook to make fine pewter objects here. Although there are recorded pewterers like Thomas Paschall and Somon Edgell who worked in Philadelphia in the late 17th and early 18th centuries, most of the surviving colonial pieces were made toward the end of the period.

These represent almost always a simpler version of models established by contemporary silversmiths. Thus a teapot by William Kirby, active in New York around 1760 (*Plate 265*), has the Dutch domed top and pear shape traditional in the city's early 18th-century silver. A flagon by his

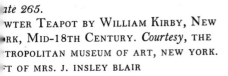

Plate 266. PEWTER FLAGON BY HENRY WILL, NEW YORK, LATE 18TH CENTURY. *Courtesy*, YALE UNIVERSITY ART GALLERY, MABEL BRADY GARVAN COLLECTION. Colonial pewterers employed many of the regional forms created by American silversmiths.

colleague Henry Will (*Plate 266*) is a characteristic late 18th-century mid-banded version of a silver communion vessel introduced by English examples presented to certain churches by William and Mary. The coffee pots of the famous Philadelphia pewterer William Will show the bands of beading common to late colonial silver made in that city. In Lancaster, German patterns were sometimes used in pewter plates, mugs and chalices.

A similar tendency to use Germanic ornament is found in the iron plates called "firebacks" made at Pennsylvania furnaces to help throw out the heat from fireplaces and also in the earliest iron stoves. The recurrence of such motifs as a prancing stag in New England iron suggests Pennsylvania influence in what was the major expression of folk art in our colonial metalwork (*Plate 267*).

Plate 267. IRON FIREBACK,
PROBABLY MASSACHUSETTS, 1781.
Courtesy, HENRY FRANCIS DU PONT WINTERTHUR
MUSEUM, WINTERTHUR, DEL.

BIBLIOGRAPHY

INDEX

BIBLIOGRAPHY

From Wilderness to Republic, 1607–1787

ANDREWS, CHARLES M., *The Colonial Period of American History.* New Haven, 1934–38.

BAXTER, W. T., *The House of Hancock: Business in Boston, 1724–1775.* Cambridge, Mass., 1945.

BEVERLEY, ROBERT, *The History and Present State of Virginia (1705).* Edited by Louis B. Wright. Chapel Hill, 1947.

BOORSTIN, DANIEL J., *The Americans: The Colonial Experience.* New York, 1958.

BRIDENBAUGH, CARL, *Cities in Revolt: Urban Life in America, 1743–1776.* New York, 1955.

———, *Cities in the Wilderness: The First Century of Urban Life in America, 1625–1742.* New York, 1938; reissued, 1955.

———, *The Colonial Craftsman.* New York, 1950.

———, *Peter Harrison: First American Architect.* Chapel Hill, 1949.

BRIDENBAUGH, CARL and JESSICA, *Rebels and Gentlemen: Philadelphia in the Age of Franklin.* New York, 1942.

BRIGHAM, CLARENCE S., *History and Bibliography of American Newspapers, 1690–1820.* 2 vols. Worcester, Mass., 1947.

———, *Journals and Journeymen: A Contribution to the History of Early American Newspapers.* Philadelphia, 1950.

BYRD, WILLIAM, *The Secret Diary of William Byrd of Westover, 1709–1712.* Edited by Louis B. Wright and Marion Tinling. Richmond, Va., 1941.

———, *Another Secret Diary of William Byrd of Westover, 1739–1741, with Letters & Literary Exercises, 1696–1726.* Edited by Maude H. Woodfin and Marion Tinling. Richmond, Va., 1942.

———, *William Byrd of Virginia: The London Diary (1712–1721) and Other Writings.* Edited by Louis B. Wright and Marion Tinling. New York, 1958.

CRANE, VERNER, *Benjamin Franklin and a Rising People.* Boston, 1954.

CROCE, GEORGE C., and WALLACE, DAVID H., (ed.), *Dictionary of Artists in America, 1564–1860.* New Haven, 1957.

CURTI, MERLE, *The Growth of American Thought.* New York, 1943.

FITHIAN, PHILIP VICKERS, *The Journal of Philip Vickers Fithian.* Edited by Hunter Dickinson Farish. Williamsburg, Va., 1943.

GIPSON, LAWRENCE H., *The British Empire before the American Revolution.* 10 vols. New York, 1936–

GRAHAM, IAN C. C., *Colonists from Scotland: Emigration to North America, 1707–1783.* Ithaca, 1956.

HEDGES, JAMES B., *The Browns of Providence Plantations: Colonial Years.* Cambridge, Mass., 1952.

HINDLE, BROOKE, *The Pursuit of Science in Revolutionary America, 1735–1789.* Chapel Hill, 1956.

KNIGHT, EDGAR W. (ed.), *A Documentary History of Education in the South Before 1860,* Vol. I, *European Inheritances.* Chapel Hill, 1949.

KRAUS, MICHAEL, *The Atlantic Civilization: Eighteenth-Century Origins.* Ithaca, 1949.

LEYBURN, JAMES G., *The Scotch-Irish: A Social History.* Chapel Hill, 1962.

MARCUS, JACOB RADAR, *Early American Jewry: The Jews of New York, New England, and Canada, 1649–1794.* Philadelphia, 1951.

MIDDLETON, ARTHUR P., *Tobacco Coast: A Maritime History of the Chesapeake Bay in the Colonial Era.* Newport News, Va., 1953.

353

Bibliography

Montgomery, Charles F. (ed.), *America's Arts and Skills*. New York, 1957.

Morgan, Edmund S., *The Puritan Family: Essays on Religion and Domestic Relations in Seventeenth-Century New England*. Boston, 1944.

———, *Virginians at Home: Family Life in the Eighteenth Century*. Williamsburg, Va., 1952.

Morison, Samuel Eliot, *The Puritan Pronaos*. New York, 1935.

Morris, Richard B., *Government and Labor in Early America*. New York, 1946.

Nagel, Charles, *American Furniture, 1650–1850: A Brief Background and an Illustrated History*. New York, 1949.

Schneider, Herbert W., *A History of American Philosophy*. New York, 1946.

Shryock, Richard H., *Medicine and Society in America, 1660–1860*. New York, 1960.

Sweet, William Warren, *Religion in Colonial America*. New York, 1942.

Tolles, Frederick B., *James Logan and the Culture of Provincial America*. Boston, 1957.

Watkins, L. W., *Early New England Potters and Their Wares*. Cambridge, 1950.

Wertenbaker, Thomas J., *The Founding of American Civilization*. 3 vols. New York, 1938–47.

Wright, Louis B., *The Cultural Life of the American Colonies, 1607–1763*. New York, 1957.

———, *The First Gentlemen of Virginia: Intellectual Qualities of the Early Colonial Ruling Class*. San Marino, Calif., 1940; reissued, 1949.

Architecture

Although emphasis and interpretation differ in some respects, a number of the examples cited in the section on Architecture were suggested by Hugh Morrison's *Early American Architecture* (New York, 1952), a convenient source of reference as well as the best general statement on the colonial architecture of America that has appeared to date. Most of the other books listed below deal with more restricted fields or topics; to these the author is also indebted and to them and the bibliographies they contain the reader is referred for a fuller treatment of the subject.

GENERAL

Andrews, Wayne, *Architecture, Ambition and Americans*. New York, 1955.

Gowans, Alan, *Images of American Living*. Philadelphia, 1964.

Howells, John M., *Lost Examples of Colonial Architecture*. New York, 1931.

Kimball, Fiske, *Domestic Architecture of the American Colonies and the Early Republic*. New York, 1922.

Pratt, Richard, *A Treasury of Early American Homes*. New York, 1949.

———, and Pratt, Dorothy, *Second Treasury of Early American Homes*. New York, 1954.

Shurtleff, Harold R., *The Log Cabin Myth*. Cambridge, Mass., 1939.

Waterman, Thomas T., *The Dwellings of Colonial America*. Chapel Hill, 1950.

SPANISH AND FRENCH COLONIES

Hannaford, Donald R., and Edwards, Revel, *Spanish Colonial or Adobe Architecture of California, 1800–1850*. New York, 1931.

Kirker, Harold, *California's Architectural Frontier*. San Marino, Calif., 1960.

Kubler, George, *The Religious Architecture of New Mexico*. Colorado Springs, Colo., 1940.

LAUGHLIN, CLARENCE J., *Ghosts Along the Mississippi*, New York, 1948.

MANUCY, ALBERT, *The Houses of St. Augustine, 1565–1821*. St. Augustine, Fla., 1962.

NEWCOMB, REXFORD, *The Old Mission Churches and Historic Houses of California*. Philadelphia, 1925.

———, *Spanish Colonial Architecture in the United States*. New York, 1937.

NEW ENGLAND COLONIES

BRIDENBAUGH, CARL, *Peter Harrison: First American Architect*. Chapel Hill, 1949.

BRIGGS, MARTIN S., *The Homes of the Pilgrim Fathers in England and America*. New York, 1932.

CADY, JOHN HUTCHINS, *The Civic and Architectural Development of Providence, 1636–1950*. Providence, 1957.

CONGDON, HERBERT W., *Old Vermont Houses*. Brattleboro, 1940.

DOWNING, ANTOINETTE F., *Early Homes of Rhode Island*, Richmond, Va., 1937.

———, and SCULLY, JR., VINCENT J., *The Architectural Heritage of Newport, Rhode Island, 1640–1915*. Cambridge, Mass., 1952.

GARVAN, ANTHONY N. B., *Architecture and Town Planning in Colonial Connecticut*. New Haven, 1951.

HITCHCOCK, JR., Henry-Russell, *Rhode Island Architecture*. Providence, 1939.

KELLY, J. FREDERICK, *The Early Domestic Architecture of Connecticut*. New Haven, 1924.

———, *Early Connecticut Meeting Houses*. New York, 1948.

KIMBALL, FISKE, *Mr. Samuel McIntire, Carver, The Architect of Salem*. Portland, 1940.

PLACE, CHARLES A., *Charles Bulfinch, Architect and Citizen*. Boston, 1925.

MIDDLE COLONIES

BAILEY, ROSALIE FELLOWS, *Pre-Revolutionary Dutch Houses and Families in Northern New Jersey and Southern New York*. New York, 1936.

DORNBUSCH, CHARLES H., *Pennsylvania German Barns*. Allentown, Pa., 1958.

EBERLEIN, HAROLD DONALDSON, and HUBBARD, CORTLANDT VAN DYKE, *Portrait of a Colonial City: Philadelphia, 1670–1838*. Philadelphia, 1939.

———, *Historic Houses and Buildings of Delaware*. Dover, Del., 1962.

———, *Historic Houses of the Hudson Valley*. New York, 1942.

HAMLIN, TALBOT, *Benjamin Henry Latrobe*. New York, 1955.

REYNOLDS, HELEN WILKINSON, *Dutch Houses in the Hudson Valley Before 1776*. New York, 1929.

SHELTON, WILLIAM H., *The Jumel Mansion*. Boston, 1916.

SHOEMAKER, ALFRED L. (ed.), *The Pennsylvania Barn*. Kutztown, Pa., 1959.

SWEENEY, JOHN A. H., *Grandeur on the Appoquinimink; the House of William Corbit at Odessa, Delaware*. Newark, Del., 1959.

WERTENBAKER, THOMAS JEFFERSON, *The Founding of American Civilization: The Middle Colonies*. New York, 1938.

SOUTHERN COLONIES

ARMES, ETHEL M., *Stratford Hall: The Great House of the Lees*. Richmond, Va., 1936.

BEIRNE, ROSAMOND RANDALL, and SCARFF, JOHN HENRY, *William Buckland, 1734–1774, Architect of Virginia and Maryland*. Baltimore, 1958.

BROCK, HENRY IRVING, *Colonial Churches in Virginia*. Richmond, Va., 1930.

DAVIS, DEERING, *Annapolis Houses, 1700–1775*. New York, 1947.

FORMAN, HENRY CHANDLEE, *The Architecture of the Old South: The Medieval Style, 1585–1850*. Cambridge, Mass., 1948.

———, *Early Manor and Plantation Houses of Maryland, 1634–1800*. Easton, 1934.

———, *Tidewater Maryland Architecture and Gardens*. New York, 1956.

355

Bibliography

FRARY, IHNA T., *Thomas Jefferson, Architect and Builder*. Richmond, Va., 1931.

MASON, GEORGE CARRINGTON, *Colonial Churches of Tidewater Virginia*. Richmond, Va., 1945.

RAVENEL, BEATRICE S. J., *Architects of Charleston*. Charleston, 1945.

WATERMAN, THOMAS T., *The Mansions of Virginia, 1706–1776*, Chapel Hill, 1946.

———, and JOHNSTON, FRANCES BENJAMIN, *The Early Architecture of North Carolina*, Chapel Hill, 1941.

WHIFFEN, MARCUS, *The Eighteenth-century Houses of Williamsburg*, Williamsburg, Va., 1960.

———, *The Public Buildings of Williamsburg*, Williamsburg, Va., 1958.

Painting

BARKER, VIRGIL, *American Painting: History and Interpretation*. New York, 1950.

DUNLAP, WILLIAM, *A History of the Rise and Progress of the Arts of Design in the United States* (1834). New edition, edited by Frank W. Bayley and Charles E. Goodspeed. Boston, 1918.

FLEXNER, JAMES THOMAS, *America's Old Masters*. New York, 1939.

———, *American Painting: First Flowers of Our Wilderness*. Boston, 1947.

———, *The Light of Distant Skies*. New York, 1954.

FOOTE, HENRY WILDER, *John Smibert, Painter*. Cambridge, Mass., 1950.

———, *Robert Feke, Colonial Portrait Painter*. Cambridge, Mass., 1930.

HAGEN, OSKAR, *The Birth of the American Tradition of Art*. New York, 1940.

LARKIN, OLIVER, *Art and Life in America*. New York, 1949.

LITTLE, NINA FLETCHER, *American Decorative Wall Painting, 1700–1856*. New York, 1952.

PARKER, BARBARA N., and WHEELER, ANNE B., *John Singleton Copley, American Portraits in Oil, Pastel and Miniature*. Boston, 1938.

RICHARDSON, EDGAR PRESTON, *Painting in America*. New York, 1956.

SELLERS, CHARLES COLEMAN, *Charles Willson Peale*. Philadelphia, 1947.

SIZER, THEODORE, *The Works of Colonel John Trumbull, Artist of the American Revolution*. New Haven, 1950.

STOKES, I. N. PHELPS, and HASKELL, D. C., *American Historical Prints, Early Views of American Cities, etc., from the Phelps Stokes and Other Collections*. New York, 1933.

WHITLEY, WILLIAM T., *Gilbert Stuart*. Cambridge, Mass., 1932.

The Decorative Arts

GENERAL

COMSTOCK, HELEN (ed)., *The Concise Encyclopedia of American Antiques*. New York, 1958.

CERAMICS

BARBER, EDWIN ATLEE, *Tulip Ware of the Pennsylvania-German Potters: An Historical Sketch of the Art of Slip-Decoration in the United States*. Philadelphia, 1903.

CLEMENT, ARTHUR W., *Our Pioneer Potters*. New York, 1947.

FURNITURE

BJERKIE, ETHEL HALL, *The Cabinetmakers of America*. Garden City, N. Y., 1957.

BOSTON MUSEUM OF FINE ARTS, *Eighteenth-century American Arts: the M. and M. Karolik Collection of Paintings, Drawings, Engravings, Furniture, Silver, Needlework & Incidental Objects*. Cambridge, Mass., 1941.

COMSTOCK, HELEN, *American Furniture: Seventeenth, Eighteenth, and Nineteenth Century Styles*. New York, 1962.

Downs, Joseph, *American Furniture in the Henry Francis duPont Winterthur Museum*. New York, 1952.

Hornor, William MacPherson, *Blue Book, Philadelphia Furniture*. Philadelphia, 1935.

Nutting, Wallace, *Furniture Treasury*. 3 vols. Framingham, Mass., 1928–1933.

GLASSWARE

Daniel, Dorothy, *Cut and Engraved Glass, 1771–1905*. New York, 1950.

McKearin, George Skinner, *American Glass*. New York, 1948.

METALS

Brass:

Kauffman, Henry, *Early American Copper, Tin and Brass*. New York, 1950.

Ironwork:

Sonn, Albert H., *Early American Wrought Iron*. New York, 1928.

Wallace, Philip B., *Colonial Ironwork in Old Philadelphia*. New York, 1930.

Pewter:

Laughlin, Ledlie Irwin, *Pewter in America, Its Makers and Their Marks*. Boston, 1940.

Silver:

Avery, Clara Louise, *Early American Silver*. New York, 1930.

Boston Museum of Fine Arts, *Colonial Silversmiths, Masters & Apprentices*. Boston, 1956.

Buhler, Kathryn C., *American Silver*. Cleveland, 1950.

Fales, Martha Gandy, *American Silver in the Henry Francis duPont Winterthur Museum*. Winterthur, Del., 1958.

Phillips, John Marshall, *American Silver*. New York, 1949.

TEXTILES

Little, Frances, *Early American Textiles*. New York, 1931.

INDEX

Index